THE COMPLETE BOOK
OF HIGH ALTITUDE BAKING

The
Book
High
Baking

by Donna Miller Hamilton

Complete

of

Altitude

and Beverly Anderson Nemiro

SAGE BOOKS, *Chicago*

Fifth Printing, 1975

Sage Books are published by
The Swallow Press Incorporated
1139 South Wabash Avenue
Chicago, Illinois 60605

ISBN 0-8040-0054-9
LIBRARY OF CONGRESS CATALOG CARD NUMBER 61-18656

PREFACE

We really had no intention of writing a high altitude baking book. When the idea was presented to us, it seemed a bit overwhelming. We have had some experience in professional writing, but we don't pretend to be professional home economists. However, upon research we found that our inherited and collected family-tested, time-tested, and kitchen-tested recipes *are* the best for high altitude baking; and these we had in abundance!

For years we've read cookbooks like novels and collected high altitude recipes wherever and whenever we ran across them. These came from family, friends, neighbors, local papers and periodicals, old church and guild cookbooks, professional bakeries, and private clubs. Some were written on time-yellowed slips of paper, some on kitchen smudged and stained leaves of an old recipe notebook. And almost anytime we encountered a delicious baked dish, we "asked for the recipe."

We have been using the family heirlooms just as they were handed down to us. We hadn't thought anything unusual about using a "lump" of butter, a "scant quart" of flour, "stoned" dates, butter "the size of an egg," "one tablespoon less of Johnstown sugar," "enough flour to make dough stiff," or baking in a "dripping pan." These were all comfortable terms that we understood. But when it came to compiling recipes for a cookbook, they looked amusingly old fashioned.

The big job then was not collecting recipes, as we had to eliminate some from our years-old collection. Our project was to interpret what we had into a modern day, functional format.

These old and acquired gems fulfilled our general requirements, but left untouched the modern phases we have incorporated in our baking habits the last few years. Cooks now have packaged mixes at their fingertips. We have children who want to bake. We have husbands on specialized diets. And the freezer plays an ever-important role in our daily lives.

As a complete bake book was our goal, it was necessary to add a comprehensive, practical collection of recipes of all these types.

We felt that a complete collection of baking recipes should spare the reader from experimenting, perhaps unsuccessfully, with the conversion of sea-level recipes to high altitudes. We included recipes for doughnuts, hot cakes, waffles, and fritters, because even though they are not baked, their batter composition is affected by altitude.

If you are an experienced cook, turn to the recipe of your choice and start on your way to successful baking. If you are a beginner, we suggest that you read "Steps to Good Baking" and "Suggestions for Successful Baking" at the beginning of each chapter.

We thank our publisher for asking us to write the book, our understanding husbands and families who were so patient while it was being written, and Mrs. E. Ray Campbell, for her knowledgeable assistance. To all we dedicate our work.

It is with a great deal of relief that at last we have all our ever-loved and used jottings, clippings, dog-eared pieces of paper between book covers and categorized, where, at last, we can find them in a minute.

August 23, 1961

DONNA MILLER HAMILTON
BEVERLY ANDERSON NEMIRO

CONTENTS

Preface   5

Introduction: Why High Altitude Baking Is Different   9
    Adjustments of Recipes in This Book   10
    High Altitude Cities and Towns   11
    High Altitude Cooking Definitions   14
    Steps to Good Baking   16
    General Rules for Freezing Baked Goods   17
    Freezer Chart   17
    Tables of Equivalents   20
    Ingredient Substitutions   22
    Oven Temperatures   23
    Interpreting Foreign Measurements   23
    Standard Can Sizes   24
    Types of Baking Powder   26

Yeast Breads   27
    Breads   33
    Rolls   43
    Sweet Rolls and Coffee Cakes   50

Quick Breads   59
    Biscuits   61
    Muffins   65
    Breads and Coffee Cakes   73
    Popovers and Corn Breads   85
    Pancakes, Cornbread, and Waffles   89
    Doughnuts, Fritters, and Dumplings   101

Cakes   107
    Creamed Cakes   115
        White Cakes   115
        Yellow Cakes   121
        Chocolate Cakes   124
        Assorted Creamed Cakes   134
        Cup Cakes   146
        Fruit Cakes   150
    Sponge Cakes   154

Frostings and Fillings 163
    Frostings 164
    Fillings 173

Cookies 177
    Drop Cookies 182
    Refrigerator Cookies 204
    Rolled or Molded Cookies 211
    Bars and Squares 221
    Uncooked Cookies 232

Pies 239
    Pie Crusts 248
    Meringues 254
    Berry or Fruit Pies 255
    Cream or Custard Pies 264
    Chiffon and Uncooked Fillings 277

Desserts 287

Diet Baking 307

Modern Marvels 315

Easy to Make Recipes for Junior Bakers 331

Index 357

INTRODUCTION

WHY HIGH ALTITUDE BAKING IS DIFFERENT

If favorite baking recipes from your home town, or recipes taken from national publications or cookbooks, have led to failures at higher elevations, blame the altitude, not the recipe, or the cook.

High altitude baking *is different.* Particularly the baking of cakes, yeast breads, quick breads, and some types of cookies.

Baking problems at high altitude are caused by lower atmospheric pressure. As altitude increases, atmospheric pressure decreases. This causes water to boil at *202° F. at 5,000 feet rather than 212° F. as it does at sea level.* Because of these differences brought about by lower atmospheric pressure, baking temperatures must be increased 10 to 15 degrees in using a sea level recipe at higher elevations. Baking time usually remains the same.

Ingredient balance must be maintained when converting low elevation recipes to high altitudes. More liquids are necessary to compensate for greater evaporation. The right amount of sugar is necessary as too little sugar makes a cake that is dry and coarse. Too much sugar results in a tough, crumbly cake. Yeast breads rise faster, and leavening agents react differently at high altitude.

All of this contributes to the ticklish, mercurial problem of how successfully to convert a recipe written for low altitude to a well-balanced recipe for high altitude.

Rules and conversion tables are varied, contradictory, and oftentimes confusing to those other than a professional home economist. Even if you follow a rule or table for adapting a recipe to high elevations, the results might be unsatisfactory and discouraging, as changing the amounts of ingredients is experimental at best. For example: unless a recipe to be adjusted to higher elevations contains the maximum amount of sugar relative to the other ingredients, the rule for using less sugar cannot be accurately applied. To determine whether or not a recipe contains the maximum amount of sugar probably would not be easy for most homemakers, and any change she made would be guesswork.

Moisture-holding liquids are important in the ingredient structure at high altitudes. Liquids with these qualities, such as sour milk, buttermilk, and cream, are not so frequently used at lower elevations as they are in recipes written for high altitude.

It is generally conceded by most baking authorities and home economists that time-tested, family-tested recipes, or recipes written and tested for high altitude, are best for baking at elevations over 2,500 feet.

This collection of recipes represents three generations of tested baking at high altitudes. Every recipe is adapted for use at elevations from 4,000 to 6,000 feet.

Careful attention has been given to making this collection a representative cross section of most types of recipes for baking, so that converting lower elevation recipes will not be a necessity.

The directions are specific because baking can be successful if done according to directions.

If you wish to convert low elevation recipes for use at altitudes 4,000 to 6,000 feet, here are recommended ingredient changes.

1. Use 2 level teaspoons additional flour per cup.
2. Decrease sugar content 1/2 tablespoon per cup for each 1,000 feet rise in elevation.
3. Decrease shortening 1/2 teaspoon per cup for each 1,000 feet rise in elevation.
4. Decrease baking powder, soda, or cream of tartar 1/4 to 1/2 teaspoon or 1/4 given amount.
5. Increase liquid 2 to 3 tablespoons per cup.

(When two amounts are given, try the smaller adjustment first.)

ADJUSTMENTS OF RECIPES IN THIS BOOK
for altitudes lower than 4,000 feet, and higher than 6,000 feet

	2,500 to 4,000 feet	over 6,000 feet
Baking powder per each teaspoon used	increase 1/4 teaspoon	decrease 1/4 teaspoon
Liquid per each cup used	decrease 1 to 2 tablespoons	increase 2 to 4 tablespoons
Sugar per each cup used	no change	decrease 1/4 cup
Baking temperature	decrease 10 to 15 degrees	increase 10 to 15 degrees

ARIZONA

Bisbee	5300	Holbrook	5080
Clifton	3440	Kingman	3328
Douglas	3955	Nogales	3857
Flagstaff	6895	Prescott	5320
Globe	3509	Winslow	4856

COLORADO

Akron	4654	Greeley	4649
Alamosa	7536	Gunnison	7820
Aspen	7844	Hot Sulphur Springs	7665
Boulder	5347	Julesburg	3467
Burlington	4250	La Junta	4052
Canon City	5332	Lamar	3500
Colorado Springs	5985	Las Animas	4050
Craig	6174	Leadville	10,200
Cortez	6198	Limon	5280
Del Norte	7880	Longmont	4941
Delta	4980	Loveland	4986
Denver	5183	Montrose	5801
Durango	6517	Pueblo	4658
Estes Park	7500	Rocky Ford	4176
Fort Collins	4994	Salida	7038
Fort Morgan	4338	Springfield	4400
Georgetown	8507	Steamboat Springs	6683
Glenwood Springs	5758	Sterling	3922
Grand Junction	4579	Trinidad	5982
Grand Lake	8380	Walden	8300
	Walsenburg	6187	

IDAHO

Boise	2775	Moscow	2569
Blackfoot	4497	Pocatello	4471
Burley	4350	Sun Valley	6000
Idaho Falls	4699	Twin Falls	3746

MONTANA

Anaconda	5288	Butte	5544
Billings	3117	Deer Lodge	4519
Bozeman	4754	Great Falls	3331

11

Havre	2480	Livingston	4491
Helena	4009	Missoula	3197
Kalispell	2946	Red Lodge	5537
Lewiston	3960	Whitefish	8000

NEBRASKA

Alliance	3958	North Platte	2803
McCook	2509	Scottsbluff	4662
	Sidney	4085	

NEW MEXICO

Albuquerque	4950	Las Cruces	3900
Carlsbad	3100	Las Vegas	6435
Clayton	5050	Los Alamos	7370
Clovis	4260	Raton	6660
Deming	4335	Roswell	3600
Farmington	5300	Santa Fe	7000
Gallup	6500	Taos	6950
Hobbs	3625	Tucumcari	4085

NEVADA

Carson City	4675	Ely	6421
Fallon	3970	Reno	4484
Elko	5067	Tonopah	6033
	Winnemucca	4317	

OREGON

Baker	3449	Klamath Falls	4112
Bend	3623	La Grande	2787
	Lakeview	4800	

SOUTH DAKOTA

Custer	5301	Lead	5089
Deadwood	4543	Hot Springs	3443
	Rapid City	3196	

TEXAS

Amarillo	3615	Lamesa	2975
Dalhart	3985	Lubbock	3241
El Paso	3710	Plainview	3366
	Rio Grande	3461	

Brigham City	431		ˌcello	7066
Eureka	646		ˌay	4310
Duchesne	55ˌ		ˌen	4307
Fillmore	57		ˌ City	6970
Heber	5ˌ		ˌvo	4532
Lehi	4		ˌlt Lake City	4390
Logan			ˌrnal	5331
Buffalo			ˌaramie	7153
Casper			Lusk	5017
Cody			Newcastle	4332
Cheyenne			Rawlins	6787
Evanston			Rock Springs	6265
Kemmerer			Sheridan	3745
Green River			Torrington	4098
Gillette			Wheatland	4747
Lander	5377		Worland	4059

FOREIGN CITIES AND TOWNS

Afghanistan, Kandahar	3310	Cali	3139
Alaska, Summit	2409	Cartago	2950
Algeria, Telergma	2484	Medellin	4915
Austria, Innsbruck	2900	Costa Rica, San Jose	3021
Bolivia, La Paz	13,402	Ecuador, Quito	9226
Canada		Ethiopia	
Aishihik, Y.T.	3176	Addis Ababa	7749
Banff, Alb.	4537	Asonara	7615
Beatton River, B.C.	2743	Germany, Kaufbeuren	2390
Calgary, Alb.	3557	Guatemala,	
Kimberly, B.C.	3005	Guatemala City	4958
Lethbridge, Alb.	3047	Honduras,	
Penhold, Alb.	2967	Tegucigalpa	3250
Swift Current, Sask.	2680	India	
Williams Lake, B.C.	3085	Bangalore	2914
China		Darjeeling	6982
Gartak, Tibet	14,240	Iran	
Jiachan, Tibet	15,870	Hamadan	5732
Lanchow	5185	Isfahan	5207
Colombia		Tehran	3950
Bogota	8355	Israel, Jeruselum	4160

Jordan, Amman	2550	Peru, Arequipa	8460
Kenya, Nairobi	5327	Saudi Arabia, Taif	4500
Mexico		Spain	
Cananea	5200	Granada	2300
Chihuahua	4444	Salamanca	2602
Durango	6200	S. Africa, Johannesburg	5689
Guadalajara	5007	Switzerland, St. Moritz	6037
Leon	6004	Turkey	
Mexico City	7340	Ankara	3122
Nogales	4010	Ayfas	3309
Parral	5990	Konya	3366
Torreon	3750	Malatya	3015
Zacatecas	8010	Murted	2755
Mongolia, Ulan Bator	4160	Venezuela, Caracas	3164

HIGH ALTITUDE COOKING DEFINITIONS

Preheat:	Heat oven to the degree given in the recipe before placing the batter or dough in oven.
Ingredients:	The substances that are used in the recipe. Always have ingredients at *room* temperature.
To Beat:	To mix with vigorous strokes with a circular motion.
To Blend:	To combine all ingredients until they are mixed thoroughly.
To Cream:	Combine shortening and sugar with a slotted spoon, with the hands, or with electric mixer until these ingredients are thoroughly blended and fluffy like whipped cream.
To Measure Brown Sugar:	Pack *firmly* in cup.
To Measure Shortening:	Pack firmly in cup or use water displacement method. Water displacement method: To measure 1/2 cup shortening, fill glass measuring cup one-half full of cold water. Then spoon in shortening until the water level reaches mark of one cup.

14

To Cut In:	Combine shortening with flour by cutting the shortening into the flour with two knives or a pastry blender until the ingredients are blended together and are like small grains of corn meal in texture.
To Dredge:	To coat the ingredients, such as nuts and fruits, completely with flour or crumbs.
To Fold In:	To fold one mixture into another mixture by a downward and over action which incorporates or encloses all the air possible until the ingredients are blended. This usually applies to ingredients into which air has been beaten and in which you wish to retain the air.
To Grease:	To spread baking pans or tins with *unsalted* butter or shortening.
To Knead:	To press ball of dough with the heels of the hand; then with fingers grasp outer edge of dough, pulling it to the center and pushing from the center outward with the heel of the hand. Keep rotating the dough and repeating action until dough feels very tight, compact, and elastic-like.
To Stir:	To mix with a spoon in a circular motion.
To Whip:	To beat with circular over and over motion to enclose as much air as possible into the ingredients. This usually applies to egg whites or cream.
To Work:	To combine rather stiff ingredients with a spoon or the hands until they hold together.
To Blanche Almonds:	Pour boiling water over shelled almonds. Permit them to stand for 5 minutes. Drain. Pour cold water over them and slip off their skins.

15

To Pour or Fill: To transfer batter from mixing bowl to baking pan. Fill pan only one-half to two-thirds full as breads, cakes, and the like, rise to fill remainder of pan.

STEPS TO GOOD BAKING

1. Follow a recipe exactly. Do not change ingredient amounts or make substitutions unless it is listed under "Ingredient Substitutions."
2. Preheat oven to required baking temperature.
3. Before beginning to bake, gather all mixing and measuring utensils together.
4. Have correct size baking pan prepared according to directions before beginning to mix ingredients.
5. Have all ingredients assembled and at room temperature (with the exceptions stated in individual recipes such as "boiling water").
6. Use standard measuring cups and spoons. Measure accurately. All spoon measurements are level with spoon edge. All cup measurements are level with measuring lines.
7. Sift flour once before measuring. Do not shake or press down in cup.
8. Pack brown sugar or shortening into cup or spoon for accurate measurement.
9. Melt chocolate over simmering, not boiling, water.
10. Cream butter and sugars thoroughly. You cannot overmix these two basic ingredients.
11. A long handled wooden spoon makes mixing, stirring, and beating more effective.
12. Cut raisins, figs, gum drops, marshmallows, dates, and so forth with scissors dipped in hot water.
13. Dredge fruits and nuts in a little flour reserved from the amount called for in the recipe.
14. When using electric mixer, scrape down sides and along bottom of bowl often with pliable rubber scraper.
15. Use medium or medium high speeds of mixer to cream shortening and sugar.
16. Use low speed to mix in dry ingredients.

17. Whip egg whites at high speed.
18. See special "Suggestions for Successful Baking" at the beginning of each baking classification.
19. These recipes are family and kitchen tested. However, ingredients differ such as egg sizes, quality of molasses, and so forth, and these variances make a difference in baking results. It will help always to use the best of ingredients such as high quality margarines and pure vanilla extract.

GENERAL RULES FOR FREEZING BAKED GOODS

1. Keep a record of what you place in the freezer: date item was baked and frozen, number of servings, and any special instructions.
2. Do not keep frozen foods longer than they will safely store in the freezer. See the Freezer Chart on pages 17-20 for the length of time frozen foods will keep safely.
3. Never keep *any* item in the freezer longer than 12 months.
4. Always use proper packaging to avoid freezer burn. Use only moisture-vaporproof wrapping. Be sure to expel all air. Most baked goods store successfully in waxed freezer wrap paper, cellophane, aluminum, or plastic bags.
5. Label every item you place in the freeezr. Don't trust your memory.
6. Always freeze item immediately after packaging.
7. Always completely *cool* any item before placing in freezer.
8. Never re-freeze after a product is thawed.

FREEZER CHART

Product	To Freeze	To Use
Yeast Bread & Rolls	Bake as usual. Cool on rack. Slice bread if desired. Wrap in moisture-vapor-proof wrap. Will keep up to 12 months.	Thaw at room temperature; or toast unthawed bread slices. Frost rolls before serving, if desired.

17

Quick Breads (Muffins, biscuits, and rolls made without yeast)	Bake as usual. Cool completely. Quick freeze in pans or in trays. Wrap in moisture-vaporproof wrap or package in plastic bags. Seal. Will keep up to 12 months.	Place, unwrapped and unthawed, in 375°F. oven for 15 minutes. Or thaw and serve cold. Heat waffles, unthawed, in pop-up toaster.
Cookies	All cookies freeze well. Bake as usual. Quick freeze on trays first, then package in bags or metal containers to avoid breakage. Store unbaked cookies in long roll. Wrap in moisture-vaporproof wrap. Will keep well up to 3 months.	Thaw baked cookies at room temperature. Serve. Defrost unbaked dough just enough to slice. Bake as usual.
Cakes	Bake as usual. Cool on rack. Quick freeze. Then wrap in moisture-vaporproof wrap. Will keep up to 12 months. Halves, fourths, or slices may be frozen successfully. Use sponge or spice cakes within 1 month. Do not freeze upside-down cake.	Thaw at room temperature for 1 to 2 hours. Best not to warm in oven.

Frostings & Fillings	Prepare as usual. Cream frostings freeze well. Do not freeze cream or custard fillings. Boiled frostings collapse in freezer.	
Pie Crusts, Unbaked	Make as usual. Do not prick dough. Leave in pan. Quick freeze. Wrap in moisture-vapor-proof wrap. Place again in freezer. Stack with cushions of crushed waxed paper between pie shells.	Unwrap. Bake at 450°F. for 5 minutes. Remove. Prick bottom. Return to oven for about 15 minutes more.
Pie Crusts, Baked	Bake. *Cool.* May be stored in or out of pan. Wrap in moisture-vaporproof wrap. Stack with cushions of crushed waxed paper between shells. Use within 6 weeks.	Unwrap. Bake at 375°F. for 10-15 minutes.
Berry, Fruit, Mincemeat, and Pumpkin Pies	Best to freeze unbaked. Freeze in pan you will bake it in. Wrap in moisture-vaporproof wrap. Use pumpkin pie within 6 weeks.	Remove wrap. Cut vent holes or prick top crust. Bake *unthawed* at 475°F. for 15-20 minutes. *Reduce* heat to 375°F. and bake 20-30 minutes more, or until done.

Chiffon Pies	Almost all freeze well. Wrap in moisture-vaporproof wrap. Quick freeze.	Thaw unwrapped for about 1 hour. Serve.

TABLES OF EQUIVALENTS

Dash	⅛ teaspoon
60 drops	1 teaspoon
3 teaspoons	1 tablespoon
2 tablespoons	1 liquid ounce
4 tablespoons	¼ cup
16 tablespoons	1 cup
2 cups	1 pint
2 pints	1 quart
4 quarts	1 gallon
8 quarts	1 peck
4 pecks	1 bushel
4 ounces	¼ pound
8 ounces	½ pound
16 ounces	1 pound

Almonds	¼ pound	=	1 cup, shelled
Apples, fresh	1 pound (3 to 4 apples)	=	3 cups, sliced
Apples, dried	1 pound dried	=	5 cups, cooked
Apricots, dried	1 pound dried	=	3 cups, cooked
Apricots, fresh	1 pound	=	about 5 to 10
Bananas	1 pound or 3 medium	=	2½ cups, sliced
Berries	1 quart	=	3½ cups
Butter	1 pound	=	2 cups
Butter	1 cube	=	½ cup
Chocolate	1 ounce	=	1 square
Chocolate, grated	1 ounce	=	6 tablespoons
Cocoa	1 pound	=	4 cups
Coconut	1 pound	=	6 cups, shredded
Cheese	1 pound	=	4½ cups, grated
Cornmeal	1 pound	=	3 cups

Cottage Cheese	1 pound	=	2 cups
Cream, heavy	½ pint (1 cup)	=	2 cups, whipped
Cream Cheese	3 ounce package	=	6 tablespoons
Dates	1 pound	=	2 cups, pitted
Eggs	1 cup	=	5 whole eggs
Egg Whites	1 cup	=	8 to 10
Egg Yolks	1 cup	=	about 14
Figs	1 pound	=	3 cups, chopped
Flour, all-purpose	1 ounce	=	4 tablespoons
Flour, all-purpose	1 pound	=	4 cups
Flour, cake, sifted	1 pound	=	4½ cups
Flour, graham	1 pound	=	3½ cups
Lard	1 pound	=	2 cups
Lemon	1 lemon, juiced	=	2 to 3 tablespoons juice
Lemon Rind, grated	1 lemon, rind of	=	3 teaspoons grated rind
Lime	1 lime, juiced	=	1 to 2 teaspoons juice
Macaroni	1 pound	=	3 cups, uncooked
Macaroni	1 cup, uncooked	=	2 cups, cooked
Marshmallows	¼ pound	=	16 regulation size
Milk	1 quart	=	16 ounces or 4 cups
Milk, sweetened condensed	1 14-ounce can	=	1¼ cups
Milk, evaporated	1 14-ounce can	=	1⅔ cups
Milk, evaporated	1 6-ounce can	=	¾ cup
Molasses	1 cup raw	=	1¼ cups, cooked
Noodles	1 cup, uncooked	=	1¼ cups, cooked
Nut meats	4-ounce package	=	1 cup
Oats, rolled	1 pound	=	5 cups
Orange	1 orange, juiced	=	6 to 8 tablespoons juice
Orange Rind, grated	1 orange, rind of	=	2 tablespoons grated rind
Peanuts	½ pound, shelled	=	1 cup, chopped
Pecans	1 pound, unshelled	=	4 cups, shelled
Prunes	1 pound	=	2½ cups, dried
Raisins	1 pound	=	2½ cups, seeded

21

Raisins, seedless	1 pound	=	3 cups
Rice	1 cup, raw	=	3 to 4 cups cooked
Rice	1 pound	=	2⅓ cups, uncooked
Saccharin	¼ grain	=	1 teaspoon sugar
Salt	1 pound	=	2 cups
Shortening	1 pound	=	2⅜ cups
Sugar, granulated	1 pound	=	2 cups
Sugar, powdered	1 pound	=	3½ cups, sifted
Sugar, brown	1 pound	=	2¼ cups, firmly packed
Sugar, loaf	1 pound	=	50 to 70 lumps
Tapioca, pearl	1 pound	=	2½ cups
Walnuts, black	5½ pounds, unshelled	=	3 cups, chopped
Walnuts, English	2½ pounds, unshelled	=	4 cups, chopped
Yeast	1 ounce	=	1 small compressed square
Yeast	2 ounces	=	1 large family size compressed square

INGREDIENT SUBSTITUTIONS

Measurement			Equivalent
Baking Powder (double-acting)	1 teaspoon	=	1⅓ teaspoons tartrate or calcium phosphate baking powder
Baking Powder (double-acting)	1 teaspoon	=	¼ teaspoon soda plus ½ teaspoon cream of tartar
Baking Powder (double-acting)	1 teaspoon	=	¼ teaspoon soda plus ½ cup sour milk or cream
Bread Crumbs	1 cup	=	¾ cup cracker crumbs
Chocolate, unsweetened	1 ounce	=	⅓ cup cocoa plus 1 tablespoon butter
Cornstarch	1 tablespoon	=	2 tablespoons flour
Cream, thick sour	1 cup	=	⅔ cup sour milk plus ⅓ cup butter
Cream, thin sour	1 cup	=	¾ cup sour milk plus 3 tablespoons butter

Egg Yolks	2 Yolks =	1 whole egg
(for custards and puddings)		
Egg	1 egg =	2 yolks plus 1 tablespoon water
(for cookies)		
Egg Whites	2 =	1 whole egg
Egg (used to thicken	1 =	1½ tablespoons flour OR
custards or sauces)		¾ tablespoon cornstarch
Flour, cake	1 cup =	1 cup all-purpose flour minus
		2 tablespoons
Flour, bread	1 tablespoon =	⅔ tablespoon arrow root
Milk, fresh	1 cup =	½ cup evaporated milk plus
		½ cup water
Milk, fresh	1 cup =	4 tablespoons milk powder plus
		1 cup water
Milk, evaporated	1 cup =	3 cups, whipped
Milk, sour or	1 cup =	1 cup sweet milk plus 1 table-
buttermilk		spoon lemon juice or white
		vinegar
Tapioca, pearl	1 cup =	⅔ cup quick-cooking tapioca

OVEN TEMPERATURES

Degrees Fahrenheit

250 to 300	Slow Oven
300 to 400	Moderate Oven
400 to 450	Hot Oven
450 to 550	Very Hot Oven

INTERPRETING FOREIGN MEASUREMENTS

1 pound or 16 ounces = 454 grams
A scant ¾ cup bread flour = 100 grams
A scant cup cake flour = 100 grams
A scant ½ cup butter = 100 grams
A scant ½ cup sugar = 100 grams
¼ pound sweet chocolate = 113 grams

STANDARD CAN SIZES

Name of Can	Net Weight	Net Product Content	Approx. Cupfuls	Products for Which It Is Used
Infant Food 5 Ounce	4¾ ounces 6 ounces	4¼ fluid ounces 6 fluid ounces	½ ¾	infant foods frozen concentrated fruit juices
Evaporated Milk	6 ounces	6 fluid ounces	⅔	evaporated milk
Small Cranberry	7 ounces	5¼ fluid ounces	⅔	cranberry sauce
8 Ounce	8 ounces	7¾ fluid ounces	1	some vegetables and fruits
No. 1 Picnic	10½ ounces	9½ fluid ounces	1¼	vegetables, some fruit juices, meat, and fish
Evaporated Milk		14½ fluid ounces	1⅔	evaporated milk
Chocolate Syrup	1 pound	13 fluid ounces	1½	chocolate syrup
No. 300	15½ ounces	13½ fluid ounces	1¾	some fruit, juices, soups, vegetables, meat, and fish
No. 1 Tall	1 pound	15 fluid ounces	2	fruits, some

No. 303 Cylinder	1 pound, 5 ounces	1 pint, 3 fluid ounces	2½	tables, some fruits and juices, soups
No. 1 Flat	9 ounces	8 fluid ounces	1	tomato and fruit juices, soups
No. 2	1 pound, 14 ounces	1 pint, 2 fluid ounces	2½	pineapple vegetables, fruit, meat
Shortening	1 pound		2⅜	shortening
No. 1¼	14½ ounces	12½ fluid ounces	1½	pineapple
No. 2½	1 pound, 13 ounces	1 pint, 10 fluid ounces	3½	fruits, some vegetables, some juices
No. 3 Cylinder	3 pounds, 2 ounces	1 quart, 14 fluid ounces	5¾	fruit juices, tomato juice, chicken
Vacuum Coffee	1 pound		5	coffee
Vacuum Coffee	2 pounds		10	coffee
Shortening	3 pounds		7	shortening
No. 5	3 pounds, 10 ounces	1 quart, 1 pint, 4 fluid ounces	6½	fruits, juices, vegetables, specialties
No. 10	6 pounds, 9 ounces	3 quarts	12	vegetables, fruits, juices, some meat and fish products, soups, specialties

TYPES OF BAKING POWDERS

There are three types of baking powders, classified according to ingredients. The label of the baking powder can clearly states which type it is.

Double-acting baking power has been used in testing these high altitude recipes, but other types may be used. When substituting for double-acting powder, 1½ times as much single-action baking powder is required per given amount of double-acting baking powder.

Double-Acting Baking Powder (Sodium aluminum sulfate baking powder)

> Reacts slowly in cold mixture. Releases most of its leavening in baking.
>> Calumet
>> K.C.
>> Davis
>> Clabber Girl
>> and others

Tartrate Baking Powder

> Begins action at room temperature as soon as liquid is added.
>> Royal
>> and others

Calcium Phosphate Baking Powder

> Reacts slowly and requires heat to start leavening action.
>> Rumford
>> Prices
>> and others

Your baking powder is fresh enough for successful use if it bubbles vigorously when mixed with hot water.

YEAST BREADS

Suggestions for Successful Yeast Bread Baking   28
Ingredient Definitions   28
Tips for Handling Ingredients   29
Mixing Tips   29
Pan Preparation   30
How to Shape Rolls   30
Baking Problems and Solutions   31
Removing from Pan and Cooling   32
Tips for Freezing Yeast Breads   32

BREADS

Mrs. Bell's Orange Bread   33
French Bread   34
Multi-Flour Health Bread   35
High Protein Bread   36
White Bread   38
Mother Miller's Whole Wheat Bread or Rolls   40
Rye Bread   42

ROLLS

English Muffins   43
Garlic and Herb Rolls   44
Feathery-Light Rolls   46
Mother Anderson's Wonderful Rolls   47
Brioche   48
Refrigerator Rolls   49

SWEET ROLLS AND COFFEE CAKES

Citrus Roll-Ups   50
Coconut Breakfast Rings   52
German Coffee Cake   53
Foundation Sweet Dough   54
Afternoon Tea Bread   56
Kolački   57

Spaces for Notes pages 37, 39, 41, 45, 58

SUGGESTIONS FOR
SUCCESSFUL YEAST BREAD BAKING

Don't let the modern-day rush keep you from the satisfying age-old, but always new, experience of smelling and eating freshly baked breads.

Baking yeast breads is basically simple. Mixing time is short, but 4 to 5 hours must be allowed for bread to rise and be made ready to bake.

INGREDIENT DEFINITIONS

Use high grade emulsifier-type or hydrogenated-type shortenings (all vegetable or combination vegetable and meat fat oils), if possible.

Use high quality margarine when margarine is specified. In some recipes the flavor will be jeopardized if margarine is substituted for butter.

Use whole sweet milk when milk is denoted.

Do not use soured cream when recipe calls for commercial sour cream.

Yeast is basis of yeast bread, so it is important to understand certain facts about the two varieties of yeast.

Cake yeast is a moist square wrapped in foil, found in the grocer's refrigerated case. It may be kept refrigerated at home for about 2 weeks, or if wrapped in freezer paper or sealed in plastic, it may be kept in freezer for about 4 months. It is beige-grey in color and turns brown when it gets old. Use only when fresh.

Active dry yeast, which comes in hermetically sealed package, contains little yeast granules similar to coarse sand. It may be kept unrefrigerated until date marked plainly on package. It may be used beyond expiration date if always kept in refrigerator.

We recommend refrigerating all yeasts at all times.
One package active dry yeast may be interchanged with one cake compressed yeast and vice versa.

TIPS FOR HANDLING INGREDIENTS

Lukewarm is the very key word in yeast bread and roll making. Water or milk which is too warm destroys the yeast action. Be careful to keep liquids between 75° and 85°F., so that they feel a little cooler than body temperature.

Scalded milk means milk heated over low heat until tiny bubbles form around edge, or a slight froth forms on top. It does *not* mean boiled milk. Rinse pan in water before adding milk. This will prevent milk from sticking during scalding. The reason for scalding is to quicken cooking in cases of custards, etc.

Melting shortening may often be accomplished by adding it to scalded milk, then letting the two cool to lukewarm together.

MIXING TIPS

The first beating of batter (when 1/3 of flour has been added to yeast and liquid ingredients) is most important. Do not stop beating until there are no lumps, and the dough has begun to take shape.

Add remaining flour gradually, *changing from spoon or mixer to hands* as dough becomes stiffer.

After the addition of all ingredients, kneading is usually necessary. Read your recipe carefully for the exceptions.

The technique of kneading starts with pressing the dough with the heels of the hand. Then with fingers grasp outer edge of dough, pulling it to the center and pushing from the center outward with the heel of the hand. Keep rotating the dough and repeating this action until the dough feels very tight, compact, and elastic-like. It will no longer stick to kneading surface, and there will be no stray bits of flour or dough, as the dough will have picked them all up and absorbed them in the kneading process. We find that if you start your mixing in a large, crock-like bowl, you can mix and knead in it as well, thus saving the use of extra equipment.

Put dough in *greased bowl* to rise. Lightly grease exposed surface of dough, or, in some cases, brush with milk. This prevents dough from sticking to cloth and/or a dry crust forming during the rising periods.

Yeast rises more quickly at high altitudes.

Place dough in warm place to rise means at a temperature of

75° to 85°F. The temperature should be even. Drafts, sunlight, or extra heat from radiators and stoves should be avoided. In cold weather a pre-warmed bowl helps the dough rise. Another "tip" is to set dough in pan of water no warmer than 85°F.

Time varies for different doughs to double in bulk. Press top with fingertips. If imprint remains, the dough is probably ready to punch down.

To punch down, make fist of hand and gently press center of dough. With fingers grasp outer edges of dough and work edges of dough to center. Turn dough bottom side up and knead very lightly.

To shape loaves it sometimes helps to wait a few minutes after the punching-down and kneading steps. When making loaves, divide dough into equal parts (in halves for two loaves, into fourths for four loaves, and so forth). Form balls, then press down and pull out to shape loaves. Place in prepared pans and lightly grease tops of loaves before covering with damp cloth. Let rise until center of dough is well rounded above pan.

PAN PREPARATION

Use only unsalted and waterless fats. Hydrogenated shortenings may be used but emulsified shortenings are not as satisfactory because of the liquid in them.

HOW TO SHAPE ROLLS

Cloverleaf: (a) form dough into rolls about 1 inch in diameter, (b) with sharp knife, or by pinching with greased fingertips, cut off 1 inch, (c) roll in palm of hand to ball shape and dip in melted butter or margarine, (d) place 3 balls in each greased muffin pan cup.

Clothespin: (a) on lightly floured surface roll dough to 1/4 inch thickness, (b) cut into strips 1/2 inch wide, (c) wrap dough lightly around greased clothespins (not spring type), (d) let double in bulk and bake as directed.

Breadsticks: (a) roll and cut in strips as for clothespin rolls, (b) gently roll strips back and forth between palms of hand until dough is 10 inches in length, (c) place sticks 1 inch apart on greased cookie sheet.

Crescents: (a) roll dough 1/4 inch thick, the shape and size of a pie pan, (b) brush dough well with melted butter or margarine, (c) cut into six or eight pie-shaped wedges, (d) roll each piece from the wide end, stretching dough gently as it is rolled until all dough is used, (e) place with point down and gently curve into crescent on greased cookie sheet.

Parkerhouse: (a) roll dough 1/4 inch thick, (b) cut with *floured* cookie cutter to desired size round, (c) place dab of butter in center and fold in half, (d) brush lightly with butter and place on greased cookie sheet.

Old-Fashioned: (a) with greased fingers, pinch off about 2 tablespoons of dough, (b) shape into ball by rolling between palms of hands, (c) dip in melted butter or margarine and place in greased layer or oblong pan.

Butterfly: (a) roll dough 1/8 inch thick into rectangular shape, (b) brush with melted butter or margarine, (c) cut into strips 1½ inches wide, (d) place 6 or 7 strips on top of one another, (e) with sharp knife, cut into 1½ inch wide squares, (f) place with cut side up in greased muffin pan cups.

Cover rolls with damp cloth and let rise until doubled in bulk.

BAKING PROBLEMS AND SOLUTIONS

If bread is too high on one side: (a) pans are too near sides of oven, causing uneven rising and browning. If bread is too brown on top: (a) pans are placed too near top of oven, (b) oven too hot. If bread is too brown on sides: (a) oven too hot, (b) oven too full, (c) pans are too close to oven sides.

Use only one rack of oven when baking bread. (We learned this the hard way. The bread rises too high to use more than one rack.) If pans smaller than 10"x5"x4" are used, it may be possible to place up to four pans on one rack. If so, do not crowd pans together or place too near oven sides. Half way through baking, it is well to reverse pans from front to back of oven and inside edge to outside edge. This helps loaves to brown more evenly.

REMOVING FROM PAN AND COOLING

Bread is done when the loaf shrinks from sides of pan. When removed from pan and tapped on the bottom, the loaf will sound "hollow" if done. If bread is not done, it may be returned to oven for more baking.

When bread is done turn out of pans *immediately.* Cool on wire rack or across top of pans.

For *crisp* crust, do not grease loaf tops when removed from oven. For *very crisp* crusts, place pan of boiling water in lowest shelf of oven during baking. For *soft tender* crust, brush loaves with butter or margarine upon removal from oven. For *glazed* crust, brush with milk before baking, or mix 1 tablespoon water and 1 egg together and brush on unbaked loaves (French bread).

To cut bread evenly it should be cool to cold, but we heartily recommend eating warm bread with butter and honey, even though the slices are rough and what's left of the loaf (maybe none) looks crudely cut!

TIPS FOR FREEZING YEAST BREADS

Almost all yeast breads freeze handsomely.

Always *cool* any baked yeast bread before placing in the freezer. If wrapped in moisture-vaporproof (film, foil, or freezer paper) wrapper, most yeast breads will keep successfully for up to 12 months.

Freezing *unbaked* yeast breads or rolls is usually less satisfactory than freezing a baked yeast product. However, if you choose to freeze unbaked yeast products, prepare dough as recipe directs, letting it double in bulk for the final time. Place in greased pan in which it is to be baked, grease top, wrap well, and freeze. Store up to two weeks only.

Freeze partially baked yeast products this way. Let rise only half way, then bake at about 325°F. for half the regular time, or until pale beige-tan in color. *Cool.* Wrap properly for freezer and freeze. Store up to 2 to 3 weeks only.

Breads

MRS. BELL'S ORANGE BREAD

Mrs. Bell's generosity in sharing this recipe is greatly appreciated.

Oven temperature: preheat to
  400°F.
Baking time: about 45 minutes

Yield: 3 small loaves
Pan: three 7"x4"x3" pans,
  well greased

1 cake yeast
1 cup *lukewarm* water
1½ cups *lukewarm* orange
  juice
few drops orange food
  coloring, if desired

⅓ cup shortening
⅔ cup granulated sugar
8 cups all-purpose flour, sifted
2 teaspoons salt
4 tablespoons grated orange
  rind

1.   In bowl large enough to accommodate raised dough, stir yeast into *lukewarm* water. Add *lukewarm* orange juice and food coloring.
2.   Cream shortening and sugar together. Add to yeast mixture.
3.   Sift flour once before measuring.
4.   Add 3 cups of flour to yeast mixture. With electric mixer or spoon, beat batter until smooth and satiny.
5.   Grease bowl. Put dough in it. Lightly grease exposed surface of dough. Cover bowl with damp cloth, leaving edges on outside of bowl. Away from drafts, let dough rise in warm place (about 80°F.) until light (about 1½ hours).
6.   Punch down the dough when it is light. Add remaining flour, salt, and orange rind, changing from spoon or mixer to hands as dough becomes stiffer. Knead lightly. Re-cover with damp cloth. Let rise until doubled in bulk.
7.   Punch down the dough when it is doubled in bulk. Work the edges to center, turn the bottom side up and knead very lightly. Divide dough into 3 equal parts.
8.   Shape dough into loaves. Place in three well greased 7"x4"x3" pans.
9.   Brush tops with melted butter or margarine. Re-cover with damp cloth. Let rise until center of dough is well rounded above pan.
10. Bake at 400°F. for about 45 minutes, or until done.
11. Turn out immediately to cool on wire rack or across pans.

FRENCH BREAD

Theories are legion regarding ingredients and methods best for making REAL French Bread. Opinions are always the same. This type bread is most popular.

Oven temperature: preheat to 350°F.
Baking time: 50 to 60 minutes

Yield: 1 large loaf or 2 small loaves
Pan: greased cookie sheet

1 package active dry yeast
1 tablespoon granulated sugar
1¼ cups *lukewarm* water
¼ cup scalded milk

1½ teaspoons salt
4 cups all-purpose flour, sifted
1 egg white mixed in 1 tablespoon water

1. In bowl large enough to accommodate raised dough, stir yeast and sugar into *lukewarm* water to dissolve.
2. Scald milk. Add salt. Cool to *lukewarm*. Add to yeast mixture.
3. Sift flour once before measuring.
4. Add 1/3 of flour. With electric mixer or spoon, beat batter until smooth and satiny. Add remaining flour gradually, changing from spoon or mixer to hands as the dough becomes stiffer.
5. Turn dough onto floured board. Knead until elastic (tight-feeling), smooth, and no longer sticky enough to adhere to board, *OR* continue to knead in mixing bowl until all flour and dough are cleaned from sides of bowl by kneading process.
6. Put dough in bowl. Cover with damp cloth, leaving edges on outside of bowl. Let rise in warm place (about 80°F.) until dough is a little more than doubled in bulk.
7. Punch dough down when it is a little more than doubled in bulk. Pat out dough on lightly floured board into one or two oblongs (depending on whether or not 1 or 2 loaves are desired). Roll the dough toward you, pressing outward and shaping the dough as you do, until a long, thin roll is formed.
8. Place loaf, or loaves, on greased cookie sheet. With scissors cut diagonal slashes across top. Brush tops with warm milk. Recover with damp cloth and let rise until dough is a little more than doubled in bulk.
9. Brush with egg white mixed with water.
10. Bake at 350°F. for 50 to 60 minutes.
Note: A pan of boiling water set in oven during baking makes bread crustier.

11. Turn out immediately to cool on wire rack or across top of pans.

MULTI-FLOUR HEALTH BREAD

Nutritional combination of graham, rye, and white flours.

Oven temperature: preheat to 375°F.
Baking time: 45 to 55 minutes

Yield: 2 loaves
Pan: two 9″x5″x3″ loaf pans, greased

1 package active dry yeast
3 cups *lukewarm* water
¼ cup melted butter
⅓ cup molasses
1 tablespoon salt

6¼ cups all-purpose flour, sifted
1½ cups graham flour
1½ cups rye flour

1. In bowl large enough to accommodate raised dough, stir yeast into *lukewarm* water to dissolve.
2. Stir butter, molasses, and salt into yeast mixture.
3. Sift all-purpose flour before measuring. Mix flours together.
4. Add 1/3 of flour. With electric mixer or spoon, beat batter until smooth and satiny. Add remaining flour gradually, changing from spoon or mixer to hands as the dough becomes stiffer.
5. Turn dough onto floured board. Knead until elastic (tight-feeling), smooth, and no longer sticky enough to adhere to board, OR continue to knead in mixing bowl until all flour and dough are cleaned from sides of bowl in kneading process.
6. Grease bowl. Put dough in it. Lightly grease exposed surface of dough. Cover bowl with damp cloth, leaving edges on outside of bowl. Let rise in warm place (about 80°F.) until dough is doubled in bulk.
7. Punch down the dough when it is doubled in bulk. Work the edges to center, turn dough bottom side up, and knead very lightly. Divide dough into 2 equal parts.
8. Shape dough into loaves. Place in two greased 9″x5″x3″ loaf pans.
9. Brush tops with melted butter. Re-cover with damp cloth. Let rise until center of dough is well rounded above pan.
10. Bake at 375°F. for 45 to 55 minutes, or until done.
11. Turn out immediately to cool on wire rack or across tops of pans.

HIGH PROTEIN BREAD

Three energy-giving flours make this bread rate high with nutritionists.

Oven temperature: preheat to
    375°F.
Baking time: 45 minutes

Yield: 2 large or 4 small loaves
Pan: two 10″x6″x3″ loaf pans,
    or four 7″x4″x3″ loaf pans,
    greased

2 packages active dry yeast
½ cup *lukewarm* water
2 cups scalded milk
½ cup non-fat dry milk
    powder
1 tablespoon melted butter or
    margarine

2 tablespoons honey or
    molasses
2 teaspoons salt
4 cups 100 percent whole
    wheat flour
2 cups coarse graham flour
1 cup Roman meal

1.   In bowl large enough to accommodate raised dough, stir yeast into *lukewarm* water to dissolve.

2. Scald milk. Stir in butter or margarine, dry milk powder, honey or molasses, and salt.

3.   Add 2 cups whole wheat flour to yeast mixture. With electric mixer or spoon, beat batter until smooth and satiny. This makes what is known as a sponge.

4.   Set in warm place (about 80°F.) until light and full of bubbles.

5. When sponge is light and bubbly, add remaining 2 cups whole wheat flour, graham flour and Roman meal gradually, changing from mixer or spoon to hands as dough becomes stiffer.

6.   Turn dough onto floured board. Knead until elastic (tight-feeling), smooth, and no longer sticky enough to adhere to board, *OR* continue to knead in mixing bowl until all flour and dough are cleaned from sides of bowl by kneading process.

7.   Grease bowl. Put dough in it. Lightly grease exposed surface of dough. Cover with damp cloth, leaving edges on outside of bowl. Let rise in warm place (about 80°F.) until dough is doubled in bulk.

8.   Punch down the dough when it is doubled in bulk. Work the edges to center, turn the bottom side up and knead very lightly. Divide dough into 2 or 4 equal parts.

9. Shape dough into loaves. Place in two greased 10"x4"x3" or four 7"x4"x3" pans.

10. Brush tops with melted butter or margarine. Re-cover with damp cloth. Let rise until center of dough is well rounded above pan.

11. Bake at 375°F. for 45 minutes, or until done.

12. Turn out immediately to cool on wire rack or across top of pans.

NOTES

WHITE BREAD

The boys are always lined up at the oven when it is time to take the bread out. Armed with honey and butter, they polish off a loaf or two in no time.

Oven temperature: preheat to 425°F.
Baking time: 45 to 50 minutes

Yield: 2 loaves
Pan: two 9"x5"x3" loaf pans, well greased

1 package active dry yeast
1¼ cups *lukewarm* water
1 cup scalded milk
1 tablespoon melted shortening

1 tablespoon melted butter
2 tablespoons granulated sugar
2 teaspoons salt
6 cups all-purpose flour, sifted

1. In bowl large enough to accommodate raised dough, stir yeast into ¼ cup *lukewarm* water to dissolve.
2. Scald milk. Stir in shortening, butter, sugar, salt, and 1 cup water. Cool to *lukewarm*. Add to yeast mixture.
3. Sift flour once before measuring.
4. Add 1/3 of flour. With electric mixer, or spoon, beat batter until smooth and satiny. Add remaining flour gradually, changing from spoon or mixer to hands as the dough becomes stiffer.
5. Turn dough onto floured board. Knead until elastic (tight-feeling), smooth, and no longer sticky enough to adhere to board, *OR* continue to knead in mixing bowl until all flour and dough are cleaned from sides of bowl by kneading process.
6. Grease bowl. Put dough in it. Lightly grease exposed surface of dough. Cover bowl with damp cloth, leaving edges on outside of bowl. Let rise in warm place (about 80°F.) until doubled in bulk.
7. Punch down the dough when it is doubled in bulk. Work the edges to center, turn dough bottom side up, and knead very lightly.
8. Lightly grease, re-cover with damp cloth, and let rise again until almost doubled in bulk.
9. Punch dough down and divide into 2 equal parts.
10. Shape dough into loaves. Place in two well greased 9"x5"x3" loaf pans.
11. Brush tops with melted butter or margarine. Re-cover with

damp cloth. Let rise until center of dough is well rounded above pan.

12. Bake at 425°F. for 15 minutes. REDUCE oven temperature to 350°F. and bake 30 to 35 minutes longer, or until done.

13. Turn out immediately to cool on wire rack or across top of pans.

NOTES

MOTHER MILLER'S WHOLE WHEAT BREAD OR ROLLS

This makes wonderfully healthful bread and the crunchiest toast imaginable.

Oven temperature: preheat to 350°F.

Baking time: 50 to 60 minutes

Yield: 2 loaves, or 2 dozen rolls

Pan: two 9"x5"x3" loaf pans or 2½"x1¼" muffin pans, well greased

1 cake yeast
1 cup *lukewarm* water
1 cup scalded milk
2 tablespoons melted butter or shortening

4 tablespoons molasses or brown sugar, firmly packed
1 teaspoon salt
3 cups whole wheat, or graham flour, sifted
2 cups all-purpose flour, sifted

1. In bowl large enough to accommodate raised dough, stir yeast into *lukewarm* water to dissolve.
2. Scald milk. Stir in butter or shortening, sugar or molasses, and salt. Cool to *lukewarm*. Add to yeast mixture.
3. Sift flour once before measuring.
4. Add 1/3 of flour. With electric mixer or spoon, beat batter until smooth and satiny. Add remaining flour gradually, changing from spoon or mixer to hands as the dough becomes stiffer.
5. Turn dough onto floured board. Knead until elastic (tight-feeling), smooth, and no longer sticky enough to adhere to board, OR continue to knead in mixing bowl until all flour and dough are cleaned from sides of bowl by kneading process.
6. Grease bowl. Put dough in it. Lightly grease exposed surface of dough. Cover bowl with damp cloth. Let rise in warm place (about 80°F.) until doubled in bulk.
7. Punch down the dough when it is doubled in bulk. Work the edges to center, turn dough bottom side up, and knead very lightly.
8. Shape dough into two loaves, or rolls. (See pages 30-31.)
9. Place in well greased 9"x5"x3" loaf pans or 2½"x1¼" muffin pan cups.
10. Brush tops with melted butter or margarine. Re-cover with damp cloth. Let rise until center of dough is well rounded above

center of pan, or until rolls are almost doubled in bulk.

11. Bake at 350°F. for 50 to 60 minutes, loaves; or 25 minutes, rolls.

Note: 1 cup all-purpose flour and 4 cups whole wheat or graham flours may be substituted for flours specified above.

NOTES

RYE BREAD

Homemade rye bread and a baked ham dinner were made for each other.

Oven temperature: preheat to
  400°-425°F.
Baking time: 50 to 60 minutes

Yield: 2 loaves
Pan: two 9″x5″x3″ loaf pans,
  well greased

1 cake yeast
¾ cup *lukewarm* water
1 cup milk
1 tablespoon melted
  shortening
2 tablespoons molasses

1 tablespoon salt
4 cups rye flour, sifted
2 cups all-purpose flour, sifted
1 tablespoon caraway seeds,
  if desired

1.   In bowl large enough to accommodate raised dough, stir yeast into *lukewarm* water to dissolve.
2.   Scald milk. Stir in shortening, molasses, and salt. Cool to *lukewarm*. Add to yeast mixture.
3.   Sift flours once before measuring. Mix and sift flours together.
4.   Add 1/3 of flour. With electric mixer or spoon, beat batter until smooth and satiny. Add remaining flour gradually, changing from spoon or mixer to hands as the dough becomes stiffer. Blend in caraway seeds, if desired.
5.   Turn dough onto floured board. Knead lightly.
6.   Grease bowl. Put dough in it. Lightly grease exposed surface of dough. Cover bowl with damp cloth. Let rise in warm place (about 80°F.) until dough is doubled in bulk.
7.   Punch down the dough when it is doubled in bulk. Work the edges to the center, turn dough bottom side up, and knead very lightly.
8.   Lightly grease, re-cover with damp cloth, and let rise again until almost doubled in bulk.
9.   Punch dough down and divide into 2 equal parts.
10.   Shape dough into loaves. Place in two well greased 9″x5″x3″ pans.
11.   Brush tops with melted butter or margarine. Re-cover with damp cloth. Let rise until center of dough is well rounded above pan.
12.   Bake at 400°-425°F. for 50 to 60 minutes.

Rolls

ENGLISH MUFFINS

Split and toast before serving.

Yield: about 24 muffins

Pan: griddle or skillet, ungreased

2 packages active dry yeast
½ cup *lukewarm* water
1½ cups scalded milk
2 tablespoons melted butter
  or margarine

2 tablespoons granulated
  sugar
1½ teaspoons salt
4½ cups all-purpose flour,
  sifted
cornmeal

1.   In bowl large enough to accommodate raised dough, stir yeast into *lukewarm* water.
2.   Scald milk. Stir in butter or margarine, sugar, and salt. Cool to *lukewarm*. Add to yeast mixture. Let stand 5 minutes before stirring.
3.   Sift flour once before measuring.
4.   Add 1/3 of flour to yeast mixture. With electric mixer or spoon, beat batter until smooth and satiny. Add remaining flour gradually, changing from spoon or mixer to hands as the dough becomes stiffer.
5.   Grease bowl. Put dough in it. Lightly grease exposed surface of dough. Cover bowl with damp cloth, leaving edges on outside of bowl. Let rise in warm place (about 80°F.) until doubled in bulk, or until very light.
6.   Punch down the dough when it is doubled in bulk. On lightly floured surface, roll out dough to 1/2 inch thick. Cut with 3½-inch round cutter. Lightly coat both sides of cut out dough with cornmeal. Let rise in warm place until 1 inch thick.
7.   Bake on medium hot ungreased skillet or griddle, or electric skillet set at 350°F. It will take from 5 to 7 minutes to brown each side. Place cooked muffins in oven preheated to 350°F. while cooking remaining muffins.

GARLIC AND HERB ROLLS

These hot rolls are wonderful at buffet parties. Serve them already buttered. Your guests will be back for more.

Oven temperature: preheat to 400°F.
Baking time: about 25 minutes

Yield: 32 rolls
Pan: greased cookie sheet

2 cakes yeast
2 cups *lukewarm* water
3 tablespoons melted shortening
2 tablespoons granulated sugar
2 teaspoons salt
4½ cups all-purpose flour, sifted
1½ cups all-bran cereal

3 tablespoons fresh parsley, chopped
2 teaspoons caraway seed
1 teaspoon celery seed
¼ teaspoon oregano, ground
1 cup butter or margarine
4 small cloves garlic, chopped fine or put through garlic press

1. In bowl large enough to accommodate raised dough, stir yeast into *lukewarm* water to dissolve.
2. Add shortening, sugar, and salt to yeast mixture.
3. Sift flour once before measuring. Mix flour, all-bran cereal, parsley, caraway seed, celery seed, and oregano together
4. Add 1/3 of flour. With electric mixer or spoon, beat batter until smooth and satiny. Add remaining flour gradually, changing from spoon or mixer to hands as the dough stiffens.
5. Turn dough onto floured board. Knead until elastic (tight-feeling), smooth, and no longer sticky enough to adhere to board, OR continue to knead in mixing bowl until all flour and dough are cleaned from sides of bowl by kneading process.
6. Grease bowl. Put dough in it. Lightly grease exposed surface of dough. Cover with damp cloth, leaving edges on outside of bowl. Let rise in warm place (about 80°F.) until doubled in bulk.
7. When dough is doubled in bulk, punch it down and divide into 4 equal parts.
8. Add minced garlic to soft butter or margarine for topping.
9. On lightly floured board, roll each part into round shape the size of a pie tin.

10. Brush well with butter and garlic mixture. Cut each round into 8 pie-shaped pieces with sharp knife or pastry cutter.

11. Beginning at wide end of each wedge, roll up dough, stretching it gently as it is rolled until entire wedge is rolled. Place roll on greased cookie sheet with point underneath.

12. Brush tops with melted butter or margarine (not garlic-butter mixture) and cover with damp cloth. Let rise until dough is doubled in bulk.

13. Bake at 400°F. for about 25 minutes.

14. Remove from oven. Brush immediately over the tops of each with remaining butter-garlic mixture.

NOTES

FEATHERY-LIGHT ROLLS

It is a treat to be invited out to dinner and have these light and heavenly rolls served.

Oven temperature: preheat to
375°F.
Baking time: 15 to 20 minutes

Yield: 3 dozen rolls
Pan: 2½"x1¼" muffin
pans, well greased

1 cake yeast
¼ cup *lukewarm* water
1¾ cups scalded milk
¼ cup melted butter

3 tablespoons granulated
sugar
2 teaspoons salt
2 eggs, beaten
5½ cups all-purpose flour,
sifted

1.　In bowl large enough to accommodate raised dough, stir yeast into *lukewarm* water to dissolve.
2.　Scald milk. Stir in butter, sugar, and salt.
3.　Add beaten eggs.
4.　Sift flour once before measuring.
5.　Add 1/3 of flour. With electric mixer or spoon, beat batter until smooth and satiny. Add remaining flour gradually, changing from spoon or mixer to hands as dough becomes stiffer.
6.　Grease bowl. Put dough in it. Lightly grease exposed surface of dough. Cover bowl with damp cloth, leaving edges on outside of bowl. Let rise in warm place (about 80°F.) until dough is doubled in bulk.
7.　Punch down the dough when it is doubled in bulk. Work the edges to center, turn dough bottom side up, and knead very lightly.
8.　With a spoon or greased fingertips, fill well greased 2½"x1¼" muffin pan cups 1/2 full.
9.　Brush tops with melted butter or milk. Re-cover with damp cloth. Let rise until doubled in bulk.
10.　Bake at 375°F. for 15 to 20 minutes.

MOTHER ANDERSON'S WONDERFUL ROLLS

Mother says, "If you ever taste these, you will never buy a roll."

Oven temperature: preheat to
  400°F.
Baking time: 8 minutes

Yield: 3 dozen rolls
Pan: greased cookie sheet

2 cakes yeast
1½ cups scalded milk
½ cup melted butter
½ cup granulated sugar

½ teaspoon salt
3 eggs, beaten
5 cups all-purpose flour, sifted

1. Place yeast in bowl large enough to accommodate raised dough.
2. Scald milk. Stir in butter, sugar, and salt. Cool to *lukewarm*. Add ½ cup milk to yeast mixture. Stir to dissolve. Add remaining milk.
3. Add slightly beaten eggs.
4. Sift flour once before measuring.
5. Add 1/3 of flour. With electric mixer or spoon, beat batter until smooth and satiny. Add remaining flour gradually, changing from spoon or mixer to hands as dough becomes stiffer.
6. Grease bowl. Put dough in it. Lightly grease exposed surface of dough. Cover bowl with damp cloth, leaving edges on outside of bowl. Let rise in warm place (about 80°F.) until dough is doubled in bulk.
7. Punch dough down and form rolls.
8. Divide dough into 6 equal parts.
9. Roll each part into a round shape the size of a pie pan.
10. Brush dough well with melted butter, then cut into 6 pie-shaped wedges. Roll each wedge from the wide end, stretching dough gently as it is rolled until the entire wedge is rolled. Place roll on greased cookie sheet with point on bottom.
11. Brush tops with melted butter or margarine. Re-cover with damp cloth. Let rise until dough is doubled in bulk.
12. Bake at 400°F. for 8 minutes.

BRIOCHE

A slightly sweet breakfast roll that is delicious served warm with butter and jelly.

Oven temperature: preheat to 400°F.
Baking time: about 20 minutes

Yield: 30 to 36 rolls
Pan: 2½"x1¼" muffin pans, greased

1 cup scalded milk
¾ cup melted butter or margarine
½ cup granulated sugar
1 teaspoon salt
2 cakes yeast
4 eggs, beaten
2 egg yolks, beaten

4½ cups all-purpose flour, sifted
½ teaspoon lemon extract OR 1 teaspoon lemon rind, grated
6 tablespoons granulated sugar dissolved in 2 table-spoons milk

1.   Scald milk. Stir in butter or margarine, sugar, and salt. Cool to *lukewarm.*
2.   In bowl large enough to accommodate raised dough, stir yeast into *lukewarm* milk.
3.   Add beaten eggs and egg yolks and lemon extract or rind.
4.   Sift flour once before measuring.
5.   Add 1/3 of flour. With electric mixer or spoon, beat batter until smooth and satiny. Add remaining flour gradually.
6.   Knead dough thoroughly. Dough may be sticky.
7.   Grease bowl. Put dough in it. Lightly grease exposed surface of dough. Cover bowl with damp cloth, leaving edges on outside of bowl. Let rise in warm place (about 80°F.) for six hours.
8.   Punch down the dough and refrigerate overnight; *OR* punch down dough and shape.
9.   Dough may be rolled into 1½-inch balls and placed in greased 2½"x1¼" muffin pan cups, or greased muffin pan cups may be filled 1/3 full with dough. Brush tops of rolls with melted butter. Re-cover with damp cloth. Let rise until doubled in bulk.
10.   Brush with 2 tablespoons of milk mixed with 6 tablespoons sugar.
11.   Bake at 400°F. for about 20 minutes.

REFRIGERATOR ROLLS

This is the way to have fresh-baked rolls every day without fuss or muss.

Oven temperature: preheat to
   400°F.
Baking time: 8 to 12 minutes

Yield: 2 to 3 dozen rolls
Pan: 2½"x1¼" muffin
   pans, greased

1 cake yeast
1 cup *lukewarm* water
⅔ cup melted butter or
   margarine
½ cup granulated sugar

1 teaspoon salt
3 eggs, beaten
4½ cups all-purpose flour,
   sifted

1. In bowl large enough to accommodate raised dough, stir yeast into *lukewarm* water to dissolve.
2. Add butter or margarine, sugar, salt, and eggs to yeast mixture.
3. Sift flour once before measuring.
4. Add 1/3 of flour. With electric mixer or spoon, beat batter until smooth and satiny. Add remaining flour gradually, changing from spoon or mixer to hands as dough becomes stiffer. Knead until all flour and dough are cleaned from sides of bowl by kneading process.
5. Grease bowl. Put dough in it. Lightly grease exposed surface of dough.
6. Cover dough with damp cloth. Put dough in refrigerator from 12 to 24 hours. When dough has doubled in bulk, punch it down to permit gases to escape.
7. With greased fingers or spoon, take out quantity needed 4 hours before baking.
8. Place the dough in greased 2½"x1¼" muffin pan cups, filling each cup 1/2 full. Brush the tops of rolls with melted butter. Cover with damp cloth and let rise until doubled in bulk.
9. Bake at 400°F. for 8 to 12 minutes. Brush with butter upon removal from oven.
Note: These rolls may be shaped into any of the conventional types of individual rolls. (See pages 30-31.)

Sweet Rolls and Coffee Cakes

CITRUS ROLL-UPS

These orange-flavored rolls are worth the time it takes to make them.

Oven temperature: preheat to
  425°F.
Baking time: 15 minutes

Yield: 18 to 24 rolls
Pan: well greased cookie sheet

1 cake yeast
¾ cup *lukewarm* water
¾ cup scalded milk
½ cup minus 1 tablespoon
  melted butter

⅓ cup granulated sugar OR
  ¼ cup honey
1 teaspoon salt
2 eggs, beaten
4 cups all-purpose flour, sifted

1.   In bowl large enough to accommodate raised dough, stir yeast into *lukewarm* water to dissolve.
2.   Scald milk. Stir in butter, sugar or honey, and salt. *Cool to lukewarm.* Add to yeast mixture.
3.   Add well beaten eggs, mixing thoroughly.
4.   Sift flour once before measuring.
5.   Add 1/3 of flour. With electric mixer or spoon, beat batter until smooth and satiny. Add remaining flour gradually, changing from spoon or mixer to hands as dough becomes stiffer. Knead lightly.
6.   Grease bowl. Put dough in it. Lightly grease exposed surface of dough. Cover bowl with damp cloth, leaving edges on outside of bowl. Let dough rise in warm place (about 80°F.) until it is doubled in bulk.
7.   Punch down the dough when it is doubled in bulk. Work the edges to center, turn dough bottom side up, and knead very lightly.
8.   Lightly grease, re-cover with damp cloth, and let rise again until almost doubled in bulk.
9.   Roll out on lightly floured board to about 1/4 inch thick.
10. Spread with filling.

¼ cup melted butter
4 tablespoons granulated
  sugar

¼ cup minus 2 teaspoons
  orange juice
1 teaspoon lemon juice
1 teaspoon cinnamon

11. Combine all ingredients. Mix thoroughly.
12. Spread filling on rolled out dough.
13. Roll rectangle as for jelly roll, starting with wide side. Seal edge of dough by moistening and pinching it to main roll. Cut into 3/4 inch slices and place on well greased cookie sheet.
14. Cover roll with damp cloth and let rise until almost doubled in bulk.
15. Bake at 425°F. for 15 minutes. Cool and frost.

3 tablespoons butter
3 tablespoons granulated
  sugar
1 cup plus 1 tablespoon
  powdered sugar, sifted
¼ teaspoon salt

3 tablespoons cream
3 tablespoons orange juice
1 teaspoon lemon juice
2 tablespoons orange rind,
  grated

1. Combine all ingredients and beat to a smooth consistency.
2. Spread on cooled rolls.

COCONUT BREAKFAST RINGS

More thoughtful and party-like than toast, these are rich and pretty to serve at a brunch.

Oven temperature: preheat to 375°F.
Baking time: 15 minutes

Yield: 12 large rolls
Pan: greased cookie sheet

2 packages active dry yeast
¼ cup *lukewarm* water
¾ cup scalded milk
¼ cup melted butter or margarine

½ cup granulated sugar
1 teaspoon salt
2 eggs, beaten
5 cups all-purpose flour, sifted

1. In bowl large enough to accommodate raised dough, stir yeast into *lukewarm* water to dissolve.
2. Scald milk. Stir in butter, sugar, and salt. Cool to *lukewarm*. Add to yeast mixture.
3. Add beaten eggs.
4. Sift flour once before measuring.
5. Add 1/3 of flour. With electric mixer or spoon, beat batter until smooth and satiny. Add remaining flour gradually, changing from spoon or mixer to hands as dough stiffens.
6. Continue to knead in mixing bowl until elastic.
7. Lightly grease exposed surface of dough. Cover with damp cloth, leaving edges on outside of bowl. Let rise in warm place (about 80° F.) until doubled in bulk.
8. Make filling.

FILLING

½ cup butter
½ cup powdered sugar, sifted

1 cup grated coconut
½ teaspoon almond extract
½ teaspoon salt

9. Mix all ingredients together. Set aside.
10. Punch down the dough when it is doubled in bulk. Knead very lightly.

11. Turn dough onto floured board. Roll out to form rectangle about 1/2 inch thick. Spread one-half of rectangle with filling; fold other half over it and pinch edges together.

12. Cut rectangle into 24 equal strips about 1 inch wide. Pinch ends of two strips together and twist. Join ends into ring and pinch to seal and hold together. Repeat, making 12 rings.

13. Place rings on greased cookie sheet. Brush tops lightly with melted butter. Cover with damp cloth. Let rise until doubled in bulk.

14. Bake at 375°F. for about 15 minutes.

15. While still warm, glaze.

GLAZE

1 cup powdered sugar, sifted	1 tablespoon coffee cream
	½ teaspoon vanilla

Mix all ingredients thoroughly. Spread on warm rolls.

GERMAN COFFEE CAKE

Old-fashioned and apple-filled, this coffee cake is one you will want to be sure to serve.

Oven temperature: preheat to 375°F.
Baking time: 35 to 40 minutes

Yield: 8 to 12 servings
Pan: 13"x9"x2" oblong pan, greased

1 package active dry yeast	1 teaspoon salt
2 tablespoons *lukewarm* water	1 egg, unbeaten
½ cup scalded milk	2½ cups all-purpose flour, sifted
2 tablespoons melted butter	
2 tablespoons granulated sugar	

TOPPING

3 cups apples, pared and sliced ¼ inch thick	2 tablespoons butter
1 cup granulated sugar	1 egg, beaten
½ teaspoon cinnamon	⅓ cup coffee cream

1.   In bowl large enough to accommodate raised dough, stir yeast into *lukewarm* water to dissolve.
2.   Scald milk. Stir in butter, sugar, and salt. Cool to *lukewarm*. Add to yeast mixture. Add egg.
3.   Sift flour once before measuring.
4.   Add 1/3 of flour. With electric mixer or spoon, beat batter until smooth and satiny. Add remaining flour gradually, changing from spoon or mixer to hands as dough becomes stiffer.
5.   Grease bowl. Put dough in it. Lightly grease exposed surface of dough. Cover bowl with damp cloth, leaving edges on outside of bowl. Let rise in warm place (about 80°F.) until doubled in bulk.
6.   Punch down the dough when it is doubled in bulk. Spread it in greased 13"x9"x2" oblong pan.
7.   Arrange pared and sliced apples in rows, covering top of cake completely.
8.   Combine sugar, cinnamon, and butter thoroughly. Reserve 2 tablespoons. Sprinkle remainder over apples.
9.   Cover with damp cloth. Let rise until dough is doubled in bulk.
10.   Bake at 375°F. for 20 to 25 minutes, or until light golden brown.
11.   Blend egg and coffee cream together. Pour over coffee cake and bake about 15 minutes longer.
12.   When done sprinkle with remaining cinnamon and sugar mixture. Serve warm.

FOUNDATION SWEET DOUGH

There is nothing better than a freshly baked, still-warm-from-the-oven cinnamon roll.

Oven temperature: preheat to
   375°-400°F.
Baking time: 20 to 25 minutes

Yield: 3½ to 4 dozen rolls
Pan: 12"x8"x2" oblong pan,
   well greased

2 cakes yeast
½ cup plus 1 tablespoon
   granulated sugar
1 cup *lukewarm* water
1 cup scalded milk
6 tablespoons melted
   shortening

1 teaspoon salt
3 eggs, beaten
7 cups all-purpose flour, sifted
butter,
brown sugar
cinnamon
raisins and/or nuts, if desired

54

1. In bowl large enough to accommodate raised dough, stir yeast and 1 tablespoon of sugar into *lukewarm* water to dissolve.
2. Scald milk. Stir in shortening, ½ cup sugar, and salt. Cool to *lukewarm*. Add to yeast mixture.
3. Add beaten eggs.
4. Sift flour once before measuring.
5. Add 1/3 of flour. With electric mixer or spoon, beat batter until smooth and satiny. Add remaining flour gradually, changing from spoon or mixer to hands as the dough becomes stiffer.
6. Continue to knead in mixing bowl until elastic.
7. Lightly grease exposed surface of dough. Cover bowl with damp cloth, leaving edges on outside of bowl. Let rise in warm place (about 80° F.) until doubled in bulk.
8. Punch down the dough when it is doubled in bulk.
9. Roll out dough in one large rectangle, 1/4 inch thick. Brush the dough generously with butter. Sprinkle generous amounts of brown sugar and cinnamon over butter. Raisins and/or nuts may be scattered over dough, too.
10. Roll rectangle as for jelly roll, starting with wide side. With sharp knife, cut into 3/4 inch slices and place in well greased 12"x8"x2" oblong pan.
11. Let rise until dough is almost doubled in bulk.
12. Bake at 375°-400°F. for 20 to 25 minutes.

VARIATION

For caramel buns, cream 6 tablespoons shortening and 6 table-spoons brown sugar, firmly packed. Spread mixture over dough and sprinkle with chopped nut meats, if desired.

ICING

4 tablespoons *lukewarm* water   ½ teaspoon vanilla
1 cup powdered sugar, sifted

1. Mix all ingredients together until smooth.
2. Spread on slightly warm rolls.

AFTERNOON TEA BREAD

Our children love this for a snack after school. The candied fruits and nuts make it wonderful to serve to company, too.

Oven temperature: preheat to 400°F.

Baking time: about 1 hour

Yield: 1 large loaf or 2 small loaves

Pan: two 7"x4"x3" loaf pans, or one 10"x6"x3" loaf pan, well greased

1 package active dry yeast
¼ cup *lukewarm* water
1 cup scalded milk
2 tablespoons melted butter or margarine
3 tablespoons honey or brown sugar, firmly packed

3½ cups all-purpose flour, sifted
1 teaspoon salt
½ cup walnut or pecan meats, chopped
½ cup candied fruit, chopped, OR 1 cup raisins

1. In bowl large enough to accommodate raised dough, stir yeast into *lukewarm* water to dissolve.
2. Scald milk. Stir in butter or margarine, honey or brown sugar, and salt. Cool to *lukewarm*. Add to yeast mixture.
3. Sift flour once before measuring.
4. Add 1/3 of flour. With electric mixer or spoon, beat batter until smooth and satiny. Add remaining flour gradually, changing from spoon or mixer to hands as the dough becomes stiffer. Add nuts and fruit peels or raisins.
5. Continue to knead until elastic.
6. Grease bowl. Put dough in it. Lightly grease exposed surface of dough. Cover bowl with damp cloth, leaving edges on outside of bowl. Let rise in warm place (about 80°F.) until dough is doubled in bulk.
7. Punch down the dough when it is doubled in bulk. Work the edges to center, turn dough bottom side up, and knead very lightly.
8. Divide dough into 2 equal parts if making two loaves.
9. Shape dough into loaf or loaves. Place in well greased 10"x6"x3" loaf pan, or two 7"x4"x3" loaf pans.

10. Brush tops of loaves with melted butter or margarine. Recover with damp cloth. Let rise until center of dough is well rounded above pan.

11. Bake at 400°F. for about 1 hour, or until done.

12. Turn out immediately to cool on wire rack or across top of pans.

KOLAČKI
(Sour Cream Rolls)

If you try only one recipe, make it this one. These take much less time than most sweet rolls, yet flavor isn't sacrificed for taste.

Oven temperature: preheat to 375°F.
Baking time: 15 to 20 minutes

Yield: 2 to 3 dozen rolls
Pan: greased cookie sheet

1 package active dry yeast
¼ cup *lukewarm* water
1 cup scalded sour cream
2 tablespoons melted shortening

3½ tablespoons granulated sugar
½ teaspoon salt
⅛ teaspoon baking soda
1 egg, beaten
3 cups all-purpose flour, sifted

1. In bowl large enough to accommodate raised dough, stir yeast into *lukewarm* water to dissolve.

2. Scald cream. Stir in shortening, sugar, salt, and soda. Cool to *lukewarm*. Add to yeast mixture.

3. Add beaten egg.

4. Sift flour once before measuring.

5. Add 1/3 of flour. With electric mixer or spoon, beat batter until smooth and satiny. Add remaining flour gradually, changing from spoon or mixer to hands as dough becomes stiffer.

6. Turn dough onto floured board. Knead until elastic (tight-feeling), smooth, and no longer sticky enough to adhere to board, OR continue to knead in mixing bowl until all flour and dough are cleaned from sides of bowl by kneading process.

7. Grease bowl. Put dough in it. Lightly grease exposed surface of dough. Cover bowl with damp cloth, leaving edges on outside of bowl. Leave for 5 minutes.

8. On lightly floured board, roll dough out to 1/4 inch thickness. Brush with melted butter. Spread with filling.

⅓ cup granulated sugar
1 egg, beaten
1 teaspoon cinnamon

1 cup nut meats, chopped
enough milk to form thick paste of spreading consistency

1. Boil filling mixture about 1 minute to blend well.
2. Spread nut mixture on rolled out dough. Cut dough into 3-inch squares. Roll like small jelly rolls. Place on greased cookie sheet.
3. Bake at 375°F. for 15 to 20 minutes.

NOTES

QUICK BREADS

Tips for Freezing Quick Breads 60
BISCUITS
Suggestions for Successful Biscuits 61
Basic Biscuits 61
Cream Biscuits 62
Buttermilk Biscuits 63
Biscuit Mix 64
Cheese Straws 65
MUFFINS
Suggestions for Successful Muffins 66
Muffin Mix 67
Bran Muffins 68
Apple Muffins 68
Blueberry Muffins 69
Sally Lunn 70
Orange Muffins 70
Whole Wheat Muffins 71
Streusel Smacks 72
BREADS AND COFFEE CAKES
Suggestions for Successful Quick Breads 73
Boston Brown Bread 73
Apricot Bread 74
Date Nut Bread 74
Date and Cheese Bread 75
Mrs. Lil's Banana Nut Bread 76
Grandma Grace's Coffee Cake 76
Nut Bread 77
White Gingerbread 78
Deluxe Coffee Cake 78
Mother's Nut Bread 79
Cinnamon Buttermilk Coffee Cake 80
Orange Marmalade Coffee Cake 80
Prune Bread 82
Cranberry Bread 82
Walnut Bread 83
Orange Bread 84
Individual Coffee Cakes 84
POPOVERS AND CORN BREADS
Suggestions for Baking Popovers 85

Suggestions for Baking Corn Breads   85
Popovers   86
Spoon Bread   86
Corn Bread or Muffins   87
Raisin Corn Meal Muffins   88
Sour Cream or Buttermilk Bread   88

PANCAKES, CORN BREAD, AND WAFFLES

Suggestions for Successful Pancakes   89
Suggestions for Successful Waffles   89
Pancakes   90
Corn Meal Griddle Cakes   91
Pancakes for Two   92
Dorothy's French Pancakes   93
Buckwheat Cakes   94
Whole Wheat or Graham Griddle Cakes   95
Leila's Butterfly Griddle Cakes   96
Buttermilk Pancakes   97
Oatmeal Pancakes   98
Chocolate Waffles   98
Buttermilk Waffles   99
Waffles   100

DOUGHNUTS, FRITTERS, AND DUMPLINGS

New England Doughnuts   101
Orange Drop Doughnuts   102
Raised Doughnuts   103
Sour Cream Doughnuts   104
Corn Fritters   105
Fruit Fritters   105
Good Dumplings for Chicken or Meat Stews   106

Space for Notes page 66

TIPS FOR FREEZING QUICK BREADS

Most quick breads freeze beautifully up to 12 months. For best preservation, bake quick breads before freezing. *Cool* before freezing. Wrap loaves in foil. Wrap rolls, pancakes, waffles and so on, in moisture-vaporproof (film, foil, or freezer paper) wrappers, seal, label, and freeze. When you wish to use them, thaw them *in wrappers* until almost at room temperature. Heat, at about 300°F. until warm. Leave loaves wrapped in foil during heating. Unwrap and serve. Waffles may be placed, frozen, in pop-up toaster to be heated.

Biscuits

SUGGESTIONS FOR SUCCESSFUL BISCUITS

All-purpose flour is best for biscuits.

Emulsified or hydrogenated shortenings or new-type lards have quick and easy blending qualities that make good biscuits.

Quick stirring and as little handling as possible when rolling out dough make lighter biscuits.

How thinly or thickly you roll out dough depends on personal preference. Thickly cut biscuits have fluffier middles. Thin biscuits are crisp almost all the way through.

Biscuits may always be baked on ungreased surface. Space apart on pan if you wish them browned all over. For soft biscuits, cut biscuits thicker and put them close together on baking sheet.

BASIC BISCUITS

The perfect Sunday dinner ... biscuits, honey, and fried chicken.

Oven temperature: preheat to 450°F.
Baking time: about 15 minutes

Yield: about 12 biscuits
Pan: ungreased cookie sheet

2 cups all-purpose flour, sifted
4 teaspoons double-acting baking powder

¾ teaspoon salt
¼ cup shortening
¾ cup milk

1. Sift flour once before measuring. Mix and sift flour, salt, and baking powder together.
2. With two table knives or pastry blender, cut shortening into dry ingredients. Blend until consistency of corn meal.
3. Make a well in center of dry ingredients. Add small amount of milk. Blend quickly. Add remaining amount of milk, using as few strokes as possible to blend two together.
4. On lightly floured board, roll or pat dough out 1/4 to 1/2 inch thick, handling as little as possible.
5. With unfloured biscuit cutter, cut into desired size rounds. Place on ungreased cookie sheet.
6. Bake at 450°F. for about 15 minutes.

CREAM BISCUITS

Richer version of basic biscuit.

Oven temperature: preheat to
   450°F.
Baking time: about 15 minutes

Yield: about 12 biscuits
Pan: ungreased cookie sheet

2 cups all-purpose flour, sifted
½ teaspoon salt

3½ teaspoons double-acting
   baking powder
¾ to 1 cup coffee cream

1.   Sift flour once before measuring. Mix and sift flour, salt, and baking powder together.
2.   Make a well in center of dry ingredients. Add small amount of cream. Blend quickly. Add remaining cream, using as few strokes as possible to blend two together.
3.   On lightly floured board, roll or pat dough out 1/4 to 1/2 inch thick, handling as little as possible.
4.   With unfloured biscuit cutter, cut into desired size rounds. Place on ungreased cookie sheet.
5.   Bake at 450°F. for about 15 minutes.

BUTTERMILK BISCUITS

Light as a feather. Cut them 25-cent size sometime.

Oven temperature: preheat to
   450°F.
Baking time: 15 to 20 minutes

Yield: about 12 biscuits
Pan: ungreased cookie sheet

2 cups all-purpose flour, sifted
½ teaspoon salt
1 teaspoon double-acting
   baking powder

½ teaspoon baking soda
5 tablespoons shortening
¾ to 1 cup buttermilk

1.   Sift flour once before measuring. Mix and sift flour, salt, baking powder, and soda together.
2.   With two table knives or pastry blender, cut shortening into dry ingredients. Blend until consistency of corn meal.
3.   Make a well in center of dry ingredients. Add small amount of buttermilk. Blend quickly. Add remaining milk, using as few strokes as possible to blend two together.
4.   On lightly floured board, roll or pat dough out 1/4 to 1/2 inch thick, handling as little as possible.
5.   With unfloured biscuit cutter, cut into desired size rounds. Place on ungreased cookie sheet.
6.   Bake at 450°F. for about 15 to 20 minutes.

BISCUIT MIX

Timesaver. Easy to prepare. Makes about 90 biscuits.

Oven temperature: preheat to
  450°F.
Baking time: about 15 minutes

Yield: 2⅓ cups mix makes
  about 12 biscuits
Pan: ungreased cookie sheet

MIX

16 cups all-purpose flour,
  sifted
½ cup double-acting baking
  powder

6 teaspoons salt
2 cups shortening

1.   Sift flour once before measuring. Mix and sift flour, baking powder, and salt together.
2.   With two table knives or pastry blender, cut shortening into dry ingredients. Blend until consistency of corn meal.
3.   Store in tightly covered jar in refrigerator.

BISCUITS

2⅓ cups mix

7/8 cup milk

1.   Make a well in center of biscuit mix. Add small amount of milk. Blend quickly. Add remaining amount of milk, using as few strokes as possible to blend two together.
2.   On lightly floured board, roll dough out to 1/2 inch thick, handling as little as possible.
3.   With unfloured biscuit cutter, cut into desired size rounds. Place on ungreased cookie sheet.
4.   Bake at 450°F. for about 15 minutes.

VARIATIONS

1.   *Cheese:* Melt 1 eight-ounce package of soft cheddar cheese with 1 cube butter. Pour over unbaked biscuit tops.
2.   *Herb:* ½ teaspoon each savory and thyme, or ¼ teaspoon curry powder. Add to mix.
3.   *Seed:* 1¼ teaspoon caraway seed, celery seed, or poppy seed. Add to mix.
4.   *Greens:* ¼ cup parsley, chopped; or ¼ cup chives, chopped; or ¼ cup green onion, chopped. Add to mix.

CHEESE STRAWS

Perfect accompaniment to most luncheon salads.

Oven temperature: preheat to
  400°F.
Baking time: 5 minutes

Yield: approximately 2 dozen
Pan: greased cookie sheet

2 tablespoons butter
1 cup New York sharp
  cheese, grated
1 cup all-purpose flour, sifted

1 teaspoon double-acting
  baking powder
½ teaspoon salt
¼ teaspoon paprika
6 to 7 tablespoons cold water

1. Mix butter and cheese well.
2. Sift flour once before measuring. Mix and sift flour, baking powder, salt, and paprika together.
3. Combine dry ingredients with cheese mixture.
4. Add cold water to make easily rolled dough.
5. Knead dough lightly and roll out 1/8 inch thick on well floured surface.
6. Cut into strips 1/2 inch wide and 4 inches long. Place on greased cookie sheet.
7. Bake at 400°F. for about 5 minutes.

Muffins

SUGGESTIONS FOR SUCCESSFUL MUFFINS

Blend liquid and dry ingredients together quickly, using just enough strokes to moisten. Do not beat or over-mix as muffins will be coarse-grained.

Fill muffin pans 2/3 full. If there is not enough batter to fill all cups of muffin pan, put water in unfilled cups.

Run knife or spatula around edge of muffin to loosen when done. If muffins are done before rest of meal, loosen and tip in pans. This will prevent muffins from becoming soggy.

Muffins baked in too hot oven form uneven tops. If oven is not hot enough, muffins do not rise properly.

NOTES

MUFFIN MIX

Makes 100 muffins. May be stored in tightly covered jar in refrigerator.

Oven temperature: preheat to 425°F.
Baking time: about 15 minutes

Yield: 2 cups mix makes 24 small muffins
Pan: 2½"x1¼" muffin pan, well greased

MIX

16 cups all-purpose flour, sifted
2 cups granulated sugar

⅔ cup double-acting baking powder
5 teaspoons salt
1½ cups shortening

1. Sift flour once before measuring. Mix and sift flour, sugar, baking powder, and salt together.
2. With two table knives or pastry blender cut shortening into dry ingredients. Blend until consistency of corn meal.
3. Store in tightly covered jar in refrigerator.

MUFFINS

2 cups plus 3 tablespoons muffin mix

1 egg, beaten
1 cup milk

1. Make a well in center of muffin mix. Beat egg with milk. Add small amount of milk. Blend quickly. Add remaining milk, using as few strokes as possible to blend two together.
2. Fill well greased 2½"x1¼" muffin pan cups 2/3 full.
3. Bake at 425°F. for about 15 minutes.

VARIATIONS

1. *Orange:* Add 2 tablespoons sugar and 2 tablespoons grated orange rind. Use ½ cup milk and ½ cup orange juice.
2. *Fruit:* Add to batter ⅔ cup raisins or 1 cup dates, cut up.
3. *Nut:* Add to batter 1 cup nut meats, finely chopped.
4. *Spice:* Add to batter ½ teaspoon cinnamon and ½ teaspoon nutmeg.
5. *Fruit-Nut:* Add to batter ½ cup nut meats, chopped; and ½ cup raisins, or apples, chopped, or dates, cut up.

BRAN MUFFINS

Quick, easy, and wholesome.

Oven temperature: preheat to
    425°F.
Baking time: 20 to 25 minutes

Yield: 12 to 16 muffins
Pan: 2½"x1¼" muffin
    pan, well greased

2 eggs, beaten
6 tablespoons molasses
1 cup milk
1 cup all-purpose flour, sifted

¼ teaspoon salt
1 teaspoon baking soda
2 cups ready-to-eat bran
    cereal

1.   Beat eggs. Blend in molasses and milk.
2.   Sift flour once before measuring. Mix and sift flour, salt, and soda together. Combine bran cereal and flour.
3.   Add dry ingredients to liquid mixture a little at a time, mixing thoroughly after each addition.
4.   Fill well greased 2½"x1¼" muffin pan cups 2/3 full.
5.   Bake at 425°F. for 20 to 25 minutes.

APPLE MUFFINS

Try these for Sunday breakfast.

Oven temperature: preheat to
    425°F.
Baking time: 25 minutes

Yield: 12 large muffins
Pan: 3"x1½" muffin pan,
    greased and floured

1 egg, beaten
½ cup plus 2 tablespoons
    granulated sugar
4 tablespoons shortening,
    melted
1 cup milk
2¼ cups all-purpose flour,
    sifted

3½ teaspoons double-acting
    baking powder
½ teaspoon salt
½ teaspoon cinnamon
½ teaspoon nutmeg
1 cup apples, finely chopped
½ cup nut meats, chopped
    if desired

1.   Beat egg. Blend in ½ cup sugar, melted shortening, and milk.

2.   Sift flour once before measuring. Mix and sift flour, baking powder, salt, ¼ teaspoon cinnamon, and ¼ teaspoon nutmeg together.
3.   Make a well in center of dry ingredients. Add small amount of liquid mixture. Blend quickly. Add remaining liquid mixture, using as few strokes as possible to blend the two together completely.
4.   Stir in apples and nuts, if desired.
5.   Fill greased and floured 3"x1½" muffin pan cups 2/3 full.
6.   Mix remaining cinnamon, nutmeg, and sugar together.
7.   Sprinkle batter with sugar and spice mixture.
8.   Bake at 425°F. for 25 minutes.

BLUEBERRY MUFFINS

In this wonderful era of fresh frozen fruit, it is possible to have this delicacy the year 'round.

Oven temperature: preheat to 425°F.
Baking time: 20 to 25 minutes

Yield: 12 to 16 muffins
Pan: 2½"x1¼" muffin pan, well greased

1 egg, beaten
2 tablespoons granulated sugar
3 tablespoons butter or shortening, melted
1½ cups milk

2½ cups all-purpose flour, sifted
5 teaspoons double-acting baking powder
1 teaspoon salt
1 cup fresh, frozen, or canned blueberries

1.   Beat egg. Blend in sugar, melted shortening, and milk.
2.   Sift flour once before measuring. Mix and sift flour, baking powder, and salt together.
3.   Make a well in center of dry ingredients. Add small amount of liquid mixture. Blend quickly. Add remaining liquid mixture, using as few strokes as possible to blend the two together completely.
4.   Stir fresh, frozen, or *drained* canned blueberries into batter.
5.   Fill well greased 2½"x1¼" muffin pan cups 2/3 full.
6.   Bake at 425°F. for 20 to 25 minutes.

SALLY LUNN

A sweet quick bread or muffin.

Oven temperature: preheat to
  425°F.
Baking time: about 30 minutes

Yield: 6 servings
Pan: 12″x8″x2″ oblong pan,
  greased

½ cup shortening
½ cup granulated sugar
3 eggs, beaten
2 cups all-purpose flour, sifted

½ teaspoon salt
2 teaspoons double-acting
  baking powder
1 cup milk

1. Cream shortening with sugar until light and fluffy.
2. Add eggs one at a time and beat well.
3. Sift flour once before measuring. Mix and sift flour, salt, and
baking powder together.
4. Add dry ingredients alternately with milk, mixing slightly
after each addition.
5. Pour batter into greased 12″x8″x2″ oblong pan.
6. Bake at 425°F. for about 30 minutes.
Note: Muffin pans instead of oblong pan may be used.
Bake muffins 20 minutes.

ORANGE MUFFINS

*These muffins are good fresh from the oven, warmed over, or
split and toasted the next day.*

Oven temperature: preheat to
  400°F.
Baking time: 30 minutes

Yield: 16 large muffins
Pan: 3″x1½″ muffin pan,
  well greased

1 egg, beaten
1 cup granulated sugar
3 tablespoons shortening,
  melted, or cooking oil
1 cup milk
2½ cups all-purpose flour,
  sifted

4 teaspoons double-acting
  baking powder
½ teaspoon salt
1 medium orange (pulp and
  rind, ground finely)

1. Beat egg. Blend in sugar, cooking oil or melted shortening,
and milk.

70

2. Sift flour once before measuring. Mix and sift flour, baking powder, and salt together.
3. Make a well in center of dry ingredients. Add small amount of liquid mixture. Blend quickly. Add remaining liquid mixture, using as few strokes as possible to blend the two together completely.
4. Stir in ground orange.
5. Fill well greased 3"x1½" muffin pan cups 2/3 full.
6. Bake at 400°F. for 30 minutes.

WHOLE WHEAT MUFFINS

So good on a cold winter's morn!

Oven temperature: preheat to 425°F.
Baking time: about 20 minutes

Yield: 12 to 16 muffins
Pan: 2½"x1¼" muffin pan, well greased

1 egg, beaten
1 tablespoon honey or brown sugar
2 tablespoons butter, melted
1 cup milk
2 cups whole wheat flour

2 teaspoons double-acting baking powder
½ teaspoon salt
½ cup raisins or dates, cut up
½ cup nut meats, if desired

1. Beat egg. Blend in honey or brown sugar, melted butter, and milk.
2. Mix flour, baking powder, and salt together.
3. Make a well in center of dry ingredients. Add small amount of liquid mixture. Blend quickly. Add remaining liquid mixture, using as few strokes as possible to blend the two together completely.
4. Stir in raisins or dates, and nuts, if desired.
5. Fill well greased 2½"x1¼" muffin pan cups 2/3 full.
6. Bake at 425°F. for about 20 minutes.

STREUSEL SMACKS

Classically European.

Oven temperature: preheat to
400°F.
Baking time: 20 to 25 minutes

Yield: 12 to 15 muffins
Pan: 2½″x1¼″ muffin
pan, greased and floured

STREUSEL MIXTURE

½ cup brown sugar,
firmly packed
2 tablespoons butter, melted
2 tablespoons all-purpose
flour

2 teaspoons cinnamon
½ cup pecan meats,
chopped

1. Blend all ingredients except nuts to make dry and crumbly mixture.
2. Add chopped pecans. This mixture is used for bottoms and tops of muffins.

BATTER

⅓ cup shortening
½ cup granulated sugar
1 egg, unbeaten
¾ cup milk
2 cups all-purpose flour, sifted

½ teaspoon salt
¼ teaspoon cream of tartar
2 teaspoons double-acting
baking powder
1 cup dates, chopped

1. Cream shortening with sugar until light and fluffy.
2. Beat in egg. Add milk. Beat very well.
3. Sift flour once before measuring. Mix and sift flour, salt, cream of tartar, and baking powder together.
4. Add dry ingredients to creamed mixture a little at a time, mixing thoroughly after each addition.
5. Stir in dates.
6. Sprinkle generous teaspoonful streusel mixture into cup bottoms of greased 2½″x1¼″ muffin pan.
7. Pour batter over streusel mixture, filling cups 2/3 full.
8. Sprinkle additional teaspoonful streusel mixture over batter.
9. Bake at 400°F. for 20 to 25 minutes.

Note: Streusel mixture may be made in larger quantities and stored in refrigerator.

Breads

SUGGESTIONS FOR SUCCESSFUL QUICK BREADS

Most quick, or baking powder, breads require speedy blending of liquid and dry ingredients.

It is best to let these breads set a few hours or overnight before slicing. They are best thinly sliced. A very sharp knife is helpful in achieving uniformly thin slices.

To keep quick breads from drying out, wrap them in foil, plastic, or plio film.

BOSTON BROWN BREAD

Bite into it and you will know why the Bostonians ate it every Saturday night.

Oven temperature: preheat to 350°F.
Baking time: 1 hour

Servings: about 12 slices
Pan: 9"x5"x3" loaf pan, greased and floured

1 cup brown sugar, firmly packed
2 cups hot water
1 cup molasses
½ cup all-purpose flour, sifted
1 cup cornmeal, unsifted

3 cups graham flour, unsifted
1 teaspoon salt
1 teaspoon double-acting baking powder
½ cup raisins
½ cup nut meats, chopped

1. Dissolve brown sugar in hot water. Add molasses.
2. Sift all-purpose flour once before measuring. Measure, then take out 2 tablespoons to dredge raisins and nut meats.
3. Mix remainder of all-purpose flour, corn meal, graham flour, salt, and baking powder together very well.
4. Add dry ingredients to molasses mixture a little at a time, mixing thoroughly after each addition.
5. Stir in raisins and nut meats dredged in flour.
6. Pour batter into greased and floured 9"x5"x3" loaf pan.
7. Bake at 350°F. for 1 hour.

APRICOT BREAD

Apricot devotées will certainly enjoy an unusual blending of apricots with other fruits.

Oven temperature: preheat to
  350°F.
Baking time: 50 to 60 minutes

Yield: 10 to 12 servings
Pan: 9"x5"x3" loaf pan,
  greased and floured

½ cup dried apricots
boiling water
1 large orange
½ cup raisins
2 tablespoons butter or
  margarine
1 cup granulated sugar
1 egg, unbeaten

1 teaspoon vanilla
2 cups all-purpose flour, sifted
2 teaspoons double-acting
  baking powder
½ teaspoon baking soda
½ teaspoon salt
½ cup nut meats, chopped

1. Put apricots in dish. Add water to them, just covering the fruit. Soak 1/2 hour.
2. Squeeze juice from orange. Put in measuring cup and add enough boiling water to make 1 cupful liquid. Save orange rinds.
3. Grind pre-soaked apricots, raisins, and orange rinds together.
4. Cream butter or margarine with sugar until light and fluffy.
5. Beat in egg. Add vanilla. Blend in ground fruits.
6. Sift flour once before measuring. Mix and sift flour, baking powder, soda, and salt together.
7. Add dry ingredients alternately with liquid, mixing thoroughly after each addition.
8. Stir in nuts.
9. Pour batter into greased and floured 9"x5"x3" loaf pan.
10. Bake at 350°F. for 50 to 60 minutes.

DATE NUT BREAD

Most of us have a weakness for a good loaf cake that isn't too sweet. Here is one of the best we have ever eaten.

Oven temperature: preheat to
  350°F.
Baking time: about 1 hour

Yield: approximately
  12 servings
Pan: 9"x5"x3" loaf pan,
  greased and floured

74

1 cup dates, chopped	1 teaspoon vanilla
1 teaspoon baking soda	1½ cups all-purpose flour,
1 cup boiling water	sifted
1 cup granulated sugar	¼ teaspoon salt
1 tablespoon butter	½ cup walnut meats,
1 egg, beaten	chopped

1. Sprinkle dates over soda. Add boiling water, sugar, and butter. Let stand until cool.
2. Add beaten egg and vanilla.
3. Sift flour once before measuring. Mix and sift flour and salt.
4. Add dry ingredients to liquid mixture a little at a time, mixing thoroughly after each addition. Stir in nuts.
5. Pour batter into greased and floured 9"x5"x3" loaf pan.
6. Bake at 350°F. for about 1 hour.

Note: This cake freezes beautifully.

DATE AND CHEESE BREAD

Nice to have on hand.

Oven temperature: preheat to
   325°F.
Baking time: about 50 minutes

Yield: 8 to 10 servings
Pan: 10"x5"x3" loaf pan,
   greased and floured

¼ cup boiling water	1 teaspoon baking soda
1 cup dates, finely chopped	¼ teaspoon salt
1 egg, beaten	¼ cup granulated sugar
1 cup grated American cheese	¼ cup brown sugar, firmly
1¾ cups all-purpose flour,	packed
sifted	

1. Pour boiling water over dates. Let stand 5 minutes.
2. Combine egg and cheese with date-liquid mixture.
3. Sift flour once before measuring. Mix and sift flour, soda, salt, and sugars together. Sift again.
4. Add dry ingredients to date mixture a little at a time, mixing thoroughly after each addition.
5. Pour batter into greased and floured 10"x5"x3" loaf pan.
6. Bake at 325°F. for about 50 minutes.

MRS. LIL'S BANANA NUT BREAD

The type of bread to serve on a dozen occasions.

Oven temperature: preheat to
  325°F.
Baking time: about 1 hour

Yield: approximately 12 slices
Pan: 10"x4"x3" loaf pan,
  well greased and floured

½ cup butter
1 cup granulated sugar
2 eggs, unbeaten
2 cups all-purpose flour, sifted
½ teaspoon salt

1 teaspoon baking soda
2 large or 3 small ripe
  bananas, mashed
½ cup nut meats, chopped,
  if desired

1. Cream butter with sugar until light and fluffy.
2. Add eggs one at a time and beat well.
3. Sift flour once before measuring. Mix and sift flour, salt, and soda together.
4. Add dry ingredients to creamed mixture a little at a time, mixing thoroughly after each addition.
5. Blend in mashed bananas and nuts.
6. Pour batter into well greased and floured 10"x4"x3" loaf pan. Place high in oven.
7. Bake at 325°F. for about 1 hour.
8. Cool overnight before slicing.

GRANDMA GRACE'S COFFEE CAKE

This is such a treat that our children always want it for their birthday breakfasts.

Oven temperature: preheat to
  350°F.
Baking time: 30 to 35
  minutes

Yield: approximately 6 to
  9 servings
Pan: 9"x9"x2" square pan,
  greased and floured

¼ cup butter
½ cup granulated sugar
1 egg, beaten
1½ cups all-purpose flour,
  sifted

1½ teaspoons double-acting
  baking powder
½ teaspoon salt
⅔ cup milk
cinnamon
brown sugar

76

1. Cream butter with sugar until light and fluffy.
2. Add egg and beat well.
3. Sift flour once before measuring. Mix and sift flour, baking powder, and salt together.
4. Add dry ingredients alternately with milk, mixing thoroughly after each addition.
5. Pour batter into greased and floured 9"x9"x2" square pan.
6. Sprinkle top of batter with cinnamon and sugar. Sprinkle again with brown sugar.
7. Bake at 350°F. for 35 minutes.

ALTERNATE TOPPING

4 tablespoons granulated sugar	2 tablespoons flour
2 tablespoons butter	2 teaspoons cinnamon

Mix all ingredients together and crumble over top of unbaked batter.

NUT BREAD

Sweet milk version of a fine old bread.

Oven temperature: preheat to 350°F.	Yield: approximately 20 servings
Baking time: approximately 1 hour	Pan: two 9"x5"x3" loaf pans, greased

3 cups all-purpose flour, sifted	1 cup granulated sugar
3 teaspoons double-acting baking powder	1 cup milk
1 teaspoon salt	1 egg, beaten
	1 cup nut meats, chopped

1. Sift flour once before measuring. Mix and sift flour, baking powder, salt, and sugar together.
2. Add milk and beaten egg to dry ingredients a little at a time, mixing thoroughly after each addition.
3. Stir in nuts.
4. Pour batter into two greased 9"x5"x3" loaf pans.
5. Bake at 350°F. for about 1 hour.

WHITE GINGERBREAD

Dress up a brunch or luncheon with a completely different bread.

Oven temperature: preheat to
   350°F.
Baking time: 35 to 40 minutes

Yield: approximately 8 to
   10 servings
Pan: 12"x8"x2" oblong pan,
   buttered

4 cups all-purpose flour, sifted	1 teaspoon baking soda
1 cup butter	½ teaspoon salt
2 cups granulated sugar	1 teaspoon nutmeg
2 eggs, beaten	½ teaspoon cinnamon
1 cup sour milk	1 teaspoon ginger

1.   Sift flour once before measuring. Put in mixing bowl.
2.   With mixer or hands combine flour with butter to make crumb-like mixture.
3.   Add sugar to the crumbed mixture and blend well. Set aside 2 cupfuls.
4.   To the remainder of crumbled mixture, add beaten eggs, sour milk, soda, salt, nutmeg, cinnamon and ginger. Blend thoroughly.
5.   Butter a 12"x8"x2" oblong pan. Spread one cup of reserved crumbs on bottom.
6.   Pour batter over crumbs. Top batter with second cup of crumbs.
7.   Bake at 350°F. for 35 to 40 minutes.

DELUXE COFFEE CAKE

Entertaining at a brunch or coffee? Bake this compliment-winner.

Oven temperature: preheat to
   350°F.
Baking time: 1 hour

Yield: approximately
   16 servings
Pan: 10"x4" tube pan,
   greased and floured

½ cup butter	1 cup sour cream
½ cup shortening	2 cups cake flour, sifted
1¼ cups granulated sugar	½ teaspoon salt
2 eggs, unbeaten	1 teaspoon baking powder
½ teaspoon baking soda	1 teaspoon vanilla

1. Cream butter and shortening with sugar until light and fluffy.
2. Add eggs one at a time and beat well.
3. Dissolve soda in sour cream.
4. Sift flour once before measuring. Mix and sift flour, salt, and baking powder together.
5. Add dry ingredients alternately with sour cream, mixing well after each addition.
6. Add vanilla. Mix very well.
7. Pour batter into greased and floured 10"x4" tube pan.

TOPPING

2 tablespoons granulated sugar

½ teaspoon cinnamon
½ cup nut meats, chopped

1. Mix all ingredients together thoroughly. Sprinkle mixture on top of unbaked cake batter.
2. Bake at 350°F. for 1 hour.

MOTHER'S NUT BREAD

When growing up, we always wished Mother would make this more often.

Oven temperature: 350°F.
DO NOT PREHEAT
Baking time: 50 minutes

Yield: approximately
20 servings
Pan: two 7"x4"x3" loaf pans, greased and floured

2 cups sour cream, thin
¾ cup granulated sugar
3 eggs, unbeaten
4 cups all-purpose flour, sifted

3 teaspoons double-acting baking powder
1 teaspoon baking soda
¼ teaspoon salt
¾ cup nut meats, chopped

1. Blend sour cream and sugar well.
2. Add eggs one at a time and beat well.
3. Sift flour once before measuring. Mix and sift flour, baking powder, soda, and salt together.
4. Add dry ingredients to cream mixture a little at a time, mixing thoroughly after each addition.
5. Stir in nut meats.
6. Pour batter into two greased and floured 7"x4"x3" loaf pans.
7. Put in cold oven and set heat at 350°F. Bake for 50 minutes.

CINNAMON BUTTERMILK COFFEE CAKE

This is the way to start the day out right.

Oven temperature: preheat to 350°F.
Baking time: 35 to 45 minutes

Yield: approximately 8 to 10 servings
Pan: 12"x8"x2" oblong pan, greased and floured

2⅓ cups all-purpose flour, sifted
2 cups brown sugar, firmly packed
½ cup butter
½ teaspoon salt

1 teaspoon baking soda
1 teaspoon cinnamon
1 egg, beaten
1 cup buttermilk
½ cup nut meats, chopped

1. Sift 2 cups flour once before measuring. Mix brown sugar and flour together.
2. With two table knives, cut butter into sugar and flour until mixture is consistency of corn meal. Set aside ¾ cup to be used for topping.
3. To the remaining flour and brown sugar mixture, add the other ⅓ cup flour, salt, soda, and cinnamon. Blend well.
4. Mix beaten egg and buttermilk together.
5. Make a well in center of dry ingredients and add small amount of liquid. Blend well. Add remaining liquid and mix well.
6. Pour batter into greased and floured 12"x8"x2" oblong pan. Top batter with the ¾ cup flour and brown sugar mixture to which the nut meats have been added.
7. Bake at 350°F. for 35 to 45 minutes.

ORANGE MARMALADE COFFEE CAKE

The marmalade topping sinks into the batter as it bakes, making the coffee cake rich and yummy.

Oven temperature: preheat to 350°F.
Baking time: 30 minutes

Yield: 6 to 9 servings
Pan: 9"x9"x2" square pan, greased and floured

½ cup brown sugar, firmly
  packed
½ cup all-purpose flour,
  sifted
2 tablespoons butter or
  margarine

1 tablespoon cream
¼ cup orange marmalade
¼ cup walnut meats,
  coarsely chopped

Combine all ingredients. Mix thoroughly. Set aside.

BATTER

⅓ cup shortening
½ cup granulated sugar
2 eggs, unbeaten
½ teaspoon vanilla
⅓ cup milk

1¾ cups all-purpose flour,
  sifted
2 teaspoons double-acting
  baking powder
¾ teaspoon salt

1. Cream shortening with sugar until light and fluffy.
2. Add eggs one at a time and beat well. Add vanilla and milk.
3. Sift flour once before measuring. Mix and sift flour, baking powder, and salt together.
4. Add dry ingredients a little at a time, mixing thoroughly after each addition.
5. Spread batter in greased and floured 9"x9"x2" square pan. Drop spoonfuls of topping over batter.
6. Bake at 350°F. for 30 minutes. Cut into squares and serve warm.

PRUNE BREAD

Tender, fruited bread.

Oven temperature: preheat to
  350°F.
Baking time: about 1 hour

Yield: approximately 8 to
  10 servings
Pan: 9"x5"x3" loaf pan,
  greased and floured

1 teaspoon baking soda
1 cup prunes, cut up
1 cup boiling water
1 tablespoon shortening
1 egg, unbeaten
¾ cup brown sugar, firmly
  packed

½ teaspoon vanilla
1½ cups all-purpose flour,
  sifted
¼ teaspoon salt
½ cup nut meats, chopped

1. Sprinkle soda over prunes. Cover with boiling water. Add shortening. Let stand 5 minutes.
2. Beat egg, sugar, and vanilla into prune mixture.
3. Sift flour once before measuring. Mix and sift flour and salt together.
4. Add dry ingredients to prune mixture a little at a time, mixing thoroughly after each addition. Stir in nuts.
5. Pour batter into greased and floured 9"x5"x3" loaf pan.
6. Bake at 350°F. for one hour.

CRANBERRY BREAD

Good for tea sandwiches with butter or cream cheese.

Oven temperature: preheat to
  350°F.
Baking time: about 1 hour

Servings: approximately
  12 slices
Pan: 9"x5"x3" loaf pan,
  greased

1 egg, beaten
2 tablespoons butter, melted
1 cup milk
3 cups all-purpose flour, sifted
1 teaspoon salt

4 teaspoons double-acting
  baking powder
½ cup granulated sugar
grated rind of 1 orange
½ cup nut meats, chopped
1 cup raw cranberries

1.   Blend beaten egg, melted butter, and milk together.
2.   Sift flour once before measuring. Mix and sift flour, salt, baking powder, and ¼ cup sugar together.
3.   Add orange rind and nuts to dry ingredients.
4.   Combine dry ingredients with egg and milk mixture, stirring enough only to blend the two together.
5.   Grind or chop cranberries and mix them with remaining ¼ cup sugar.
6.   Fold sweetened cranberries into batter.
7.   Pour batter into greased 9"x5"x3" loaf pan.
8.   Bake at 350°F. for about 1 hour.
Note: Bread slices best when cooled overnight.

WALNUT BREAD

Very good for breakfast. Texture and flavor improve after 12 hours.

Oven temperature: preheat to 375°F.
Baking time: 50 to 60 minutes

Yield: approximately 12 servings
Pan: 10"x5"x3" loaf pan, waxed paper lined

2 eggs, well beaten
2 cups less 2 tablespoons brown sugar, firmly packed
2 cups sour milk
4 cups all-purpose flour, sifted

1 teaspoon double-acting baking powder
½ teaspoon salt
2 teaspoons baking soda
½ teaspoon vanilla
1 cup walnut meats, chopped

1.   Beat eggs and sugar thoroughly.
2.   Add sour milk. Beat well.
3.   Sift flour once before measuring. Mix and sift flour, baking powder, salt and soda together.
4.   Add dry ingredients to sugar mixture a little at a time, mixing thoroughly after each addition.
5.   Stir in vanilla and nuts.
6.   Pour batter into waxed paper lined 10"x5"x3" loaf pan.
7.   Bake at 375°F. for 50 to 60 minutes or until done.

ORANGE BREAD

There are so many times this fits in just right . . . box lunches, brunches, luncheons, and munches.

Oven temperature: preheat to 350°F.
Baking time: about 1 hour.

Yield: approximately 12 to 24 thin slices
Pan: 9″x5″x3″ loaf pan, waxed paper-lined and greased

2 tablespoons shortening, melted
1 cup granulated sugar
1 egg, unbeaten
2 cups all-purpose flour, sifted
1 teaspoon double-acting baking powder

1 teaspoon baking soda
½ teaspoon salt
1 cup orange juice
1½ tablespoons orange rind, grated
½ cup nut meats, chopped

1. Mix melted shortening with sugar.
2. Add egg and beat well.
3. Sift flour once before measuring. Mix and sift flour, baking powder, soda, and salt together.
4. Add dry ingredients alternately with orange juice, mixing thoroughly after each addition.
5. Add orange rind. Mix well.
6. Stir in nut meats.
7. Pour batter into waxed paper-lined and greased 9″x5″x3″ loaf pan.
8. Bake at 350°F. for about 1 hour.
9. Cool 10 minutes in pan before turning out.
10. Cool overnight before slicing.

INDIVIDUAL COFFEE CAKES

A good muffin-type breakfast cake.

Oven temperature: preheat to 375°F.
Baking time: 20 to 25 minutes

Yield: approximately 8 to 12 muffin-size coffee cakes
Pan: 2½″x1¼″ muffin pan, greased or lined with paper baking cups

¼ cup butter or margarine
¾ cup plus 1 tablespoon
  granulated sugar
2 eggs, separated (beat
  whites until stiff, not dry)

1¼ cups all-purpose flour,
  sifted
2 teaspoons double-acting
  baking powder
½ teaspoon salt
½ cup milk

1. Cream butter or margarine with sugar until light and fluffy.
2. Add egg yolks and beat well.
3. Sift flour once before measuring. Mix and sift flour, baking powder, and salt together.
4. Add dry ingredients alternately with milk, mixing thoroughly after each addition.
5. With pliable rubber scraper or whisk, gently fold in stiffly beaten egg whites.
6. Fill 2½"x1¼" greased or paper-lined muffin pan cups 1/2 full.
7. Sprinkle batter with topping.

TOPPING

⅓ cup granulated sugar
1 teaspoon cinnamon

½ cup nut meats, chopped

1. Mix all ingredients together thoroughly.
2. Sprinkle on top of batter.
3. Bake at 375°F. for 20 to 25 minutes.

Popovers and Corn Breads

SUGGESTIONS FOR BAKING POPOVERS

There are varied opinions on mixing and baking popovers. One rule that applies to every system is that ingredients should be room temperature.

Do not fill cups over ½ full, allowing room for that dramatic "pop."

SUGGESTIONS FOR BAKING CORN BREAD

Blend liquids and dry ingredients quickly, using just enough strokes to completely moisten.

Some cooks prefer preheated, well greased baking pans.

POPOVERS

One of life's real eating excitements!

Oven temperature: preheat to
  450°F.
Baking time: 45 minutes

Yield: 8 or 16 popovers
Pan: 2½"x1¼" muffin
  pans, oven glass custard
  cups, or classic cast iron
  popover pans, greased

SINGLE RECIPE	DOUBLE RECIPE
1 cup all-purpose flour, sifted	2 cups all-purpose flour, sifted
½ teaspoon salt	1 teaspoon salt
2 eggs, beaten	5 eggs, beaten
1 cup milk	2 cups milk
1 tablespoon butter, melted	2 tablespoons butter, melted

1. Sift flour once before measuring. Mix and sift flour and salt together.
2. Combine eggs, milk, and melted butter.
3. Add dry ingredients to liquid mixture. Beat very well.
4. Pour batter into preheated and greased 2½"x1¼" muffin pan cups, custard cups, or popover pans, filling each cup ½ full.
5. Bake at 450°F. for 15 minutes. REDUCE heat to 350°F. and bake 20 minutes longer.

SPOON BREAD

A fine accompaniment for roast pork or roast duckling.

Oven temperature: preheat to
  350°F.
Baking time: about 45 minutes

Yield: 6 to 8 servings
Pan: 2-quart casserole,
  greased

2 cups milk, scalded
½ cup cornmeal
2 tablespoons butter, melted
3 eggs, separated (beat
  whites until stiff, not dry)

1 teaspoon salt
½ teaspoon double-acting
  baking powder

86

1.   Scald milk. Gradually stir cornmeal into milk. Cook to mush stage, stirring constantly. Remove from heat. Add butter. Cool.
2.   Beat egg yolks until light. Add egg yolks and salt to corn meal mixture.
3.   With pliable rubber scraper or whisk, fold baking powder into stiffly beaten egg whites. Gently fold egg whites into corn meal mixture.
4.   Pour batter into greased 2-quart casserole.
5.   Bake at 350°F. for about 45 minutes.
6.   Eat immediately with lots of butter.

CORN BREAD OR MUFFINS

We like this old fashioned corn bread.

Oven temperature: preheat to 400°F.
Baking time: 15 to 20 minutes, muffins; 25 to 30 minutes, bread

Yield: approximately 8 servings, bread; approximately 12 servings, muffins
Pan: 9"x9"x2" square pan or 2½"x1¼" muffin pan, greased

2 eggs, slightly beaten
1 tablespoon butter, melted
2 tablespoons granulated sugar – tiny bit
1¼ cups milk + 3T

1 cup all-purpose flour, sifted
1 cup cornmeal
3 teaspoons (double-acting) baking powder ?
1 teaspoon salt

1.   Blend slightly beaten egg, melted butter, sugar, and milk *warm* together.
2.   Sift flour once before measuring. Mix flour, cornmeal, baking powder, and salt together.
3.   Make a well in center of dry ingredients. Add small amount of liquid mixture. Blend quickly. Add remaining liquid mixture, using as few strokes as possible to blend two together.
4.   Fill greased 2½"x1¼" muffin pan cups 2/3 full or pour batter into greased 9"x9"x2" square pan.
5.   Bake at 400°F. for 15 to 20 minutes, muffins; 25 to 30 minutes, bread.
    410-415

RAISIN CORNMEAL MUFFINS

Think how good these would be with baked ham!

Oven temperature: preheat to
350°F.
Baking time: about 30 minutes

Yield: 12 to 14 muffins
Pan: 2½"x1¼" muffin pan,
well greased

1 egg, beaten
2 tablespoons granulated
sugar
2 tablespoons butter, melted
1½ cups all-purpose flour,
sifted

1½ cups milk
½ cup cornmeal
1 teaspoon salt
4 teaspoons double-acting
baking powder
¾ cup raisins

1. Beat egg. Blend in sugar, melted butter, and milk.
2. Sift flour once before measuring. Mix flour, cornmeal, baking powder, and salt together.
3. Make a well in center of dry ingredients. Add small amount of liquid mixture. Blend quickly. Add remaining liquid mixture, using as few strokes as possible to blend two together completely.
4. Stir in raisins.
5. Fill well greased 2½"x1¼" muffin pan cups 2/3 full.
6. Bake at 350°F. for about 30 minutes.

SOUR CREAM OR BUTTERMILK CORN BREAD

You will find this happily different.

Oven temperature: preheat to
425°F.
Baking time: 25 to 30 minutes

Yield: approximately
8 servings
Pan: 9"x9"x2" square pan,
greased

2 eggs, beaten
3 tablespoons shortening or
butter, melted
1 tablespoon granulated
sugar
1 cup sour cream or
buttermilk

1 cup all-purpose flour, sifted
1 cup cornmeal
¾ teaspoon salt
½ teaspoon baking soda
1 teaspoon double-acting
baking powder

1.   Blend beaten eggs, melted shortening or butter, sugar, and buttermilk or sour cream together.
2.   Sift flour once before measuring. Mix flour, cornmeal, salt, soda, and baking powder together.
3.   Make a well in center of dry ingredients. Add small amount of liquid mixture. Blend quickly. Add remaining liquid mixture, using as few strokes as possible to blend the two together.
4.   Pour batter into greased 9"x9"x2" square pan.
5.   Bake at 425°F. for 25 to 30 minutes.
Note: This batter may be used for corn sticks or muffins also. Bake them at 425°F. for about 25 minutes.

Pancakes and Waffles

SUGGESTIONS FOR SUCCESSFUL PANCAKES

Quickly blend liquid and dry ingredients.
Cool shortening before adding to batter.
Lightly grease cooking surface with salad oil or shortening.
When few drops of water sprinkled over cooking surface bounce and sputter, the griddle is ready to cook pancakes.
If batter begins to thicken and does not pour easily, add a little milk.
Always serve pancakes immediately.
If you have batter left over, put it in refrigerator and later make fritters with it by adding cut up fresh fruits and frying in deep hot oil.

SUGGESTIONS FOR SUCCESSFUL WAFFLES

Quickly blend liquid and dry ingredients.
Cool melted shortening before adding to batter.
Stiffly beaten egg whites, folded in separately, make better waffles.
Do not grease waffle iron unless it is a very old type. Most electric irons are factory treated and do not need additional greasing.
Set waffle iron for degree of doneness you prefer. The higher heat designations make browner and crisper waffles.
Do not peek during baking. It takes about 5 minutes for

waffles to bake. When steam stops coming out sides of waffle iron, it is an indication that the baking time is nearly complete.

Waffles are a delightful base for creamed chicken, fish, or vegetables. They also make a fine dessert when topped with ice cream smothered with fruit or sauce.

Waffle batter keeps well in refrigerator.

PANCAKES

We could eat these every morning.

Yield: batter to serve 4

Pan: heavy griddle, skillet or electric frypan, very lightly greased, or greaseless type griddle or skillet

5 tablespoons granulated sugar
3 eggs, beaten
4 tablespoons butter, melted
½ teaspoon vanilla, if desired
2 cups milk

2½ cups all-purpose flour, sifted
1 teaspoon salt
1 teaspoon double-acting baking powder

1. Add sugar to beaten eggs.
2. Blend in melted butter, vanilla, and milk.
3. Sift flour once before measuring. Mix and sift flour, salt, and baking powder together.
4. Put dry ingredients in pitcher or mixing bowl that pours. Make a well in center of dry ingredients. Add small amount of liquid mixture. Blend quickly. Add remaining liquid mixture, using as few strokes as possible to blend the two together completely.
5. Preheat very lightly greased griddle or skillet. When few drops of water sprinkled on hot cooking surface bounce and sputter, the temperature is right (about 400° F. on electric skillet).
6. Pour or spoon batter onto cooking surface in amount for desired size pancakes. When top of pancake is well covered with bubbles beginning to burst, turn pancake. *Turn only once.*
7. Serve immediately.

Note: Melted butter and warmed syrup or honey are well worth the time it takes to heat them.

CORNMEAL GRIDDLE CAKES

Try this wonderful diversion from ordinary pancakes.

Yield: batter to serve 4

Pan: heavy griddle, skillet or electric frypan, very lightly greased, or greaseless type griddle or skillet

1 tablespoon granulated sugar
2 eggs, beaten
3 tablespoons butter or shortening, melted
1½ cups buttermilk
½ teaspoon soda dissolved in 2 tablespoons warm water

1½ cups all-purpose flour, sifted
¾ cup yellow cornmeal, sifted
1 teaspoon salt
3 teaspoons double-acting baking powder

1. Add sugar to beaten egg.
2. Blend in melted butter or shortening, buttermilk, and soda dissolved in water.
3. Sift flour once before measuring. Mix and sift flour, cornmeal, salt, and baking powder together.
4. Put dry ingredients in pitcher or mixing bowl that pours. Make a well in center of dry ingredients. Add small amount of liquid mixture. Blend quickly. Add remaining liquid mixture, using as few strokes as possible to blend the two together completely.
5. Preheat very lightly greased griddle or skillet. When few drops of water sprinkled on hot cooking surface bounce and sputter, the temperature is right (about 400°F. on electric skillet).
6. Pour or spoon batter onto cooking surface in amount for desired size pancakes. When top of pancake is well covered with bubbles beginning to burst, turn pancake. *Turn only once.*
7. Serve immediately.
Note: Melted butter and warmed syrup or honey are well worth the time it takes to heat them.

PANCAKES FOR TWO

Brides or mothers whose chicks have left the nest will find this handy.

Yield: batter to serve 2

Pan: heavy griddle, skillet or electric frypan, very lightly greased, or greaseless type griddle or skillet

1 tablespoon granulated sugar
1 egg, beaten
2 tablespoons butter, melted
¾ cup milk

1 cup all-purpose flour, sifted
⅛ teaspoon salt
2 teaspoons double-acting baking powder

1. Add sugar to beaten egg.
2. Blend in melted butter and milk.
3. Sift flour once before measuring. Mix and sift flour, salt, and baking powder together.
4. Put dry ingredients in pitcher or mixing bowl that pours. Make a well in center of dry ingredients. Add small amount of liquid mixture. Blend quickly. Add remaining liquid mixture, using as few strokes as possible to blend the two together completely.
5. Preheat very lightly greased griddle or skillet. When few drops of water sprinkled on hot cooking surface bounce and sputter, the temperature is right (about 400°F. on electric skillet).
6. Pour or spoon batter onto cooking surface in amount for desired size pancakes. When top of pancake is well covered with bubbles beginning to burst, turn pancake. *Turn only once.*
7. Serve immediately.
Note: Melted butter and warmed syrup or honey are well worth the time it takes to heat them.

DOROTHY'S FRENCH PANCAKES

The elite of all pancakes. Fill them with creamed chicken.

Yield: batter to serve 4 to 6

Pan: 6-inch skillet, very
lightly greased

4 eggs, well beaten
4 teaspoons butter or
margarine, melted
2 cups milk

1⅓ cups all-purpose flour,
sifted
½ teaspoon salt
¼ to ½ cup nut meats,
chopped

1.   Blend beaten eggs, melted butter or margarine, and milk together.
2.   Sift flour once before measuring. Mix and sift flour and salt together.
3.   Put dry ingredients in pitcher or mixing bowl that pours. Make a well in center of dry ingredients. Add small amount of liquid mixture. Blend quickly. Add remaining liquid mixture, using as few strokes as possible. Batter will be slightly lumpy.
4.   Stir in chopped nuts.
5.   Preheat very lightly greased 6-inch skillet. When few drops of water sprinkled on hot cooking surface bounce and sputter, the temperature is right.
6.   Pour about ¼ cup batter into skillet. Tip skillet back and forth and to sides. Brown and turn. *Turn only once.*
Note: For dessert, spread pancake with jelly, roll like jelly roll and sprinkle with powdered sugar.

BUCKWHEAT CAKES

Batter keeps well.

Yield: batter to serve 4

Pan: heavy griddle, skillet or electric frypan very lightly greased, or greaseless type griddle or skillet

1 tablespoon granulated sugar or molasses
1 egg, beaten
2 tablespoons shortening or butter, melted
2¼ cups milk
½ teaspoon salt

½ cup all-purpose flour, sifted and 1½ cups buckwheat flour, *OR* 1 cup all-purpose flour, sifted and 1 cup buckwheat flour
4 teaspoons double-acting baking powder

1. Add sugar or molasses to beaten egg.
2. Blend in melted shortening or butter and milk.
3. Sift flour once before measuring. Mix salt, flour, baking powder, and buckwheat flour together very well.
4. Put dry ingredients in pitcher or mixing bowl that pours. Make a well in center of dry ingredients. Add small amount of liquid mixture. Blend quickly. Add remaining liquid mixture, using as few strokes as possible to blend the two together completely.
5. Preheat very lightly greased griddle or skillet. When few drops of water sprinkled on hot cooking surface bounce and sputter, the temperature is right (about 400°F. on electric skillet).
6. Pour or spoon batter onto cooking surface in amount for desired size pancakes. When top of pancake is well covered with bubbles beginning to burst, turn pancake. *Turn only once.*
7. Serve immediately.
Note: Melted butter and warmed syrup or honey are well worth the time it takes to heat them.

WHOLE WHEAT OR GRAHAM GRIDDLE CAKES

*These are made with yeast and should be made the night before
you have need for them.*

Yield: batter to serve 4

Pan: heavy griddle, skillet or
electric frypan, very lightly
greased, or greaseless type
griddle or skillet

2 cups milk, scalded
1 tablespoon butter or
margarine, melted
1 tablespoon granulated
sugar
1 teaspoon salt

½ cake yeast
1 cup all-purpose flour, sifted
1 cup whole wheat or graham
flour
¼ teaspoon soda dissolved
in 2 tablespoons milk

1.   Scald milk. Stir in butter or margarine, sugar, and salt. Cool
to *lukewarm.*
2.   In bowl large enough to accommodate raised dough, stir
yeast into *lukewarm* milk.
3.   Sift all-purpose flour once before measuring. Mix all-purpose
and graham flour together.
4.   Put dry ingredients in pitcher or mixing bowl that pours.
Make a well in center of dry ingredients. Add small amount of
yeast mixture. Beat well. Add remainder of yeast mixture. Beat
well again.
5.   Cover bowl with damp cloth, leaving edges on outside of
bowl. Refrigerate overnight.
6.   In morning add soda dissolved in milk to batter.
7.   Preheat very lightly greased griddle or skillet. When few
drops of water sprinkled on hot cooking surface bounce and sputter, the temperature is right (about 400°F. on electric skillet).
8.   Pour or spoon batter onto cooking surface in amount for desired size pancakes. When top of pancake is well covered with
bubbles beginning to burst, turn pancake. *Turn only once.*
9.   Serve immediately.
Note: Melted butter and warmed syrup or honey are well worth
the time it takes to heat them.

LEILA'S BUTTERFLY GRIDDLE CAKES

A very talented cook dreamed these up.

Yield: batter to serve 2 to 3

Pan: heavy griddle, skillet or electric frypan, very lightly greased, or greaseless type griddle or skillet

3 eggs, separated (beat whites until stiff, not dry)
½ cup milk
¾ cup all-purpose flour, sifted

½ teaspoon salt
¼ cup commercial sour cream
3 tablespoons butter, melted

1.   Beat egg yolks in pitcher or mixing bowl that pours. Add milk.
2.   Sift flour once before measuring. Mix and sift flour and salt together.
3.   Gradually add dry ingredients to liquid mixture, using as few strokes as possible to blend the two together completely.
4.   Blend in sour cream and melted butter.
5.   With pliable rubber scraper or whisk, gently fold in stiffly beaten egg whites.
6.   Preheat very lightly greased griddle or skillet. When few drops of water sprinkled on hot cooking surface bounce and sputter, the temperature is right (about 400°F. on electric skillet).
7.   Pour or spoon batter onto cooking surface in amount for desired size pancakes. When top of pancake is well covered with bubbles beginning to burst, turn pancake. *Turn only once.*
Note: Melted butter and warmed syrup or honey are well worth the time it takes to heat them.

BUTTERMILK PANCAKES

So light they will melt in your mouth.

Yield: batter to serve 3 to 4

Pan: heavy griddle, skillet or electric frypan, very lightly greased or greaseless type griddle or skillet

1 tablespoon granulated sugar
1 egg, beaten
1 tablespoon butter, melted
1¼ cups buttermilk

1½ cups all-purpose flour, sifted
½ teaspoon salt
½ teaspoon baking soda

1. Add sugar to beaten egg.
2. Blend in melted butter and buttermilk.
3. Sift flour once before measuring. Mix and sift flour, salt, and soda together.
4. Put dry ingredients in pitcher or mixing bowl that pours. Make a well in center of dry ingredients. Add small amount of liquid mixture. Blend quickly. Add remaining liquid mixture, using as few strokes as possible to blend the two together completely.
5. Preheat very lightly greased griddle or skillet. When few drops of water sprinkled on hot cooking surface bounce and sputter, the temperature is right (about 400°F. on electric skillet).
6. Pour or spoon batter onto cooking surface in amount for desired size pancakes. When top of pancake is well covered with bubbles beginning to burst, turn pancake. *Turn only once.*
7. Serve immediately.
Note: Melted butter and warmed syrup or honey are well worth the time it takes to heat them.

OATMEAL PANCAKES

This recipe was passed on to us by an old Coloradan.

Yield: batter to serve 4

Pan: heavy griddle, skillet or electric frypan, very lightly greased, or greaseless type griddle or skillet

2 cups milk
1½ cups quick-cooking rolled oats
2 tablespoons granulated sugar
⅓ cup shortening or butter, melted

2 eggs, beaten
1 cup all-purpose flour, sifted
½ teaspoon salt
2½ teaspoons double-acting baking powder

1. In pitcher or mixing bowl that pours, blend milk and rolled oats together. Let stand 5 minutes.
2. Add sugar and melted butter or shortening to beaten eggs. Combine with oats and milk mixture.
3. Sift flour once before measuring. Mix and sift flour, salt, and baking powder together.
4. Add dry ingredients to oats and milk mixture a little at a time. Blend quickly after each addition, using as few strokes as possible.
5. Preheat very lightly greased griddle or skillet. When few drops of water sprinkled on hot cooking surface bounce and sputter, the temperature is right (about 400°F. on electric skillet).
6. Pour or spoon batter onto cooking surface in amount for desired size pancakes. When top of pancake is well covered with bubbles beginning to burst, turn pancake. *Turn only once.*
7. Serve immediately.

Note: Melted butter and warmed syrup or honey are well worth the time it takes to heat them.

CHOCOLATE WAFFLES

Attention, all chocolate lovers!

Yield: batter to serve 6

Pan: waffle iron, preheated to temperature desired

2 ounces chocolate, melted
2 tablespoons shortening, melted
3 tablespoons granulated sugar
2 eggs, separated (beat whites until stiff, not dry)

1½ cups milk
½ teaspoon vanilla
2 cups cake flour, sifted
1 teaspoon salt
3 teaspoons double-acting baking powder

1. Melt chocolate and shortening over simmering water. Cool.
2. Add sugar to beaten egg yolks. Blend in milk and vanilla.
3. Sift flour once before measuring. Mix and sift flour, salt, and baking powder together.
4. Put dry ingredients in pitcher or mixing bowl that pours. Make a well in center of dry ingredients. Add small amount of liquid mixture. Blend quickly. Add remaining liquid mixture. Add and mix chocolate mixture.
5. With pliable rubber scraper or whisk, gently fold in stiffly beaten egg whites.
6. Fill preheated waffle iron 2/3 full. Bake approximately 5 minutes, or until done.

BUTTERMILK WAFFLES

Children say "Oh, boy!" when these are on the breakfast menu.

Yield: batter to serve 4

Pan: waffle iron, preheated to temperature desired

½ cup butter or shortening, melted
1¼ cups buttermilk
2 eggs, separated (beat whites until stiff, not dry)

1¾ cups all-purpose flour, *OR* 2 cups cake flour, sifted
½ teaspoon salt
2 teaspoons double-acting baking powder
½ teaspoon baking soda

1. Blend melted butter or shortening, buttermilk, and egg yolks.
2. Sift flour once before measuring. Mix and sift flour, salt, baking powder, and soda together.
3. Put dry ingredients in pitcher or mixing bowl that pours. Make a well in center of dry ingredients. Add small amount of liquid mixture. Blend quickly. Add remaining liquid mixture, using as few strokes as possible to blend together completely.
4. With scraper or whisk, gently fold in stiffly beaten egg whites.
5. Fill preheated waffle iron 2/3 full. Bake approximately 5 minutes.

WAFFLES

Fit for a king, the head of the house, or Sunday night company.

Yield: batter to serve 6

Pan: waffle iron, preheated to temperature desired

2 tablespoons granulated sugar

2 eggs, separated (beat whites until stiff, not dry)

½ cup butter or shortening, melted

2 cups all-purpose flour, sifted

½ teaspoon salt

4 teaspoons double-acting baking powder

1¾ cups milk

1. Add sugar to beaten egg yolks.
2. Blend in melted butter and milk.
3. Sift flour once before measuring. Mix and sift flour, salt, and baking powder together.
4. Put dry ingredients in pitcher or mixing bowl that pours. Make a well in center of dry ingredients. Add small amount of liquid mixture. Blend quickly. Add remaining liquid mixture, using as few strokes as possible to blend the two together completely.
5. With pliable rubber scraper or whisk, gently fold in stiffly beaten egg whites.
6. Fill preheated waffle iron 2/3 full. Bake approximately 5 minutes.
7. Serve immediately.

Note: Melted butter and warmed syrup or honey are well worth the time it takes to heat them.

Doughnuts, Fritters, and Dumplings

NEW ENGLAND DOUGHNUTS

The good old spiced cake doughnut we love so well.

Yield: 3 dozen doughnuts
Pan: heavy sauce pan, or
   skillet at least 3 inches
   deep

Cooking temperature: melted
   shortening or cooking oil
   heated to 360°-375°F.

1 cup granulated sugar
2 eggs, beaten
4 tablespoons shortening
   melted
1 cup milk
4 cups all-purpose flour, sifted

3 teaspoons double-acting
   baking powder
½ teaspoon salt
¼ teaspoon nutmeg or
   cinnamon

1. In mixing bowl, gradually add sugar to beaten eggs.
2. Blend in melted shortening and milk.
3. Sift flour once before measuring. Mix and sift flour, baking powder, salt, and nutmeg or cinnamon together.
4. Add dry ingredients to liquid mixture and stir until blended.
5. Dough may be chilled until manageable. If manageable it is not necessary to chill dough.
6. On well floured surface, roll dough out 3/8-inch thick. Cut with doughnut cutter. Cut out doughnuts that are dried for 15 minutes before cooking absorb less fat when cooking.
7. Fry doughnuts in deep melted shortening or cooking oil heated to 360°-375°F., or hot enough to brown bread cube in 1 minute. Have sufficient fat to float doughnuts while cooking.
8. Brown doughnuts on one side. Turn and brown on other, about 3 minutes in all.
9. Drain on paper toweling, or other absorbent paper, or place in oven at 375°F. until crisp and dry.
10. Roll in powdered sugar, or sprinkle with mixture of 2 teaspoons cinnamon and ⅔ cup granulated sugar. Doughnuts may be shaken in paper bag containing either of these coatings.

ORANGE DROP DOUGHNUTS

Serve warm with milk or coffee, and the day will be off to a good start.

Cooking temperature: melted shortening or cooking oil heated 360°-375°F.

Yield: 2 dozen doughnuts
Pan: heavy sauce pan, or skillet at least 3 inches deep

2 tablespoons shortening
½ cup granulated sugar
2 eggs, beaten
1 tablespoon orange rind, grated
2 cups all-purpose flour, sifted

2½ teaspoons double-acting baking powder
½ teaspoon salt
½ teaspoon nutmeg
½ cup orange juice

1. Cream shortening with sugar until light and fluffy.
2. Add beaten eggs and orange rind. Blend well.
3. Sift flour once before measuring. Mix and sift flour, baking powder, salt, and nutmeg together.
4. Add dry ingredients alternately with orange juice, mixing thoroughly after each addition.
5. Drop dough by teaspoonful into deep melted shortening or cooking oil, heated to 360°-375°F., or hot enough to brown bread cube in 1 minute. Have sufficient oil to float doughnuts.
6. Brown doughnuts on one side. Turn and brown on other, about 3 minutes, or less, in all.
7. Drain on paper toweling or other absorbent paper, or place in oven at 375°F. until crisp and dry.
8. Roll in powdered sugar, or sprinkle with mixture of 2 teaspoons cinnamon and ⅔ cup granulated sugar. Doughnuts may be shaken in paper bag containing either of these coatings. Very good served warm with syrup or honey.
Note: For plain drop doughnuts, omit orange rind. Substitute ½ cup milk for orange juice.

RAISED DOUGHNUTS

These light, fluffy doughnuts either glazed or sugared are the first choice at our houses.

Cooking temperature: melted shortening or cooking oil heated to 360°-375°F.

Yield: 2 dozen doughnuts
Pan: heavy sauce pan, or skillet at least 3 inches deep

1 cup milk, scalded
¼ cup granulated sugar
1 teaspoon salt
¼ cup shortening

1 cake yeast
3½ to 3¾ cups all-purpose flour, sifted

1. Scald milk. While it is still hot, dissolve in it sugar, salt, and shortening.
2. When milk mixture is *lukewarm,* add yeast and stir until it is dissolved.
3. Sift flour once before measuring.
4. Stir flour thoroughly into milk mixture until it becomes too stiff to stir easily, then, with hands, knead remaining flour into dough.
5. Enough kneading is achieved when there are no scraps of dough or flour, and the bowl sides are clean.
6. Cover dough with cloth and set in warm place to rise.
7. When it is doubled in bulk, roll dough out on well floured surface 1/2-inch thick. Cut with doughnut cutter.
8. Fry the doughnuts in deep melted shortening or cooking oil, heated 360°-375°F., or hot enough to brown bread cube in 1 minute. Have sufficient cooking oil to float doughnuts.
9. Brown doughnuts on one side. Turn and brown on other, about 3 minutes in all.
10. Drain doughnuts on paper toweling or other absorbent paper.

SOUR CREAM DOUGHNUTS

Some Sunday morning, treat your family to something special like these.

Cooking temperature: melted shortening or cooking oil heated 360°-375°F.

Yield: about 4 dozen doughnuts

Pan: heavy sauce pan or skillet at least 3 inches deep

2 eggs, beaten
1 cup granulated sugar
¾ cup sour cream
¾ cup sour milk or butter-milk
4½ cups all-purpose flour, sifted

½ teaspoon salt
1 teaspoon baking soda
1¾ teaspoons double-acting baking powder
1 teaspoon nutmeg

1.   To beaten eggs, gradually add sugar.
2.   Blend in sour cream and sour milk or buttermilk.
3.   Sift flour once before measuring. Mix and sift flour, salt, soda, baking powder, and nutmeg together.
4.   Add dry ingredients to egg mixture and stir until blended.
5.   A little more flour may be added if dough does not seem stiff enough to roll. Chilling the dough will make it more manageable.
6.   On well floured surface, roll the dough 3/8-inch thick and cut with doughnut cutter. Cut out doughnuts that are dried 15 minutes before cooking absorb less fat when cooking.
7.   Fry the doughnuts in deep melted shortening or cooking oil heated to 360°-375°F., or hot enough to brown bread cube in 1 minute. Have sufficient cooking oil to float doughnuts.
8.   Brown doughnuts on one side. Turn and brown on other, about 3 minutes in all.
9.   Drain on paper toweling or other absorbent paper, or place in oven at 375°F. until crisp and dry.
10.   Roll in powdered sugar, or sprinkle with mixture of 2 teaspoons cinnamon and ⅔ cup granulated sugar. Doughnuts may be shaken in paper bag containing either of these coatings. Icings and glazes are good finishing touches, too.

CORN FRITTERS

Cooking temperature: melted shortening or cooking oil preheated to 360°F.

Yield: batter to serve 4
Pan: heavy sauce pan or deep edge skillet

1 egg, slightly beaten
½ cup milk
⅞ cup all-purpose flour, sifted

1 teaspoon double-acting baking powder
¾ cup canned whole kernel corn, drained

1. Blend egg and milk.
2. Sift flour once before measuring. Mix and sift flour and baking powder together.
3. Make a well in center of dry ingredients. Add small amount of liquid mixture. Blend quickly. Add remaining amount of liquid mixture, using as few strokes as possible to blend two together completely.
4. Add drained corn.
5. Drop by spoonfuls into melted shortening or cooking oil preheated to 360°F. Cook until brown. Drain on absorbent paper.
Note: Serve with maple syrup or honey.

FRUIT FRITTERS

Dip apple slices, bananas, cherries, or pineapple in this batter.

Cooking temperature: melted shortening or cooking oil preheated to 360°F.

Yield: batter to serve 4 to 6
Pan: heavy sauce pan or deep edge skillet

2 eggs, beaten
2 tablespoons granulated sugar
1 tablespoon shortening or butter, melted
½ teaspoon vanilla, if desired
½ cup milk

1½ cups all-purpose flour, sifted
½ teaspoon salt
2 teaspoons double-acting baking powder
fruit of choice, see below (steps 4 and 5)

1.   Blend beaten eggs, sugar, melted shortening or butter, vanilla, and milk together.
2.   Sift flour once before measuring. Mix and sift flour, salt, and baking powder together.
3.   Make a well in center of dry ingredients. Add small amount of liquid mixture. Blend quickly. Add remaining amount of liquid mixture, using as few strokes as possible to blend two together.
4.   Dip slices of banana, or peeled apple, or pineapple in batter. Drop into melted shortening or cooking oil preheated to 360°F. Cook until brown. Drain on absorbent paper. *OR:*
5.   Stir into batter 1 cup of apple, chopped; or 2 bananas, sliced 1/4 inch thick; or 1 cup pineapple bits, drained or 1 cup pie cherries, drained. Drop by tablespoonfuls into preheated melted shortening or cooking oil. Cook until brown. Drain on absorbent paper.
Note: Serve fritters with syrup or sprinkled with powdered sugar.

GOOD DUMPLINGS FOR CHICKEN OR MEAT STEWS

Just the sound of chicken and dumplings whets the appetite!

Yield: 12 dumplings

1 egg, slightly beaten
2 tablespoons butter, melted
1 cup milk
2 cups all-purpose flour, sifted
2 teaspoons double-acting
  baking powder

½   teaspoon salt
1 teaspoon parsley, chopped,
  OR ¼ teaspoon thyme or
  savory, if desired

1.   Blend egg, melted butter, and milk together.
2.   Sift flour once before measuring. Mix and sift together flour, baking powder, salt, and herbs, if desired.
3.   Make a well in center of dry ingredients. Add small amount of liquid mixture. Blend quickly. Add remaining liquid mixture, using as few strokes as possible to blend two together. Dough should be stiff. Add a small additional amount of flour if necessary.
4.   Drop dough by tablespoonfuls into hot broth. Cover with lid and cook 10 minutes. Uncover and cook 10 minutes more.

CAKES

Ingredient Definitions 110

Tips for Handling Ingredients 110

Mixing Tips 111

Pan Preparation 111

Baking Problems and Solutions 112

Proper Placement of Layer Cakes in Oven 112

General Tips 112

Tips for Freezing Cakes 113

CREAMED CAKES
Creamed Cake Tips 115

WHITE CAKES
Mrs. Egan's Dessert Ring 115

Poppy Seed Cake 116

Lady Baltimore White Cake 117

Chocolate Shower Cake 118

Coconut Cake 118

Powdered Sugar Cake 119

One Bowl White Sheet Cake 120

Two-Layer White Cake 120

YELLOW CAKES
Quick-Method Golden Layer Cake 121

Three-Layer Yellow Cake 122

Lazy Daisy Cake 123

Pound Cake 124

CHOCOLATE CAKES
Pete's Sour Cream Cake 124

Economy Fudge Cake 125

Betty's Elegant Chocolate Cake 126

Lee's Nut Fudge Cake 127

Grandmother Andrew's Chocolate Cake 128
Cocoa Cake 129
Salad Dressing Chocolate Cake 130
Ken's Continental Chocolate Cake 130
Spice Chocolate Mashed Potato Cake 132
Miss Dispence's Chocolate Cake 133

ASSORTED CREAMED CAKES

Applesauce Cake 134
Sour Cream Cake 134
Whipped Cream Cake 135
Party Applesauce Cake 136
Burnt Sugar Cake 137
Miss Rose's Gingerbread 138
Hallowe'en Marble Cake 139
A Man's Cake 140
Maple-Nut Cake 141
Peach or Pineapple Upside Down Cake 142
Mark's Pumpkin Cake 143
Scripture Cake 144
Spice Cake 145
Little Spice Cake 146

CUPCAKES

Cupcake Tips 146
Dee's Fudge Sponge Cup Cakes 147
Golden Cupcakes 148
Puff Cakes 148
Coffee Cupcakes 149

FRUIT CAKES

Holiday Fruit Cake 150
Chocolate Bits, Cherry, and Date Cake 151
Old Fashioned Dark Fruit Cake 152
Economy Fruit Cake 153

SPONGE CAKES

Sponge Cake Tips 154

Angel Food Cake Deluxe   155
Yellow Angel Food Cake   156
Jelly Roll   157
John's Chocolate Roll   158
Mocha Torte   159
Viennese Torte   160
Sponge Cake   161
Four-Egg Sponge Cake   162

Space for notes, Page 154

Toppings Pages 116, 123

Fillings, Pages 122, 137

Icings, Pages 123, 126, 128, 131, 136, 147

SUGGESTIONS FOR SUCCESSFUL CAKE BAKING

Unquestionably, we think that a cake made from "scratch" is well worth the few minutes more it takes to make it.

INGREDIENT DEFINITIONS

Use double-acting baking powder always in these recipes. If substitution is necessary, see "Ingredient Substitutions," page 22.

Use high grade emulsifier-type or hydrogenated-type shortenings (all vegetable or combination vegetable and meat fat oils), if possible. Do not substitute melted fats or vegetable or salad oils for these shortenings. For extra flavor, half butter and half shortening may be used where shortening is designated. Substituting shortening for butter may impair the flavor of cakes.

Butter, emulsified or hydrogenated shortenings, and margarine may be interchanged cupful for cupful.

Use high quality margarine when margarine is specified. In some recipes, the flavor will be jeopardized if margarine is substituted for butter.

Use whole, sweet milk when milk is denoted. Use unsweetened, canned milk when recipe calls for evaporated milk.

Do not use soured cream when recipe calls for commercial sour cream.

Use pure vanila extract for best flavor.

Self-rising flour does not produce satisfactory cakes at altitudes over 3,500 feet.

If using all-purpose flour to replace cake flour, use ⅞ cup instead of 1 cup.

TIPS FOR HANDLING INGREDIENTS

To dredge candied fruits, nuts, raisins, and the like, save 2 tablespoons of flour from amount called for in recipe. This is to prevent pieces sticking together, or all going to the bottom of the batter.

Use scissors dipped in hot water when cutting up dates, marshmallows, raisins, figs, and so forth.

Melt chocolate in double-boiler, or equivalent, over simmering, not boiling, water.

MIXING TIPS

For creaming shortening with sugar use medium speed on electric mixer. Scrape bottom and sides of bowl frequently so that ingredients will be blended uniformly. *Do not under-cream shortening and sugar*. Too little creaming causes coarse texture. It is practically impossible to cream too much.

If eggs are overbeaten at high altitude the cake will be too dry. *Do not overbeat when adding flour and liquid*, or after their addition. This will dry out the cake and toughen its texture. *Remember, retention of moisture is very necessary to successful high altitude baking*.

Set the mixer at high speed to beat egg whites stiffly. "Beat until stiff, not dry" means beat whites until they keep shape when beater is lifted and sharp peaks are formed. They should retain a glossy look. Too dry egg whites resemble the froth of soap suds. Egg whites are best beaten just before use.

We do not recommend the use of an electric mixer for folding in egg whites. A pliable rubber scraper or wire whisk is best. The folding-in method of adding egg whites to batter is meant to include as much air as possible in this process, so do not beat or mash the egg whites when "gently" folding them in. When folding in egg whites, keep bowl rotating with non-mixing hand. With scraper or whisk make a complete circle through the batter from upper outer edge of bowl over the top of the batter to center of bowl, down through the batter to the bottom of bowl, along bottom and up side to point of beginning.

We do not recommend using the electric mixer for stirring in nuts, chocolate bits, and fruits.

PAN PREPARATION

To determine size of cake pan, measure across top from inside edge to inside edge. Use correct size pan properly prepared.

To grease pans, spread lightly with *unsalted* fat. Salted butter burns readily and vegetable or salad oils sometimes are detrimental to the batter.

To flour pans, sprinkle greased pan lightly with flour, or gently shake flour sifter over greased surface. Use cocoa to "flour" chocolate cake pans.

To line pans with waxed paper, set pan on sheet of waxed

paper. Trace around edge of pan with sharp point. Cut out along line of tracing. Put waxed paper in bottom of cake pan.

To grease pans lined with waxed paper, gently coat waxed paper lining with shortening or unsalted margarine.

Do not grease and use spotlessly clean pan for angel food or sponge cakes.

BAKING PROBLEMS AND SOLUTIONS

If baked cake is higher on one side: (a) batter was spread unevenly in pan; (b) pans were set too close to sides of oven; (c) range was not level; (d) warped cake pans were used.

If cake burns on sides: (a) oven was too full; (b) oven was too hot; (c) pans were too close to sides of oven.

If cake cracks on top: (a) oven was too hot; (b) batter was too thick.

If cake is streaky, flour has been exposed to moisture.

If cake sticks to bottom of pan, dip a cloth in hot water, wring it out, and place it under cake pan until cake loosens.

PROPER PLACEMENT OF LAYER CAKES IN OVEN

Place cake pans at least one inch away from sides of oven.

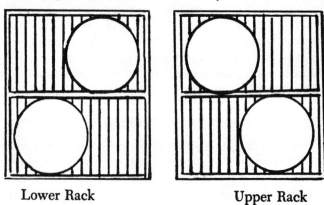

Lower Rack   Upper Rack

GENERAL TIPS

Fill pans only two-thirds full. Cut through batter with knife two or three times before putting cake in oven. This will remove air bubbles.

Cake is done when a wire cake tester, toothpick, or broomstraw comes out clean when inserted into the thickest part of cake. Another test for doneness is to press the surface of cake lightly with fingertips. If it springs back quickly, it is done. Cake will shrink away from sides of pan when done.

To cool, remove pan from oven and let it set for five minutes, then turn the cake out of the pan onto a wire rack to complete cooling. Remove waxed paper. An angel food or sponge cake must cool *completely* before being removed from pan.

Brush crumbs from any cake before icing and cut off any hard edges.

Do not ice cake until completely cool.

TIPS FOR FREEZING CAKES

Generally, it is easier and more successful to bake a cake before freezing. A frozen baked cake will be as fresh as the moment is was baked, when first defrosted; but it will dry out more quickly. If your family does not eat a whole cake soon after baking, cut the cake in half, package and freeze each half separately. Or cut it in quarters, thirds, or pieces, according to what you think you will need. Thaw all frozen baked cakes at room temperature *without* removing freezer wrapper. Always wrap any cake in moisture-vaporproof wrapping (foil, film, or freezer paper), seal, label, and date.

Creamed cakes freeze the best. A frozen fruit cake will freeze almost indefinitely because it is so solid and holds its shape so well. It seems the richer the cake batter the better the cake freezes.

Sponge and *angel cakes* freeze well, provided they are not made with cornstarch. Sponge cakes are fragile so they must be handled with caution. A baked frozen sponge cake may shrink a bit. Angel and sponge cakes freeze well up to about 3 months.

Cupcakes are so easy to freeze. Bake them in paper baking cups set in muffin pans. Cool. Do not remove paper cups. Simply place cooled cupcakes in a large plastic bag, exhaust the air, seal, and freeze. You may then remove as many as needed, re-seal the bag, and return it to the freezer.

We think it advisable to quick freeze all frosted cakes and cupcakes, immediately remove from freezer and wrap properly,

113

then return to freezer for storage. This prevents the frosting and wrapping from sticking together.

Unbaked cake batter may be frozen, though it is usually not as satisfactory or convenient as baking first. If you choose to make cake batter to freeze, be sure to use *double-acting* baking powder, and plan to bake the batter within 2 weeks of freezer time. This is because the baking powder loses its power to make the cake rise after a certain length of time, due to the intense cold. Freeze batter in the prepared pan you intend to bake it in (use only oven glass or aluminum cake pans for the freezer). Quick freeze the batter directly on a freezer shelf. Remove it immediately and properly wrap it in moisture-vaporproof wrapping. To bake, take it directly from the freezer to preheated oven. Batter frozen in an 8-inch layer pan may be baked without thawing at 375°F. for 35 to 40 minutes. Cupcakes may be baked without thawing at 275°F. for 15 minutes, then at 350°F. for 15 minutes more.

Creamed Cakes

CREAMED CAKE TIPS

Have butter soft, but not runny or melted.

Be certain butter and sugar are creamed until very light and fluffy.

Beaten egg whites should be stiff, but not dry, forming glossy peaks.

Do not overmix dry ingredients and liquid additions.

WHITE CAKES

MRS. EGAN'S DESSERT RING

Delicious sour cream cake with topping baked right on.

Oven temperature: preheat to 350°F.
Baking time: 50 to 60 minutes

Yield: 12 servings
Pan: 9"x3½" tube pan, greased and floured

¾ cup butter
1½ cups granulated sugar
2 eggs, beaten
1 cup commercial sour cream
1 teaspoon vanilla

2 cups cake flour, sifted
¼ teaspoon salt
1 teaspoon double-acting baking powder

1. Cream butter with sugar until light and fluffy.
2. Add eggs one at a time and beat well.
3. Blend in sour cream and vanilla.
4. Sift flour once before measuring. Mix and sift flour, salt, and baking powder together.
5. Add dry ingredients to creamed mixture a little at a time, mixing thoroughly after each addition.
6. Spoon batter into greased and floured 9"x3½" tube pan.

2 tablespoons brown sugar,
firmly packed
1 teaspoon instant cocoa mix

½ teaspoon cinnamon
½ cup pecan meats,
chopped

1. Mix all ingredients together thoroughly.
2. Sprinkle over top of cake batter.
3. Bake at 350°F. for 50 to 60 minutes.

POPPY SEED CAKE

This is the only dessert that a restaurant near Chicago serves because it is so lusciously different. It adjusted perfectly for high altitude baking.

Oven temperature: preheat to
375°F.
Baking time: about 35 minutes

Yield: approximately
10 servings
Pan: 2 nine-inch layer pans,
greased and floured

¼ cup poppy seeds
1 cup milk
⅔ cup butter
1½ cups granulated sugar
2 cups plus 2 tablespoons
cake flour, sifted

2 teaspoons double-acting
baking powder
½ teaspoon salt
½ teaspoon vanilla
4 egg whites, beaten until
stiff, not dry

1. Soak poppy seeds in milk for at least 5 hours in refrigerator.
2. Cream butter with sugar until light and fluffy.
3. Sift flour once before measuring. Mix and sift flour, baking powder, and salt together.
4. Add dry ingredients alternately with milk and poppy seed mixture, mixing thoroughly after each addition.
5. Add vanilla. Mix very well.
6. With pliable rubber scraper or whisk gently fold in stiffly beaten egg whites.
7. Pour batter into two greased and floured 8-inch layer pans.
8. Bake at 375°F. for about 35 minutes.
Note: Butter-Nut frosting and filling on page 165 is a delicious complement to this cake.

LADY BALTIMORE WHITE CAKE

The lovliest of traditional white birthday cakes to be decoratively iced in any color or flavor.

Oven temperature: preheat to 350°F.

Baking time: 25 to 30 minutes

Yield: approximately 16 servings

Pan: 3 eight-inch layer pans, greased and floured or waxed paper lined and greased

½ cup butter
1½ cups granulated sugar
3 cups cake flour, sifted
4 teaspoons double-acting baking powder
½ teaspoon salt
1 cup water

1 teaspoon vanilla, *OR* ½ teaspoon vanilla and ¼ teaspoon almond extract
4 egg whites, beaten until stiff, not dry

1. Cream butter with sugar until light and fluffy.
2. Sift flour once before measuring. Mix and sift flour, salt, and baking powder together.
3. Add dry ingredients alternately with water, mixing thoroughly after each addition.
4. Add vanilla, or vanilla and almond extract and mix very well.
5. With pliable rubber scraper or whisk gently fold in stiffly beaten egg whites.
6. Pour batter into three greased and floured or waxed paper lined and greased 8-inch layer pans.
7. Bake at 350°F. for 25 to 30 minutes.

Note: 1 cup walnut meats, ground, are a rich addition to this cake batter.

CHOCOLATE SHOWER CAKE

All men are crazy about this cake.

Oven temperature: preheat to
375°F.

Baking time: 25 to 30 minutes

Yield. approximately
10 servings

Pan: 2 nine-inch layer pans,
greased and floured

½ cup butter or margarine
1 cup granulated sugar
2 cups cake flour, sifted
2 teaspoons double-acting
baking powder

½ teaspoon salt
1 cup water or skim milk
1 teaspoon vanilla
⅔ cup chocolate,
coarsely shaved
3 egg whites

1. Cream butter or margarine with ½ cup sugar until light and fluffy.
2. Sift flour once before measuring. Mix and sift flour, baking powder, and salt together.
3. Add dry ingredients alternately with water or milk, mixing thoroughly after each addition.
4. Add vanilla and shaved chocolate. Mix very well.
5. Beat egg whites until very stiff. Gradually beat in the remaining ½ cup sugar.
6. With pliable rubber scraper or whisk, gently fold egg white mixture into batter.
7. Pour batter into two greased and floured 9-inch layer pans.
8. Bake at 375°F. for 25 to 30 minutes.

COCONUT CAKE

A moist, tender cake with a fascinating flavor.

Oven temperature: preheat to
375°F.

Baking time: about 25 to 30
minutes

Yield: approximately
10 servings

Pan: 2 nine-inch
layers, greased and floured

1 cup coconut, shredded
2 tablespoons milk
¾ cup butter or margarine
1¾ cups minus 1 table-
spoon granulated sugar
2¾ cups all-purpose flour,
sifted
½ teaspoon salt

2½ teaspoons double-acting
baking powder
1 cup plus 2 tablespoons
water
1 teaspoon lemon extract
4 egg whites, beaten until
stiff, not dry

1. Soak coconut in milk.
2. Cream butter or margarine with sugar until light and fluffy.
3. Sift flour once before measuring. Mix and sift flour, salt, and baking powder together.
4. Add dry ingredients alternately with water, mixing thoroughly after each addition.
5. Add lemon extract and coconut-milk mixture. Mix very well.
6. With pliable rubber scraper or whisk, gently fold in stiffly beaten egg whites.
7. Pour batter into two greased and floured 9-inch layer pans.
8. Bake at 375°F. for 30 minutes.
Note: This cake is good with a citrus flavored frosting.

POWDERED SUGAR CAKE

What a heavenly, elegant white cake . . . butter-tasty, feather-light!

Oven temperature: preheat to 350°F.

Baking time: 25 to 30 minutes

Yield: approximately 12 servings

Pan: 3 eight-inch layer pans, greased and floured or waxed paper lined and greased

2 cups powdered sugar
⅔ cup butter
2½ cups cake flour, sifted
½ teaspoon salt
2½ teaspoons double-acting baking powder

1 cup plus 1 tablespoon milk
1 teaspoon vanilla or almond extract
6 egg whites, beaten until stiff, not dry

1. Sift measured powdered sugar over butter. Cream until light and fluffy.
2. Sift flour once before measuring. Mix and sift flour, salt, and baking powder together.
3. Add dry ingredients alternately with milk, mixing thoroughly after each addition.
4. Add vanilla or almond extract. Mix very well.
5. With pliable rubber scraper or whisk gently fold in stiffly beaten egg whites.
6. Pour batter into three greased and floured, or waxed paper lined and greased 8-inch layer pans.
7. Bake at 350°F. for 25 to 30 minutes.

ONE BOWL WHITE SHEET CAKE

A family recipe originally from Mississippi. Suit your fancy as to what flavor it will be: vanilla, lemon, almond, or orange.

Oven temperature: preheat to 375°F.
Baking time: 35 minutes

Yield: twelve 3"x3" squares
Pan: 12"x8"x2" oblong pan, greased and floured

2½ cups cake flour, sifted
1¾ cups granulated sugar
2 teaspoons double-acting baking powder
⅛ teaspoon salt
½ cup shortening
3 egg whites, beaten

1¼ cups cold water
1 teaspoon vanilla, OR
1 teaspoon vanilla and ½ teaspoon lemon extract, OR
1 teaspoon orange extract, OR
½ teaspoon vanilla and ¼ teaspoon almond extract

1. Sift flour once before measuring. Mix and sift flour, baking powder, sugar, and salt together.
2. Put dry ingredients, shortening, and 1 cup cold water into mixing bowl.
3. Beat 2 minutes at medium speed.
4. Add beaten egg whites, flavoring, and remaining ¼ cup cold water. Beat 2 minutes at medium speed.
5. Pour batter into greased and floured 12"x8"x2" oblong pan.
6. Bake at 375°F. for 35 minutes.

TWO-LAYER WHITE CAKE

A wonderfully reliable, all-around cake.

Oven temperature: preheat to 350°F.
Baking time: 25 to 30 minutes

Yield: approximately 10 servings
Pan: 2 eight or nine-inch layer pans, greased and floured

½ cup butter
1 cup granulated sugar
2 cups cake flour, sifted
2½ teaspoons double-acting baking powder

¼ teaspoon salt
1 cup milk
1 teaspoon vanilla
3 egg whites, beaten until stiff, not dry

. Cream butter with sugar until light and fluffy.
. Sift flour once before measuring. Mix and sift flour and bak-
ng powder together.
. Add dry ingredients alternately with milk, mixing thoroughly
fter each addition.
Add vanilla. Mix very well.
. With pliable rubber scraper or whisk gently fold in stiffly
eaten egg whites.
. Pour batter into two greased and floured 8 or 9-inch layer
ans.
. Bake at 350°F. for 25 to 30 minutes.

YELLOW CAKES

QUICK-METHOD GOLDEN LAYER CAKE

conomical, simple to concoct, but dandy tasting.

Oven temperature: preheat to
350°F.
Baking time: 25 to 30 minutes

Yield: approximately
10 servings
Pan: 2 eight-inch layer pans,
greased and floured

2 cup shortening or butter
cup milk
teaspoon vanilla
1/4 cups all-purpose flour,
sifted

1 1/2 cups granulated sugar
3 teaspoons double-acting
baking powder
1/2 teaspoon salt
2 eggs, unbeaten

. Mix shortening, 2/3 cup milk, and vanilla until well blended.
. Sift flour once before measuring. Mix and sift flour with
ugar, baking powder, and salt.
. Add dry ingredients to shortening and milk mixture a little
t a time, mixing thoroughly after each addition.
. Beat in eggs. Add remaining 1/3 cup milk. Beat well.
. Pour batter into two greased and floured 8-inch layer pans.
. Bake at 350°F. for 25 to 30 minutes.

THREE-LAYER YELLOW CAKE

This is truly pleasing, full-flavored and congenial with a number of fillings and icings.

Oven temperature: preheat to 375°F.

Baking time: 25 to 30 minutes

Yield: approximately 12 to 16 servings

Pan: 3 eight-inch layer pans, greased and floured or waxed paper lined and greased

1 cup butter or margarine
1½ cups granulated sugar
4 eggs, separated (beat egg whites until stiff, not dry)
3 cups cake flour, sifted

2½ teaspoons double-acting baking powder
½ teaspoon salt
1 cup plus 2 tablespoons milk
2 teaspoons vanilla, *OR* 1 teaspoon lemon rind, grated

1. Cream butter or margarine with sugar until light and fluffy
2. Add egg yolks. Beat well.
3. Sift flour once before measuring. Mix and sift flour, baking powder, and salt together.
4. Add dry ingredients alternately with milk, mixing thoroughly after each addition.
5. Add vanilla or lemon rind and mix very well.
6. With pliable rubber scraper or wire whisk, gently fold in stiffly beaten egg whites.
7. Pour batter into three greased and floured, or waxed paper lined and greased, 8-inch layer pans.
8. Bake at 375°F. for 25 to 30 minutes.

FILLING

½ cup granulated sugar
1½ tablespoons cornstarch
¼ teaspoon salt
½ cup water
½ cup orange juice

2 egg yolks, beaten
1 tablespoon lemon juice
1 tablespoon butter
grated rind of one orange

1. Blend sugar, cornstarch, and salt together in saucepan.
2. Stir in water and orange juice. Bring to boil, stirring constantly over medium heat. Cook 3 minutes.
3. Blend a little of this mixture into egg yolks, then add remainder of egg yolks to orange juice mixture. Cook 1 minute more, then remove from heat.

4. Stir in lemon juice, orange rind, and butter. Cool before spreading between cake layers.

ICING

¼ cup butter

3 cups powdered sugar, sifted

¼ teaspoon salt

3 tablespoons orange juice

1. Cream butter, powdered sugar, and salt together until light and fluffy.
2. Add orange juice. Mix well and spread on cake.

LAZY DAISY CAKE

Carry it safely in its pan on a picnic, or to a potluck gathering.

Oven temperature: preheat to 350°F.

Baking time: 30 minutes

Yield: approximately 8 servings

Pan: 8"x8"x2" square pan, greased and floured

2 eggs, separated (beat whites until stiff, not dry)

1 cup granulated sugar

½ teaspoon vanilla

1 cup plus 1 tablespoon all-purpose flour, sifted

1 teaspoon double-acting baking powder

½ teaspoon salt

½ cup warm milk

1. To stiffly beaten egg whites, add yolks one at a time.
2. Gradually blend in sugar, then vanilla.
3. Sift flour once before measuring. Mix and sift flour, baking powder, and salt together.
4. Add dry ingredients alternately with warm milk, mixing thoroughly after each addition.
5. Pour batter into greased and floured 8"x8"x2" square pan.
6. Bake at 350°F. for about 30 minutes.

TOPPING

7 tablespoons brown sugar, firmly packed

4½ tablespoons butter

3 tablespoons cream, or evaporated milk

¾ cup coconut or nut meats, chopped

1. Bring brown sugar, butter, and cream to boil.
2. Add nuts or coconut. Spread on baked cake.
3. Place under broiler for about 3 minutes.

123

POUND CAKE

Versatile. It goes with so many things.

Oven temperature: preheat to
   310°F.
Baking time: 1¼ to 1½ hours

Yield: approximately
   16 servings
Pan: 10"x4" tube pan or
   10"x5"x3" loaf pan, waxed
   paper lined and greased

¾ cup butter
1 cup granulated sugar
1¾ cups cake flour, sifted
½ teaspoon double-acting
   baking powder
½ teaspoon salt

½ teaspoon nutmeg or mace
2 tablespoons brandy
4 eggs, separated (beat
   whites of 2 eggs until stiff,
   not dry)
2 teaspoons powdered sugar

1. Cream butter with sugar until light and fluffy.
2. Add 2 whole eggs and 2 egg yolks one at a time and beat well.
3. Sift flour once before measuring. Mix and sift flour, baking powder, salt, and nutmeg or mace together.
4. Add dry ingredients to creamed mixture a little at a time, mixing thoroughly after each addition. Blend in brandy. If dough seems too stiff a very small additional amount of brandy may be added.
5. Add powdered sugar to stiffly beaten egg whites. With pliable rubber scraper or whisk, gently fold in egg whites.
6. Pour batter into waxed paper lined and greased 10"x4" tube pan or 10"x5"x3" loaf pan.
7. Bake at 375°F. for 40 to 50 minutes.

CHOCOLATE CAKES

PETE'S SOUR CREAM CAKE

Childhood memories were made of this; it was Mother's recipe.

Oven temperature: preheat to
   350°F.
Baking time: 20 to 25 minutes

Yield: approximately
   10 servings
Pan: 2 eight-inch layer pans,
   greased and floured

3 ounces chocolate, melted
1 cup granulated sugar
1 cup sour cream
1 egg, unbeaten

1 teaspoon baking soda
¾ cup milk
2 cups cake flour, sifted
½ teaspoon salt

1. Melt chocolate over simmering water. Cool.
2. Cream sugar with sour cream.
3. Beat in egg. Add melted chocolate.
4. Dissolve soda in milk.
5. Sift flour once before measuring. Mix and sift flour and salt together.
6. Add dry ingredients alternately with milk, mixing thoroughly after each addition. Batter will seem thin.
7. Pour batter into two greased and floured 8-inch layer pans.
8. Bake at 350°F. for about 20 to 25 minutes.

ECONOMY FUDGE CAKE

Takes only short time to make and bake.

Oven temperature: preheat to 350°F.
Baking time: 30 minutes

Yield: approximately 8 servings
Pan: 7-inch ring mold or 8"x8"x2" square pan, greased and floured

2 ounces chocolate, melted
2 tablespoons butter
1 cup granulated sugar
1 egg, beaten
1 cup milk

1½ cups cake flour, sifted
1 teaspoon baking soda
½ teaspoon salt
1 teaspoon vanilla

1. Melt chocolate and butter together over simmering water.
2. Mix sugar and egg well. Add ½ cup milk.
3. Sift flour once before measuring. Mix and sift flour, soda, and salt together.
4. Add dry ingredients alternately with remaining ½ cup milk, mixing thoroughly after each addition.
5. Blend in chocolate-butter mixture and vanilla.
6. Pour batter into greased and floured 7-inch ring mold or 8"x8"x2" square pan.
7. Bake at 350°F. for about 30 minutes.

BETTY'S ELEGANT CHOCOLATE CAKE

You may stake your reputation on this rich, moist, elegant cake.

Oven temperature: preheat to 350°F.

Baking time: 35 minutes, oblong pan; 30 minutes, layer pans

Yield: approximately 16 servings

Pan: one 14"x9"x2" oblong pan, no smaller; or three 9-inch layer pans, greased and floured or waxed paper lined and greased

3 ounces chocolate, melted
1 cup butter
2 cups granulated sugar
5 eggs, unbeaten
1 teaspoon baking soda

1 cup buttermilk
2½ cups cake flour, sifted
½ teaspoon salt
2 teaspoons vanilla

1. Melt chocolate over simmering water. Cool.
2. Cream butter with sugar until light and fluffy.
3. Add eggs one at a time. Beat well after each addition. Blend in melted chocolate.
4. Dissolve soda in buttermilk.
5. Sift flour once before measuring. Mix and sift flour and salt together.
6. Add dry ingredients alternately with buttermilk, mixing thorougly after each addition.
7. Add vanilla. Mix very well.
8. Pour batter into greased and floured, or waxed paper lined and greased 14"x9"x2" pan, or three 9-inch layer pans.
9. Bake at 350°F. for 35 minutes, or until cake center springs back when touched with fingertips.

ICING

2 ounces chocolate, melted
4 tablespoons water
6 tablespoons butter
2 egg yolks, beaten

½ teaspoon salt
1 pound package powdered sugar

1. Melt chocolate, water, and butter together over simmering water. Cool. Add 2 beaten egg yolks and salt.

2. Cook 2 minutes after mixture comes to a boil, stirring constantly.
3. Blend in powdered sugar and beat well until consistency for easy spreading.

LEE'S NUT FUDGE CAKE

A winner in the "little" cake division.

Oven temperature: preheat to 350°F.
Baking time: about 30 minutes

Yield: 6 to 9 servings
Pan: 9″x9″x2″ square pan, or 10″x6″x2″ oblong pan,, greased and floured or waxed paper lined and greased

2 ounces chocolate, melted, OR ⅓ cup cocoa in enough hot water to make paste
½ cup butter or shortening
1 cup granulated sugar
2 eggs, separated (beat whites until stiff, not dry)

1 cup cake flour, sifted
1 teaspoon double-acting baking powder
½ teaspoon salt
½ cup milk
1 teaspoon vanilla
½ cup nut meats, chopped

1. Melt chocolate over simmering water. Cool.
2. Cream butter or shortening with sugar until light and fluffy.
3. Add egg yolks and beat well. Blend in melted chocolate or chocolate paste.
4. Sift flour once before measuring. Mix and sift flour, baking powder, and salt together.
5. Add dry ingredients alternately with milk, mixing thoroughly after each addition.
6. Add vanilla.
7. With pliable rubber scraper or whisk, gently fold in stiffly beaten egg whites. Stir in nut meats.
8. Pour batter into greased and floured, or waxed paper lined and greased 9″x9″x2″ square or 10″x6″x2″ oblong pan.
9. Bake at 350°F. for about 30 minutes.

GRANDMOTHER ANDREW'S CHOCOLATE CAKE

A treasured family heirloom. There aren't words to describe the delectable result of this recipe. From it can be made tea cakes, iced all over, or layer cake.

Oven temperature: preheat to 350°F.

Baking time: layers, 30 to 35 minutes; teacakes, 15 to 20 minutes

Yield: approximately 16 servings or 4 dozen tea cakes

Pan: 3 nine-inch layer pans, greased and floured or waxed paper lined and greased; or 1½"x1" muffin pans, well greased

3½ ounces chocolate melted

½ cup butter

1½ cups granulated sugar

4 eggs, separated (beat whites until stiff, not dry)

2 cups cake flour, sifted

½ teaspoon salt

3 teaspoons double-acting baking powder

1¼ cups milk

1 teaspoon vanilla

1. Melt chocolate over simmering water.
2. Cream butter with sugar until light and fluffy.
3. Add egg yolks and beat well. Blend in chocolate.
4. Sift flour once before measuring. Mix and sift flour with salt and baking powder.
5. Add dry ingredients alternately with milk, mixing thoroughly after each addition.
6. Add vanilla. With pliable rubber scraper or whisk, gently fold in stiffly beaten egg whites.
7. Pour batter into three greased and floured, or waxed paper lined and greased 9-inch layer pans; or fill well greased 1½"x1" muffin pan cups scant 1/2 full.
8. Bake at 375°F. 30 to 35 minutes, layers; 15 to 20 minutes, tea cakes. Frost little cakes on tops and sides. Frost layers as usual.

ICING

½ cup plus 1 tablespoon coffee cream

2½ ounces chocolate, melted

½ cup butter

½ teaspoon salt

½ teaspoon vanilla

2 cups powdered sugar, sifted

1. Over simmering water, heat cream, butter, chocolate, and sa. until chocolate and butter are melted.
2. Add vanilla.
3. Sift powdered sugar. Slowly blend it into chocolate mixture.
4. If more or less powdered sugar is needed, it will be determined by the consistency of the icing, which should be spreadable, but not too thin.
5. If icing begins to set before you are finished frosting the cake or cakes add a little more coffee cream.

COCOA CAKE

Light and luscious. If there is any left, freeze it.

Oven temperature: preheat to
  350°F.
Baking time: 30 to 35 minutes

Yield: approximately
  10 servings
Pan: 2 nine-inch layer pans,
  greased and floured or
  waxed pap   and
  greased

½ cup butter
1½ cups granulated sugar
3 eggs, beaten
⅓ cup cocoa dissolved in
  ⅓ cup hot water
1 teaspoon baking soda

1 cup mil
1¾ cups   r, sifted
½ teasp   ble-acting
  bakin   er
½ teas   lt
1 teaspo   nilla

1. Cream butter with sugar until light and fluffy.
2. Add eggs and beat well.
3. Blend in cocoa mixture.
4. Dissolve soda in milk.
5. Sift flour once before measuring. Mix and sift flour, baking powder, and salt together.
6. Add dry ingredients alternately with milk, mixing thoroughly after each addition.
7. Add vanilla. Mix very well. Batter will seem thin.
8. Pour batter into two greased and floured or waxed paper lined and greased 9-inch layer pans.
9. Bake at 350°F. for 30 to 35 minutes.

SALAD DRESSING CHOCOLATE CAKE

Moist and yummy with good-keeping qualities.

Oven temperature: preheat to
   350°F.
Baking time: 30 to 35 minutes

Yield: approximately
   10 servings
Pan: 2 nine-inch layer pans,
   greased and floured or
   waxed paper lined and
   greased

1 cup mayonnaise
1½ cups granulated sugar
2 teaspoons baking soda
1 cup plus 2 tablespoons hot
   water

2 cups all-purpose flour, sifted
½ cup cocoa
½ teaspoon salt
2 teaspoons vanilla

1. Cream mayonnaise and sugar together very well.
2. Dissolve soda in hot water.
3. Sift flour once before measuring. Mix and sift flour, cocoa, and salt together.
4. Add dry ingredients alternately with water, mixing thoroughly after each addition.
5. Add vanilla. Mix well.
6. Pour batter into two greased and floured, or waxed paper lined and greased 9-inch layer pans.
7. Bake at 350°F. for 30 to 35 minutes.
Note: Seven-minute frosting is very good with this cake.

KEN'S CONTINENTAL CHOCOLATE CAKE

This is the most sublime textured and best tasting cake you will ever put in your mouth. Ken's wife perfected the recipe.

Oven temperature: preheat to
   375°F.
Baking time: about 35 minutes

Yield: approximately
   16 servings
Pan: 3 eight-inch or nine-inch
   layer pans, waxed paper
   lined and greased

3 ounces pure milk chocolate (Swiss* is excellent), melted
1 ounce chocolate, melted
½ cup water
1 cup butter, margarine, or shortening
2 cups less 2 tablespoons granulated sugar
4 eggs, separated (beat whites until stiff, not dry)
1 teaspoon baking soda
1 cup buttermilk
2½ cups cake flour, sifted
½ teaspoon salt
1 teaspoon vanilla

1. Melt chocolates and ½ cup water over simmering water. Cool.
2. Cream butter, margarine or shortening with sugar until light and fluffy.
3. Beat in egg yolks one at a time. Blend in melted chocolate.
4. Dissolve soda in buttermilk.
5. Sift flour once before measuring. Mix and sift flour and salt together.
6. Add dry ingredients alternately with buttermilk, mixing thorougly after each addition.
7. Add vanilla and mix very well.
8. With pliable rubber scraper or whisk, gently fold in stiffly beaten egg whites.
9. Pour batter into three waxed paper lined and greased 8-inch or 9-inch layer pans.
10. Bake at 375°F. for about 35 minutes.

*European milk chocolate is best. For an interesting flavor, try mocha flavored milk chocolate.

ICING

½ cup butter
½ cup evaporated milk
½ cup top milk, or coffee cream
1 cup granulated sugar
3 egg yolks, beaten
½ teaspoon salt
1 teaspoon vanilla
1 cup coconut, shredded
1 cup nut meats, chopped

1. Combine butter, evaporated milk, top milk or cream, sugar, beaten egg yolks, and salt.
2. Cook, stirring frequently to keep mixture from sticking, until it thickens
3. Add vanilla, coconut, and nuts. Beat well until consistency for easy spreading.
4. For company, decorate top of cake with nut halves.

SPICE CHOCOLATE MASHED POTATO CAKE

Old World blending brings something different to modern day desserts.

Oven temperature: preheat to 350°F.
Baking time: 30 minutes, layer pans; 45 to 55 minutes, tube pan

Yield: approximately 10 servings
Pan: 9"x3½" tube pan, greased, or 2 nine-inch layer pans, greased and floured or waxed paper lined and greased

¾ cup butter
2 cups sugar
4 eggs, separated (beat whites until stiff, not dry)
½ cup mashed potatoes
1½ cups cake flour, sifted
½ cup cocoa
2 teaspoons double-acting baking powder

½ teaspoon salt
1 teaspoon cinnamon
½ teaspoon ground cloves
½ teaspoon nutmeg
½ cup milk
1 teaspoon vanilla
1 cup nut meats, chopped

1. Cream butter with sugar until light and fluffy.
2. Beat in egg yolks. Blend in mashed potatoes.
3. Sift flour once before measuring. Mix and sift flour, cocoa, baking powder, salt, cinnamon, cloves, and nutmeg together.
4. Add dry ingredients alternately with milk, mixing thoroughly after each addition.
5. Add vanilla. Mix very well.
6. Stir in nuts. With pliable rubber scraper or whisk, fold in stiffly beaten egg whites.
7. Pour batter into two greased and floured, or waxed paper lined and greased 9-inch pans, or greased 9"x3½" tube pan.
8. Bake at 350°F. for 30 minutes, layer pans; 45 to 55 minutes, tube pan.

MRS. DISPENCE'S CHOCOLATE CAKE

From a dear neighbor who is one of the world's best cooks.

Oven temperature: preheat to 350°F.
Baking time: 30 to 35 minutes

Yield: approximately 16 servings
Pan: 3 nine-inch layer pans, greased and floured or waxed paper lined and greased

3 ounces chocolate, melted
½ cup plus 2 tablespoons shortening
1 cup granulated sugar
1 cup brown sugar, firmly packed
4 eggs, separated (beat whites until stiff, not dry)

1 teaspoon baking soda
1½ cups milk *OR* 1 cup buttermilk
3 cups cake flour, sifted
½ teaspoon salt
1 teaspoon vanilla

1. Melt chocolate over simmering water. Cool.
2. Cream shortening with sugars until light and fluffy.
3. Add egg yolks and beat well. Blend in melted chocolate.
4. Dissolve soda in milk or buttermilk.
5. Sift flour once before measuring. Mix and sift flour and salt together.
6. Add dry ingredients alternately with milk, mixing thoroughly after each addition.
7. Add vanilla. With pliable rubber scraper or whisk, gently fold in stiffly beaten egg whites.
8. Pour batter into three greased and floured, or waxed paper lined and greased 9-inch layer pans.
9. Bake at 350°F. for 30 to 35 minutes.

APPLESAUCE CAKE

Welcome the good traveler that stays moist and tempting for a long time.

Oven temperature: preheat to 350°F.
Baking time: 35 minutes

Yield: approximately 10 servings
Pan: 2 nine-inch layer pans, greased and floured

1/2 cup shortening
2 cups granulated sugar
3 eggs, unbeaten
1 1/2 cups unsweetened applesauce
2 1/2 cups all-purpose flour, sifted
3/4 teaspoon double-acting baking powder

1/4 teaspoon baking soda
1 teaspoon salt
1 teaspoon cinnamon
1/2 teaspoon ground cloves
1/2 teaspoon allspice
3/4 cup water
1/2 to 1 cup nut meats, chopped
1 cup raisins, cut up

1. Cream shortening with sugar until light and fluffy.
2. Add eggs one at a time and beat well.
3. Blend in applesauce.
4. Sift flour once before measuring. Mix and sift flour, baking powder, soda, salt, cinnamon, cloves, and allspice together.
5. Add dry ingredients alternately with water, mixing thoroughly after each addition.
6. Stir in nut meats and raisins.
7. Pour batter into two greased and floured 9-inch layer pans.
8. Bake at 350°F. for about 35 minutes.

SOUR CREAM CAKE

Just what you have been looking for because it takes to so many different kinds of icings, sauces, and berries.

Oven temperature: preheat to 350°F.
Baking time: 25 minutes

Yield: approximately 10 servings
Pan: 2 eight-inch layer pans, greased and floured or waxed paper lined and greased

134

1 cup granulated sugar
1 egg, unbeaten
1 cup plus 1 tablespoon sour
  cream

½ teaspoon baking soda
1½ cups cake flour, sifted
½ teaspoon salt

1. Combine sugar, egg, sour cream, and soda. Mix thoroughly.
2. Sift flour once before measuring. Mix and sift flour and salt
together.
3. Add dry ingredients to sour cream mixture a little at a time,
mixing thoroughly after each addition.
4. Pour batter into two greased and floured, or waxed paper
lined and greased 8-inch layer pans.
5. Bake at 350°F. for 25 minutes.

WHIPPED CREAM CAKE

*Try putting the layers together with flavored whipped cream, and
topping the cake with fresh strawberries or peaches.*

Oven temperature: preheat to
  325°F.
Baking time: 25 to 30 minutes

Yield: approximately
  10 servings
Pan: 2 eight-inch layer pans,
  greased and floured

½ pint whipping cream
3 eggs, separated (beat
  whites until stiff, not dry)
1½ cups cake flour, sifted

1 cup granulated sugar
⅛ teaspoon salt
1 teaspoon double-acting
  baking powder

1. Chill bowl and beaters beforehand. Whip cream until almost
stiff.
2. Just before cream gets stiff, add egg yolks one at a time.
3. Sift flour once before measuring. Mix and sift flour, sugar,
salt, and baking powder together twice. Add to the cream mixture, mixing gently but thoroughly.
4. With pliable rubber scraper or whisk gently fold in stiffly
beaten egg whites.
5. Pour batter into two greased and floured 8-inch layer pans.
6. Bake at 325°F. for 25 to 30 minutes, or until done.

PARTY APPLESAUCE CAKE

A rich nut and raisin icing adds to the spicy flavor of this cake.

Oven temperature: preheat to
   375°F.
Baking time: 1½ hours

Yield: approximately
   12 servings
Pan: 10″x4″ tube pan,
   greased and floured

1 cup butter or margarine
2 cups granulated sugar
1 cup brown sugar, firmly
   packed
2 eggs, unbeaten
2 teaspoons baking soda
2¼ cups warm applesauce
3 cups cake flour, sifted
2 tablespoons cocoa

¼ teaspoon salt
¼ teaspoon ginger
¼ teaspoon mace
1 teaspoon ground cloves
¼ teaspoon allspice
1 tablespoon cinnamon
1 cup raisins, ground
2 cups pecan meats, ground

1.   Cream butter or margarine with sugars until light and fluffy.
2.   Add eggs one at a time and beat well.
3.   Dissolve soda in warm applesauce. Add to creamed ingredients.
4.   Sift flour once before measuring. Mix and sift flour, cocoa, salt, ginger, mace, cloves, allspice, and cinnamon together.
5̆.   Add dry ingredients alternately with applesauce, mixing thoroughly after each addition.
6.   Combine and grind raisins and pecans.
7.   Add raisin and pecan mixture to batter. Mix very well.
8.   Pour batter into greased and floured 10″x4″ tube pan.
9.   Bake at 375°F. for 1½ hours.

ICING

1½ cups granulated sugar
½ cup butter, softened
½ cup evaporated milk

1 cup nut meats, ground
1 cup raisins, ground

1.   Combine sugar, butter, and milk in saucepan and cook over low heat until mixture forms a soft ball when dropped into cup of cold water.
2.   Beat well until mixture is quite cool.
3.   Add ground nut meats and raisins. Mix very well.

BURNT SUGAR CAKE

For some reason, chances to taste this wonderful cake are not very frequent. It needs a revival.

Oven temperature: preheat to 350°F.

Baking time: 25 to 30 minutes

Yield: approximately 12 to 16 servings

Pan: 3 eight-inch layer pans, greased and floured or waxed paper lined and greased

2½ cups granulated sugar
1 cup hot water
½ cup butter
3 eggs, separated (beat whites until stiff, not dry)
3 cups cake flour, sifted three times

1 teaspoon double-acting baking powder
1 teaspoon baking soda
½ teaspoon salt
1 cup water
1 teaspoon vanilla

1. Put 1 cup sugar into skillet. Let melt and brown. Add 1 cup hot water and let cook to a syrup. Set aside.
2. Cream butter with 1½ cups sugar until light and fluffy.
3. Add egg yolks and beat well.
4. Sift flour once before measuring. Mix and sift flour, baking powder, soda, and salt together twice more.
5. Add dry ingredients alternately with water and ½ cup burnt sugar syrup, mixing thoroughly after each addition.
6. Add vanilla and mix very well.
7. With pliable rubber scraper or whisk, gently fold in stiffly beaten egg whites.
8. Pour batter in three greased and floured, or waxed paper lined and greased, 8-inch layer pans.
9. Bake at 350°F. for 25 to 30 minutes.

CARAMEL FILLING

3 cups brown sugar, firmly packed

¾ cup coffee cream
¾ cup butter

1. Put all ingredients in sauce pan and cook until thick.
2. Beat well until mixture is consistency for easy spreading between layers.

137

MISS ROSE'S GINGERBREAD

To our way of thinking this gingerbread is the best. Not too dark, not too light . . . just right.

Oven temperature: preheat to 350°F.
Baking time: 35 to 40 minutes

Yield: approximately 8 to 12 servings
Pan: 8″x12″x2″ oblong pan or 9″x9″x2″ square pan, greased and floured

½ cup shortening
½ cup granulated sugar
½ cup molasses
2 eggs, unbeaten
2 teaspoons baking soda
1 cup boiling water

2½ cups all-purpose flour, sifted
½ teapsoon salt
1 teaspoon ginger
½ teaspoon ground cloves

1. Cream shortening with sugar until light and fluffy.
2. Blend in molasses.
3. Add eggs one at a time and beat well.
4. Dissolve soda in boiling water.
5. Sift flour once before measuring. Mix and sift flour, salt, ginger, and cloves together.
6. Add dry ingredients alternately with water, mixing thoroughly after each addition.
7. Pour batter into greased and floured 8″x12″x2″ oblong or 9″x9″x2″ square pan.
8. Bake at 350°F. for 35 to 40 minutes.
Note: A little rum added to whipped cream topping makes this a party dessert.

HALLOWE'EN MARBLE CAKE

A combination of orange and chocolate batters produces a new taste thrill.

Oven temperature: preheat to
   350°F.
Baking time: 50 to 60 minutes

Yield: approximately
   8 to 12 servings
Pan: 9"x3½" tube pan,
   greased, waxed paper
   lined, and greased

1 ounce chocolate,
   melted
½ cup butter or margarine
1 cup minus 2 tablespoons
   granulated sugar
2 eggs, unbeaten
1¼ cups all-purpose flour,
   sifted

½ teaspoon salt
2 teaspoons double-acting
   baking powder
¾ cup milk
1 teaspoon vanilla
2 teaspoons orange rind,
   grated
¼ cup nut meats, chopped

1. Melt chocolate over simmering water. Cool.
2. Cream butter or margarine with sugar until light and fluffy.
3. Add eggs one at a time and beat well.
4. Sift flour once before measuring. Mix and sift flour, salt, and baking powder together.
5. Add dry ingredients alternately with milk, mixing thoroughly after each addition.
6. Add vanilla and mix very well.
7. Divide batter in half. Gently fold melted chocolate and nuts into one-half of the batter. Stir orange rind into the other half.
8. Spoon batters alternately into greased, waxed paper lined and greased 9"x3½" tube pan.
9. Bake at 350°F. for 50 to 60 minutes or until done. Let stand in pan for 5 minutes before removing to cool.

A MAN'S CAKE

There is something about this cake that is tantalizingly different.

Oven temperature: preheat to
  375°F.
Baking time: 25 to 30 minutes

Yield: approximately
  10 servings
Pan: 2 nine-inch layer pans,
  greased and floured or
  waxed paper lined and
  greased

½ cup shortening
1 cup granulated sugar
2 eggs, separated (beat
  whites until stiff, not dry)
2¼ cups all-purpose flour,
  sifted

2 teaspoons double-acting
  baking powder
½ teaspoon salt
1 cup cold coffee
1 teaspoon vanilla

1. Cream shortening with sugar until light and fluffy.
2. Add egg yolks and beat well.
3. Sift flour once before measuring. Mix and sift flour, baking powder, and salt together.
4. Add dry ingredients alternately with coffee, mixing thoroughly after each addition.
5. Add vanilla. Mix very well.
6. With pliable rubber scraper or wire whisk, gently fold in stiffly beaten egg whites.
7. Pour batter into two greased and floured or waxed paper lined and greased 9-inch layer pans.
8. Bake at 375°F. for 25 to 30 minutes.
Note: ½ cup walnut meats, chopped, are a nice addition to this cake batter.

MAPLE-NUT CAKE

Brown sugar and maple flavoring give special taste-appeal.

Oven temperature: preheat to
   350°F.
Baking time: 50 to 55 minutes

Yield: approximately
   10 servings
Pan: 10"x5"x3" loaf pan,
   greased and floured or
   waxed paper lined and
   greased

1 cup cake flour, sifted
6 tablespoons brown sugar,
   firmly packed
6 tablespoon granulated
   sugar
1½ teaspoons double-acting
   baking powder
¼ teaspoon salt

¼ cup salad oil
3 egg yolks, unbeaten
6 tablespoons cold water
1 teaspoon maple flavoring
4 egg whites, beaten until
   stiff, not dry
¼ teaspoon cream of tartar
½ cup walnut meats, finely
   chopped

1.   Sift flour once before measuring. Mix and sift flour, sugars, baking powder, and salt together.
2.   Make a well in center of dry ingredients and into it put salad oil, egg yolks, water, and maple flavoring. Beat until mixture is very smooth and well blended.
3.   Beat egg whites and cream of tartar until stiff, not dry. With pliable rubber scraper or whisk, gently fold in stiffly beaten egg whites, adding the nuts in this process, too.
4.   Pour batter into greased and floured or waxed paper lined and greased 10"x5"x3" loaf pan.
5.   Bake at 350°F. for 50 to 55 minutes.
Note: Bake-on icing or powdered sugar icing with nuts is very good with this cake.

PEACH OR PINEAPPLE UPSIDE DOWN CAKE

How long has it been since you have had a piece of this generations-old favorite?

Oven temperature: preheat to
  350°-375°F.
Baking time: 45 minutes

Yield: approximately
  6 to 8 servings
Pan: 8"x8"x2" square pan,
  ungreased

¼ cup butter
¼ cup brown sugar, firmly
  packed

6 to 9 peach halves or pineapple slices and maraschino
  cherries

1. Melt butter and brown sugar over low heat.
2. Arrange pineapple slices or peach halves (cut side down) on bottom of ungreased 8"x8"x2" pan, putting cherry in center of each.
3. Cover with brown sugar mixture.

BATTER

3 eggs, separated (beat
  whites until stiff, not dry
1 cup granulated sugar
1½ cups all-purpose flour,
  sifted
1 teaspoon double-acting
  baking powder

½ teaspoon salt
½ cup peach or pineapple
  juice
whipped cream for topping

1. Beat egg yolks well. Gradually add sugar.
2. Sift flour once before measuring. Sift again. Mix and sift flour, baking powder, and salt together.
3. Add dry ingredients alternately with juice, mixing thoroughly after each addition.
4. With pliable rubber scraper or whisk, gently fold in stiffly beaten egg whites.
5. Pour batter over fruit.
6. Bake at 350°-375°F. for 45 minutes.
7. Remove from pan to cake rack.
8. Serve warm with whipped cream.
Note: Good cold in lunch boxes the next day.

MARK'S PUMPKIN CAKE

Here is something out of the ordinary that would make a fine finale to autumn dinners.

Oven temperature: preheat to
  350°-375°F.
Baking time: 50 minutes

Yield: twelve 3"x3" squares
Pan: 12"x8"x2" oblong pan,
  greased and floured

½ cup butter
1¼ cups granulated sugar
2 eggs, unbeaten
1 cup canned pumpkin
2¼ cups all-purpose flour,
  sifted
3 teaspoons double-acting
  baking powder

½ teaspoon baking soda
1 teaspoon salt
3½ teaspoons pumpkin pie
  spice, *OR*
½ teaspoon cinnamon,
  ¼ teaspoon ground cloves
  and ¼ teaspoon nutmeg
¾ cup milk

1. Cream butter with sugar until light and fluffy.
2. Add eggs one at a time and beat well. Blend in pumpkin.
3. Sift flour once before measuring. Mix and sift flour, baking powder, soda, salt, and spices together.
4. Add dry ingredients alternately with milk, mixing thoroughly after each addition.
5. Pour batter into greased and floured 12"x8"x2" oblong pan. Cupcake pans, greased or paper lined, may be used also. The yield would be about 30 cupcakes.
6. Bake at 350°-375°F. for about 50 minutes. Bake cupcakes at same temperature for 25 minutes.

SCRIPTURE CAKE

A curious old recipe that has been cut in half and adjusted to high altitude, but it still nourishes the spirit as well as the body.

Oven temperature: preheat to 350°F.
Baking time: about 1 hour

Yield: 8 to 10 servings
Pan: 10"x5"x3" loaf pan, greased

½ cup butter . . . Kings, 4:22
1 cup granulated sugar . . . Jeremiah, 6:20
3 eggs, beaten . . . Isaiah, 10:14
3 tablespoons honey . . . Samuel, 14:25
2¼ cups all-purpose flour, sifted . . . I. Kings, 4:22
¼ teaspoon salt . . . Leviticus, 2:13

1 teaspoon double-acting baking powder . . . Corinthians, 5:6
Spices to taste . . . Kings, 10:10
½ cup water . . . Genesis, 24:17
1 cup raisins . . . Samuel, 30:12
1 cup figs, finely chopped . . . Samuel, 30:12
1 cup almond meats, finely chopped . . . Numbers, 17:8

1. Cream butter with sugar until light and fluffy.
2. Beat in eggs. Blend in honey.
3. Sift flour once before measuring. Mix and sift flour, salt, baking powder, and spices together.
4. Add dry ingredients alternately with water, mixing thoroughly after each addition.
5. Stir in fruits and nuts.
6. Pour batter into greased 10"x5"x3" loaf pan.
7. Bake at 350°F. for about 1 hour.

"There was a cake baken". . . I Kings, 19:6

SPICE CAKE

Don't know your guest's tastes too well? This spice cake is a sure bet.

Oven temperature: preheat to 350°F.

Baking time: 45 to 50 minutes, sheet cake; 25 minutes, layer cake

Yield: approximately 12 servings

Pan: 13"x9"x2" oblong pan or 2 nine-inch layer pans, waxed paper lined and greased

¾ cup shortening
1½ cups brown sugar, firmly packed
3 eggs, unbeaten
2½ cups cake flour, sifted
¾ teaspoon baking soda
1 teaspoon salt
1 teaspoon cinnamon

½ teaspoon nutmeg
½ teaspoon allspice
1¼ cups sour milk or buttermilk
1 cup nut meats, finely chopped
1 cup raisins, cooked, drained, and cut up

1. Cream shortening with brown sugar until light and fluffy.
2. Add eggs one at a time and beat well.
3. Sift flour once before measuring. Mix and sift flour, soda, salt, cinnamon, nutmeg, and allspice together.
4. Add dry ingredients alternately with sour milk or buttermilk, mixing thoroughly after each addition.
5. Stir in nut meats and raisins.
6. Pour batter into waxed paper lined and greased 13"x9"x2" pan, or two 9-inch layer pans.
7. Bake at 350°F. for 45 to 50 minutes, sheet cake; 25 minutes, layer cake.

LITTLE SPICE CAKE

Parents' night-out? Leave this for the children; they'll be glad you're going.

Oven temperature: preheat to 350°F.

Baking time: 25 to 30 minutes, layer cake; 30 to 35 minutes, square cake

Yield: approximately 6 to 8 servings

Pan: 8"x8"x2" square pan, greased and floured

½ cup sour cream
½ cup milk
½ teaspoon baking soda
1½ cups all-purpose flour, sifted

1 cup granulated sugar
2 teaspoons cinnamon
1 teaspoon ground cloves
½ teaspoon salt
1 egg, beaten

1.   Mix sour cream, milk, and soda together.
2.   Sift flour once before measuring. Mix and sift flour, sugar, cinnamon, cloves, and salt together.
3.   Add dry ingredients to sour cream and milk mixture a little at a time, mixing thoroughly after each addition.
4.   Add beaten egg and blend well.
5.   Pour batter into greased and floured 8"x8"x2" pan or two eight-inch layer pans.
6.   Bake at 350°F. for 25 to 30 minutes, layer cake; 30 to 35 minutes, square cake.

Note: Bake-on icing is perfect for this.

CUPCAKES

CUPCAKE TIPS

Bake cupcakes in well greased muffin pans, or in paper baking cups placed in muffin pans.

Fill each cup 1/2 to 2/3 full, no fuller.

Almost any *creamed* cake batter can be used for cupcakes.

146

DEE'S FUDGE SPONGE CUPCAKES

We traditionally take these for dessert to Red Rocks family concerts. They are one of the richest and best cupcakes we've ever tasted.

Oven temperature: preheat to 375°F.
Baking time: 15 minutes

Yield: 2 to 3 dozen cupcakes
Pan: 2½"x1¼" muffin pans, lined with paper baking cups or greased

1½ ounces chocolate, melted
1 cup milk
½ cup butter or margarine
1½ cups granulated sugar
3 eggs, well beaten

2 cups all-purpose flour, sifted
1 teaspoon baking soda
⅛ teaspoon salt
1 teaspoon vanilla
1 teaspoon lemon xtract

1. Melt chocolate in ½ cup milk over simmering ᴡᴀᴛ Cool.
2. Cream butter or margarine with sugar until lig d fluffy.
3. Add eggs one at a time and beat well.
4. Sift flour once before measuring. Mix and sift fl aking soda, and salt together.
5. Add dry ingredients alternately with remaining ½ milk, mixing thoroughly after each addition.
6. Add melted chocolate mixture, vanilla, and lemon. nd well.
7. Pour batter into greased or paper baking cup lined x 1¼" muffin pans, filling each cup 1/2 to 2/3 full.
8. Bake at 375°F. for 15 minutes. Ice with rich fudge icing.

FUDGE ICING

2 cups granulated sugar
2 ounces chocolate, melted
2 tablespoons cornstarch

1 tablespoon butter
⅔ cup evaporated milk
1 teaspoon vanilla

1. Put all ingredients together in saucepan.
2. Cook until mixture thickens and takes form when dribbled from a teaspoon into cup of cold water. Stir constantly.
3. Beat until creamy. Spread generously on top and sides of cupcakes.

147

GOLDEN CUPCAKES

e are excellent.

Oven temperature: preheat to 350°F.
Baking time: 15 to 20 minutes

Yield: approximately 2 to 3 dozen
Pan: 2½"x1¼" muffin pans, greased

⅓ cup butter or margarine
1 cup granulated sugar
2 eggs, separated (beat whites until stiff, not dry)
2 cups all-purpose flour, sifted

2 teaspoons double-acting baking powder
¼ teaspoon salt
1 cup milk
1 teaspoon vanilla, almond, lemon, or orange extract

1. Cream butter or margarine with sugar until light and fluffy.
2. Add egg yolks. Beat well.
3. Sift flour once before measuring. Mix and sift flour, baking powder, and salt together.
4. Add dry ingredients alternately with milk, mixing thoroughly after each addition.
5. Add vanilla or extract of choice. Mix very well.
6. With pliable rubber scraper or wire whisk, gently fold in stiffly beaten egg whites.
7. Pour batter into greased 2½"x1¼" muffin pans, filling each cup 1/2 to 2/3 full.
8. Bake at 350°F. for 15 to 20 minutes.

PUFF CAKES

Their texture is different. They are well-suited to a variety of icings, or make a good shortcake for fresh fruits.

Oven temperature: preheat to 350°F.
Baking time: about 20 minutes

Yield: 1 dozen cupcakes
Pan: 2½"x1¼" muffin pans, greased

1 cup minus 1 tablespoon granulated sugar
2 eggs plus enough sour cream to make 1 cup
1½ cups all-purpose flour, sifted

½ teaspoon baking soda
1 teaspoon double-acting baking powder
¼ teaspoon salt
1 teaspoon vanilla

148

1. Add sugar to sour cream and eggs. Beat very well.
2. Sift flour once before measuring. Mix and sift flour, baking soda, baking powder, and salt together.
3. Add dry ingredients to sour cream mixture a little at a time, mixing thoroughly after each addition.
4. Add vanilla. Mix very well.
5. Pour batter into greased 2½"x1¼" muffin pans, filling each cup 1/2 to 2/3 full.
6. Bake at 350°F. for about 20 minutes.

COFFEE CUPCAKES

A good barbecue dessert, one your guests will surely enjoy.

Oven temperature: preheat to 350°F.
Baking time: 20 to 25 minutes

Yield: 2 to 3 dozen cup cakes
Pan: 2½"x1¼" muffin pans, lined with paper baking cups or greased

1 cup shortening
2 cups brown sugar, firmly packed
2 eggs, unbeaten
2 cups raisins, cooked
1 teaspoon baking soda, dissolved in a little cold coffee

3½ cups all-purpose flour, sifted
1 teaspoon double-acting baking powder
1 teaspoon cinnamon
1 teaspoon nutmeg
1 teaspoon ground cloves
1 cup cold coffee

1. Cream shortening with brown sugar until light and fluffy.
2. Add eggs one at a time and beat well.
3. Add raisins and soda to creamed mixture.
4. Sift flour once before measuring. Mix and sift flour, baking powder, cinnamon, nutmeg, and cloves together.
5. Add dry ingredients alternately with coffee, mixing thoroughly after each addition.
6. Pour batter into paper baking cup lined or greased 2½"x 1¼" muffin pans, filling each cup only 1/2 to 2/3 full.
7. Bake at 350°F for about 20 minutes.

HOLIDAY FRUIT CAKE

Wrap in foil and pretty ribbon for gifts, or serve to guests who drop in during the holidays.

Oven temperature: preheat to
   300°F.
Baking time: 3 to 3¼ hours

Yield: 5 pounds
Pan: 10"x4" tube pan, waxed
   paper lined and greased

1 cup shortening
1 cup granulated sugar
1 cup honey
4 eggs, beaten
1 teaspoon vanilla
5 cups all-purpose flour,
   sifted
1½ teaspoons salt
1¼ teaspoons baking soda
½ cup orange juice
1 cup prune juice (½ cup of
   this may be whiskey, wine,
   or brandy)
1 teaspoon mace

½ teaspoon ground cloves
½ teaspoon allspice
2 teaspoons cinnamon
1 cup cooked prunes, cut up
   (half figs may be used)
1¾ cups seedless raisins
½ cup citron, cut up
½ cup candied lemon peel,
   cut up
¾ cup candied orange peel,
   cut up
½ cup candied cherries, cut
   up
1 cup walnut meats, chopped

1. Cream shortening with sugar until light and fluffy. Blend in honey.
2. Beat in eggs. Add vanilla.
3. Sift flour once before measuring. Set aside 1 cup flour. Mix and sift 4 cups flour, salt, soda, mace, cloves, allspice, and cinnamon together.
4. Add dry ingredients alternately with juices, mixing thoroughly after each addition.
5. Combine remaining 1 cup flour with fruits and nuts. Stir all into batter.
6. Pour batter into waxed paper lined and greased 10"x4" tube pan.
7. Bake at 300°F. for 3 to 3¼ hours, or until cake tester inserted in center comes out clean.

8. Store cake in wrapped foil or waxed paper. If desired brush occasionally with fruit juice, cider, port, sherry, or brandy. Refrigerate.

Note: Loaf pans may be substituted.

CHOCOLATE BIT, CHERRY, AND DATE CAKE

Rich, rich, rich. This is a contemporary version of fruit cake.

Oven temperature: preheat to 325°F.
Baking time: 1½ hours

Yield: approximately 16 servings
Pan: 9"x3½" tube pan, or 10"x5"x3" loaf pan, very well greased

3 eggs, beaten
½ teaspoon vanilla
1 cup granulated sugar
1½ cups all-purpose flour, sifted
1½ teaspoons double-acting baking powder
½ teaspoon salt

1 six-ounce package chocolate bits
2 cups nut meats, chopped
1 cup dates, chopped
1 cup maraschino cherries, halved
blanched almonds

1. Beat eggs well. Blend in vanilla. Gradually add sugar.
2. Sift flour once before measuring. Mix and sift flour, baking powder, and salt together.
3. Add dry ingredients to sugar and egg mixture a little at a time, mixing thoroughly after each addition.
4. Stir in chocolate bits, nut meats, dates, and ¾ cup cherries.
5. Place batter in *very well greased* 9"x3½" tube pan, or 10"x5"x3" loaf pan.
6. Decorate top with almonds and remaining ¼ cup cherries.
7. Bake at 325°F. for 1½ hours.

OLD FASHIONED DARK FRUIT CAKE

It would not be Christmas without this rich, heavy-with-fruit cake.

Oven temperature: preheat to 250°-300°F.
Baking time: 3 to 4 hours

Yield: 10 pounds
Pan: 9"x5"x3" loaf pans, waxed paper lined and greased

1 cup shortening, melted
1 cup brown sugar, firmly packed
1 cup molasses
1 cup jelly (any kind), melted
3 eggs, unbeaten
2 teaspoons baking soda
1 cup sour milk
6 cups all-purpose flour, sifted
2 teaspoons cinnamon
1 teaspoon ground cloves
2 teaspoons nutmeg
½ teaspoon allspice
1 pound dates, cut up

1 cup candied orange peel, cut up
¼ cup citron, cut up
1 cup candied orange peel, cut up
¼ cup candied lemon peel, cut up
1 eight-ounce bottle maraschino cherries, drained and sliced
1 cup walnut meats, chopped
1 cup almonds, blanched
1 pound raisins
1 pound currants

1. Cream shortening, brown sugar, molasses, and melted jelly together.
2. Beat in eggs.
3. Dissolve soda in sour milk. Blend in with first mixture.
4. Sift flour once before measuring. Mix and sift flour, cinnamon, cloves, nutmeg, and allspice together. Combine with fruits and nuts.
5. Stir the two mixtures together until thoroughly blended.
6. Put batter in waxed paper lined and greased 9"x5"x3" loaf pans.
7. Bake at 250°-300°F. for 3 to 4 hours.
8. Remove waxed paper and store in tightly covered tin box or foil.
Note: For brandied fruit cake, soak fruit, but not nuts, in brandy overnight. Drain off brandy and use it to baste the cakes after they are baked.

ECONOMY FRUIT CAKE

. . . or maybe you are like some of our family, who like it better because it has no candied fruits in it.

Oven temperature: preheat to 325°F.
Baking time: about 1 hour

Yield: approximately 16 servings
Pan: 9"x5"x3" loaf pan, waxed paper lined and greased

½ pound raisins
1¼ cups water
½ cup shortening
1 cup granulated sugar
1 egg, unbeaten
½ teaspoon lemon extract if desired

2 cups all-purpose flour, sifted
1 teaspoon salt
1 teaspoon cinnamon
1 teaspoon ground cloves
1 teaspoon nutmeg
1 teaspoon baking soda
½ cup nut meats, chopped

1. Boil raisins for 15 minutes in water. Set aside to cool. Drain and save juice from raisins.
2. Cream shortening with sugar until light and fluffy.
3. Beat in egg. Add lemon extract.
4. Sift flour once before measuring. Mix and sift flour, salt, cinnamon, cloves, and nutmeg together.
5. Dissolve soda in raisin juice.
6. Add dry ingredients alternately with raisin juice, mixing thoroughly after each addition.
7. Stir in nuts.
8. Pour dough into waxed paper lined and greased 9"x5"x3" loaf pan.
9. Bake at 325°F. for about one hour, or until testing straw, or knife comes out clean when inserted in thickest part of cake.

Sponge Cakes

SPONGE CAKE TIPS

Beat egg yolks until thick and lemon-colored.

Sift sugar and flour.

Use *fresh* cream of tartar.

Do not beat batter unless recipe designates.

Fold in ingredients *gently, incorporating as much air as possible* into batter.

Use *ungreased* and *spotlessly clean* cake pans.

Do not crowd in oven. Leave enough room at oven top for cake to rise well above pan.

NOTES

ANGEL FOOD CAKE DELUXE

What more can be said? It is out of this world.

Oven temperature: preheat to 325°F.

Baking time: 45 to 55 minutes

Yield: approximately 16 servings

Pan: 10"x4" tube pan, or 9"x3½" tube pan, ungreased and spotlessly clean

1¼ cups egg whites (about 10)

½ teaspoon salt

1½ teaspoons fresh cream of tartar

1 teaspoon vanilla, *OR*

½ teaspoon vanilla and ½ teaspoon almond extract

1½ cups less 1 tablespoon granulated sugar, sifted twice

1¼ cups cake flour, sifted four times

1. Beat egg whites until foamy. Add salt, cream of tartar, and vanilla, or vanilla and almond extract. Continue beating until egg whites form stiff, but moist peaks.
2. Gradually whip in ¾ cup sifted sugar.
3. Sift flour once before measuring. Mix and sift flour with remaining sugar three times.
4. Sift ¼ cup flour and sugar mixture over the batter. Rotating bowl, fold it in gently with pliable rubber scraper or whisk, using approximately 12 to 15 strokes for each addition. Repeat this until all the flour and sugar are blended with the egg-white mixture.
5. Pour batter into clean, ungreased 10"x4" or 9"x3½" tube pan. Cut through batter several times with knife, or scraper, to break up air bubbles.
6. Bake at 300°-325°F. for 45 to 50 minutes, or until cake is delicately brown and springs back when lightly touched with fingertips.
7. Overturn the pan on wire rack or inverted funnel until cold.

Note: Thanks to the refinement of flours and sugars, we do not have to sift these ingredients nine times as did our grandmothers!

YELLOW ANGEL FOOD CAKE

Act II. After a delicious angel food cake, use the yolks to bake an equally delicious yellow angel food.

Oven temperature: preheat to 325°F.
Baking time: about 50 minutes

Yield: approximately 16 servings
Pan: 10"x4" tube pan, or 9"x3½" tube pan, ungreased and spotlessly clean

12 egg yolks, beaten
½ cup hot water
1 cup granulated sugar, sifted twice
1 cup cake flour, sifted four times

2 teaspoons double-acting baking powder
¼ teaspoon salt
1 teaspoon lemon extract, *OR*
1 teaspoon vanilla, *OR*
½ teaspoon lemon or orange rind, grated

1. Beat egg yolks until thick and lemon-colored. Beat in hot water.
2. Beat in sifted sugar.
3. Sift flour once before measuring. Mix and sift flour, baking powder, and salt together three times.
4. Fold dry ingredients into egg mixture a little at a time, mixing thoroughly.
5. Blend in lemon extract, or flavoring of choice.
6. Pour batter into clean, ungreased 10"x4", or 9"x3½" tube pan.
7. Bake at 325°F. for about 50 minutes, or until lightly browned and springs back when gently touched with fingertips.
Note: For special freezer dessert, split cake in two. Spread slightly softened ice cream between layers and freeze. Serve topped with fresh fruit, chocolate or butterscotch sauce, and/or whipped cream.

JELLY ROLL

Just because they look fancy doesn't mean they are difficult to make.

Oven temperature: preheat to 400°F.
Baking time: 15 minutes

Yield: approximately 8 servings
Pan: 15″x10″x1″ jellyroll pan, (cookie sheet may be substituted) waxed paper lined and greased

4 eggs, unbeaten
1 teaspoon double-acting baking powder
½ teaspoon salt
1 cup granulated sugar
1 cup cake flour, sifted

juice of one lemon
jelly or preserves (cherry, currant, strawberry, red raspberry)
powdered sugar for coating towel and top of jelly roll

1. Put eggs, baking powder, and salt into mixing bowl. Beat 2 minutes at high speed, or until thick and lemon-colored.
2. At medium speed, gradually add sugar and beat 3 minutes. Mixture should be thick and very light colored.
3. Sift flour once before measuring.
4. Reduce to lowest speed and add lemon juice, then flour. Beat only until mixture becomes moist.
5. Pour onto waxed paper lined and greased 15″x10″x1″ pan.
6. Bake at 400°F. for 15 minutes.
7. Turn baked cake onto clean towel coated with powdered sugar and remove waxed paper from bottom. Cut off hard edges of cake.
8. Roll cake and towel coated with sugar into jelly roll shape and place to shape and cool for 10 minutes.
9. Unroll, remove towel, then spread cake with jelly or preserves.
10. Re-roll cake and wrap the roll in waxed paper. Before serving, sprinkle it with powdered sugar.

JOHN'S CHOCOLATE ROLL

Grandmother discovered it. Son John continually requested it.
We've all been gorging ourselves on it ever since.

Oven temperature: preheat to
   400°F.
Baking time: 15 minutes

Yield: approximately 8 to
   10 servings
Pan: 15"x10"x1" jelly roll pan,
   (cookie sheet may be substituted), waxed paper
   lined and greased

6 eggs, separated (beat
   whites until stiff, not dry)
1 teaspoon vanilla
2 tablespoons all-purpose
   flour, sifted
1 cup powdered sugar, sifted
2 tablespoons cocoa
½ teaspoon salt

1 pint whipping cream,
   whipped and sweetened
   with 3 tablespoons
   powdered sugar
½ cup nut meats, chopped
powdered sugar for coating
   towel

1.   Beat egg yolks until thick and lemon-colored. Add vanilla
2.   Sift flour once before measuring. Mix and sift flour, powdered sugar, cocoa, and salt together.
3.   Add dry ingredients to egg yolks a little at a time, mixing thoroughly after each addition.
4.   With pliable rubber scraper or whisk, gently fold in stiffly beaten egg whites.
5.   Pour batter onto waxed paper lined and greased 15"x10"x1" pan.
6.   Bake at 400°F. for 15 minutes. Watch carefully that edges do not get too done.
7.   Turn baked cake onto clean towel coated with powdered sugar and remove waxed paper from bottom. Cut off hard edges of cake.
8.   Roll cake and towel coated with sugar into jelly roll shape. Place to cool for 10 minutes.
9.   Unroll. Remove towel.
10. Whip whipping cream. When nearly spreading consistency add 3 tablespoons powdered sugar. Whip until ready to spread, then fold in nut meats.

11. Spread cake with whipping cream mixture. Re-roll cake and wrap the roll in waxed paper. Refrigerate.

12. Serve with chocolate sauce.

Note: Crushed peppermint candy may be substituted for nuts.

MOCHA TORTE

How to make a very good impression on your husband's boss, or anyone else, for that matter.

Oven temperature: preheat to 325°F.

Baking time: 45 to 50 minutes

Yield: approximately 16 servings

Pan: 10"x4" tube pan, or 9"x3" spring form pan with tube insert, ungreased

6 eggs, separated (beat whites until stiff, not dry)

2 tablespoons plus ½ teaspoon instant coffee

½ teaspoon salt

¾ cup granulated sugar, sifted twice

½ teaspoon vanilla

1 cup cake flour, sifted three times

½ pint whipping cream, whipped

chocolate covered crunchy butter toffee OR

nut meats, finely chopped

1. To stiffly beaten egg whites, gradually add 2 tablespoons instant coffee, salt, and sugar that have been sifted together twice.

2. Beat egg yolks until thick and lemon-colored. Gently blend yolks into egg white mixture. Add vanilla.

3. Sift flour once before measuring. Sift twice more.

4. With pliable rubber scraper or whisk, fold flour into egg mixture a little at a time.

5. Pour batter into ungreased 10"x4" tube pan, or 9"x3" spring form pan with tube insert.

6. Bake at 325°F. for 45 to 50 minutes, or until lightly browned and springs back when gently touched with fingertips.

7. Cool cake on wire rack, or inverted funnel.

8. Split cake in half and fill with chocolate filling. (See page 174.)

9. Ice cake with whipped cream flavored with remaining ½ teaspoon instant coffee.

10. Decorate top with finely chopped nut meats, or broken toffee candy.

159

VIENNESE TORTE

Jam filling and whipped cream topping make this torte excellent company fare. Chock full of calories, but worth it.

Oven temperature: preheat to 350°F.
Baking time: 25 to 30 minutes

Yield: approximately 16 servings
Pan: 3 eight-inch pans with removable sides, ungreased and spotlessly clean

4 teaspoons cake flour
¾ cup cocoa
1 teaspoon cinnamon
9 eggs, separated (beat whites until stiff, not dry)
1⅓ cups plus 1 tablespoon granulated sugar

2 tablespoons lemon rind, grated
3 tablespoons lemon juice
1 cup jam (apricot, peach, pineapple-peach)
½ pint whipping cream, whipped

1. Sift flour, cocoa, and cinnamon together three times.
2. Beat egg yolks with sugar until thick and lemon-colored.
3. Add lemon juice and lemon rind.
4. Blend flour into egg mixture a little at a time, mixing thoroughly after each addition.
5. With pliable rubber scraper or whisk, gently fold in stiffly beaten egg whites.
6. Pour batter into three clean, ungreased 8-inch pans with removable sides.
7. Bake at 350°F. for 25 to 30 minutes.
8. Cool layers on wire rack.
9. When cool, fill layers with jam and top with whipped cream.

SPONGE CAKE

Delicate, delectable cake that rises high in the pan . . . and in our opinion.

Oven temperature: preheat to 350°F.
Baking time: 45 to 55 minutes

Yield: approximately 16 servings
Pan: 10"x4" tube pan, ungreased and spotlessly clean

7 eggs, separated (beat whites until stiff, not dry)
1 cup plus 3 tablespoons granulated sugar, sifted three times
2 tablespoons water
1½ tablespoons lemon juice

1 teaspoon vanilla
1½ tablespoons lemon rind, grated
1 cup cake flour, sifted four times
¼ teaspoon salt
½ teaspoon fresh cream of tartar

1. Beat egg yolks until thick and lemon-colored. Gradually add sugar sifted three times.
2. Blend in water, lemon juice, vanilla, and lemon rind.
3. Sift flour once before measuring. Mix and sift flour, salt, and cream of tartar together three more times.
4. Add dry ingredients to the egg and sugar mixture, beating batter until it is smooth.
5. With pliable rubber scraper or whisk, gently fold in stiffly beaten egg whites.
6. Turn batter into clean, ungreased 10"x4" tube pan.
7. Bake at 350°F. for 45 to 55 minutes.
8. Overturn pan on wire rack or funnel for one hour to cool.

FOUR-EGG SPONGE CAKE

Not too many calories in this useful cake.

Oven temperature: preheat to
325°-350°F.
Baking time: 55 minutes

Yield: 12 to 16 servings
Pan: 10"x4" tube pan,
ungreased and spotlessly
clean

4 eggs, separated (beat
whites until stiff, not dry)
1½ cups granulated sugar,
sifted three times
2 teaspoons cold water
1 teaspoon vanilla
1 teaspoon lemon extract

1⅔ cups cake flour, sifted
four times
¼ teaspoon salt
½ teaspoon fresh cream of
tartar
½ teaspoon double-acting
baking powder
½ cup hot water

1. Beat egg yolks until thick and lemon-colored. Gradually add
1 cup sugar, sifted three times.
2. Blend in cold water, vanilla, and lemon extract.
3. Sift flour once before measuring. Mix and sift flour, salt,
cream of tartar, and baking powder together three more times.
4. Add dry ingredients alternately with hot water, mixing thoroughly after each addition.
5. To stiffly beaten egg whites, gradually fold in remaining
½ cup sugar. With pliable rubber scraper or whisk, gently fold
egg white mixture into batter.
6. Pour batter into clean, ungreased 10"x4" tube pan.
7. Bake at 325°-350°F. for 55 minutes.
8. Overturn pan on wire rack or inverted funnel for 1 hour
to cool.
Note: For orange-flavored sponge cake substitute orange extract
for lemon, or substitute 3 tablespoons orange juice for the lemon
extract and use 3 tablespoons less hot water.

FROSTINGS AND FILLINGS

See Index for other frostings and fillings

FROSTINGS

Apple Icing 164
Bake-on Icing 164
Banana Icing 164
Minute Fudge Icing 164
Bittersweet Icing 165
Butter-Nut Frosting and Filling 165
Caramel Icing 166
Cream Cheese-Chocolate Frosting 166
Easy Chocolate Icing or Filling 166
Orange-Almond Filling and Frosting 167
Freezer-Perfect Chocolate Icing 167
Chocolate Powdered Sugar Icing 167
Fudge Sauce or Frosting 168
Easy Lemon Icing 168
Marmalade-Butter Frosting 168
Mocha Icing 169
Orange Butter Cream 169
Blender Peanut Butter Icing 169
Penuche Icing 170
Pineapple Icing 170
Seven Minute Icing I 170
Seven Minute Icing II 171
White Icing 171
Mint Jelly Icing 171
Sea Foam Icing I 172
Sea Foam Icing II 172

FILLINGS

Heavenly Angel Food Cake Filling 173
Custard Filling 173
Quick Chocolate Cream Filling 174
Chocolate Custard Filling 174
Lemon Custard Cake Filling 174
Raisin Nut Filling 175

Space for notes, Page 176

163

Frostings

APPLE ICING

2 teaspoons lemon juice
3 tablespoons grated apple

1 cup granulated sugar
1 egg white

1.   Sprinkle lemon juice over grated apple. Cover with sugar.
2.   Beat egg white until soft peaks form. Add apple and sugar mixture. Beat until stiff peaks form, and icing is consistency for spreading.

BAKE-ON ICING

6 tablespoons butter, melted
⅔ cup brown sugar, firmly
   packed

¼ cup evaporated milk
1 cup nut meats, chopped *OR*
1 cup coconut, shredded

1.   Blend all ingredients together.
2.   When cake is baked, remove from oven. Quickly spread icing over top of cake. Return to oven and cook until icing bubbles.
Note: Icing may be spread on cooled cake and placed under broiler until it bubbles. Set cake as far away from flame or electric element as possible to prevent scorching.

BANANA ICING

1½ cups powdered sugar,
   sifted
3 tablespoons butter, softened
1½ small ripe bananas,
   mashed

1 tablespoon lemon junce
⅛ teaspoon salt
½ teaspoon vanilla

1.   Gradually add powdered sugar to butter. Blend completely.
2.   Add banana pulp, lemon juice, salt, and vanilla. Beat until consistency for spreading.

MINUTE FUDGE ICING

½ cup cocoa
¼ cup margarine
1 cup granulated sugar

¼ cup milk
½ teaspoon salt

1. In sauce pan, dissolve all ingredients over *very low*
2. When completely dissolved, increase heat. Bring mix
a boil. Cook one minute.
3. Beat until consistency for spreading.

BITTERSWEET ICING

4 ounces chocolate, melted
¼ teaspoon salt
3 tablespoons butter or
   margarine

½ cup coffee cream
2¼ cups powdered sugar,
   sifted
1 teaspoon vanilla

1. In sauce pan, melt chocolate, salt, and butter or margarine together.
2. Remove from heat. Alternately add cream and powdered sugar. Stir in vanilla.
3. Beat until consistency for spreading.

BUTTER-NUT FROSTING AND FILLING

½ cup milk
2½ tablespoons cake flour
½ cup butter
½ cup granulated sugar
¼ teaspoon salt

½ teaspoon vanilla
½ cup nut meats, coarsely
   chopped
⅞ cup powdered sugar, sifted

1. Blend milk gradually into flour. Cook over low heat, stirring constantly until mixture forms a thick paste, about 10 minutes. Cool.
2. Cream butter with sugar and salt until light and fluffy.
3. Add cooled flour and milk paste. Beat until light and fluffy.
4. Stir in vanilla and nuts.
5. Use about 1/2 of mixture for filling between layers of cake.
6. Add powdered sugar to remaining half of mixture. Mix well. Spread on top and sides of cake.

CARAMEL ICING

2 cups brown sugar, firmly packed
½ cup granulated sugar
1 cup buttermilk
½ teaspoon baking soda
⅓ cup butter
1 teaspoon vanilla

1. In saucepan, put sugars, soda, and buttermilk. Stir until completely dissolved.
2. Boil without stirring until mixture forms soft ball when dropped into a cup of cold water. Add butter. Cool.
3. When icing is cool, add vanilla. Beat until consistency for spreading. If icing begins to harden, thin with a little cream.

CREAM CHEESE-CHOCOLATE FROSTING

2 ounces chocolate, melted
1 three-ounce package cream cheese
2 tablespoons cream
2 cups powdered sugar, sifted
¼ teaspoon salt

1. Melt chocolate over simmering water.
2. Allow cream cheese to reach room temperature first. Mix thoroughly with cream.
3. Add sifted powdered sugar gradually, beating thoroughly after each addition.
4. Add melted chocolate and salt. Mix very well.
5. Spread between and over layers of 2-layer cake.

EASY CHOCOLATE ICING OR FILLING

2 ounces chocolate, melted
¾ cup granulated sugar
¾ cup water
2 tablespoons cornstarch
2 tablespoons butter
1 teaspoon vanilla

1. Melt chocolate over simmering water. Add sugar and ½ cup water.
2. Mix ¼ cup water and cornstarch together until smooth. Blend into chocolate mixture. Add butter.
3. Cook, stirring constantly, until mixture is very thick.
4. Cool. Add vanilla.
Note: This icing stays soft.

ORANGE-ALMOND FILLING AND FROSTING

For angel food cake.

5 egg yolks
¼ cup granulated sugar
¼ cup orange juice
¼ teaspoon salt
2 teaspoons orange rind,
   grated

1 teaspoon lemon juice
½ pint whipping cream
   whipped
1 cup toasted almond meats

1.   In top of double boiler, beat egg yolks until thick and lemon-colored. Blend in sugar, orange juice, salt, and orange rind.
2.   Cook over medium heat, stirring constantly, until mixture is thickened. Cool thoroughly.
3.   With pliable rubber scraper or whisk, gently fold lemon juice and whipped cream into *cooled* egg mixture.
4.   Spread between "layers" of angel food cake, and swirl on top and sides. Sprinkle almonds on top and sides of cake.

FREEZER-PERFECT CHOCOLATE ICING

3 ounces chocolate, melted
1½ cups powdered sugar,
   sifted

3 tablespoons hot water
4 tablespoons butter, melted
3 egg yolks

1.   Melt chocolate over simmering water.
2.   Stir in sugar and hot water. Mix thoroughly. Beat well if using beater or use many strokes if using spoon or whisk.
3.   Add melted butter and egg yolks alternately, beating well after each addition.
4.   Icing may be slightly thin. If so, add more powdered sugar.

CHOCOLATE POWDERED SUGAR ICING

⅔ cup coffee cream
⅓ cup granulated sugar
¼ teaspoon salt
1 teaspoon vanilla

2½ ounces chocolate,
   melted
2½ cups powdered sugar,
   sifted

1.   In sauce pan, put cream, granulated sugar, salt, and chocolate. Stir until sugar is dissolved in cream.
2.   Place mixture over low heat. Simmer until chocolate is melted.
3.   Remove from heat and gradually add powdered sugar. Beat until icing is consistency for spreading. Add vanilla.

FUDGE SAUCE OR FROSTING

1 six-ounce package
  chocolate bits
½ cup butter
3¼ cups powdered sugar,
  sifted

1½ cups evaporated milk
½ teaspoon salt
1 teaspoon vanilla

1. Melt chocolate bits and butter over low heat.
2. Remove from heat and add 2 cups powdered sugar alternately with milk. Beat well after each addition. Add salt.
3. Return to heat and bring to boil, stirring constantly. Cook and stir 8 minutes.
4. Remove from heat and add vanilla. This concludes steps for sauce.
5. For icing, cool 2 cups of sauce to room temperature and blend into it 1¼ cups powdered sugar. Beat well.

EASY LEMON ICING

2 egg yolks
4 tablespoons lemon juice
rind of 1 lemon, grated

4½ cups powdered sugar,
  sifted

1. Combine egg yolks with lemon juice and rind.
2. Gradually add powdered sugar. Beat until consistency for spreading.

MARMALADE-BUTTER FROSTING

3 cups powdered sugar, sifted
8 tablespoons butter, softened
½ cup orange marmalade

2 tablespoons lemon juice
¼ teaspoon salt

1. Cream sugar with butter until smooth.
2. Add marmalade and lemon juice. Mix thoroughly with beater or by hand.
3. Add salt. Mix well.
Note: Lemon or lime marmalade may be substituted.

MOCHA ICING

2 tablespoons strong hot coffee
2 tablespoons cocoa
¼ teaspoon salt
2 tablespoons butter, melted
1 teaspoon vanilla
1 cup powdered sugar, sifted

1. Mix coffee with cocoa until smooth. Add salt, melted butter, and vanilla.
2. Gradually add powdered sugar. Beat until consistency for spreading.

ORANGE BUTTER CREAM

2 cups powdered sugar, sifted
¼ cup butter or margarine, softened
2 teaspoons orange rind, grated
3½ tablespoons fresh orange juice (or frozen-fresh)

1. Combine powdered sugar with butter or margarine. Mix very well.
2. Add orange rind and orange juice. Beat until thick and fluffy.

BLENDER PEANUT BUTTER ICING

Also delicious on toast or bread, broiled to a golden brown.

⅓ cup cream
½ cup brown sugar, firmly packed
3 tablespoons peanut butter
3 tablespoons butter or margarine, melted
⅔ cup salted peanuts
½ teaspoon vanilla

1. Combine all ingredients in blender.
2. Blend at high speed until peanuts are ground fine.
3. Spread on top of baked and cooled cake. Then broil slowly until a rich golden brown.
Note: Evaporated milk may be substituted for cream.

PENUCHE ICING

¾ cup granulated sugar
¾ cup brown sugar, firmly
  packed
½ cup butter
½ cup shortening
½ cup milk

¼ teaspoon salt
1 tablespoon light refined
  corn syrup
1 teaspoon vanilla
1 cup nut meats, chopped

1.   In saucepan, combine sugars, butter, shortening, milk, salt, and corn syrup.
2.   Place over low heat and slowly bring to full rolling boil, stirring constantly. Let boil 2 minutes.
3.   *Cool until lukewarm.* Add vanilla. Beat until consistency for spreading. Add nuts.

PINEAPPLE ICING

2 cups powdered sugar, sifted
¼ cup butter, softened
⅔ cup crushed pineapple,
  drained (reserve juice)

1 teaspoon lemon juice
2 tablespoons pineapple juice
⅛ teaspoon salt

1.   Gradually add powdered sugar to butter. Blend completely.
2.   Add pineapple, lemon juice, pineapple juice, and salt. Beat until creamy and consistency for spreading.

SEVEN MINUTE ICING I

⅞ cup granulated sugar
1 egg white
3 tablespoons cold water

¼ teaspoon cream of tartar
½ teaspoon vanilla

1.   In top of double boiler, mix all ingredients together, and beat until well blended.
2.   Place over rapidly boiling water. Beat constantly for 7 minutes with electric mixer or egg beater. If not consistency for spreading, beat a little longer.

SEVEN MINUTE ICING II

1½ cups granulated sugar
2 egg whites
1½ teaspoons light refined
    corn syrup

¼ teaspoon cream of tartar
⅛ teaspoon salt
5 tablespoons cold water
1 teaspoon vanilla

Follow directions for Seven Minute Icing I.

VARIATIONS

1.   ½ cup coconut or nut meats OR 1 stick peppermint candy, crushed, may be added to, or sprinkled over, icing.
2.   Lemon Seven Minute Icing: Substitute 2 tablespoons lemon juice for 2 tablespoons water. Add ½ teaspoon grated lemon rind. Omit vanilla.
3.   Orange Seven Minute Icing: Substitute ¼ cup orange juice for 5 tablespoons water. Add ½ teaspoon grated orange rind. Substitute lemon extract for vanilla.

WHITE ICING

4 tablespoons hot water
3 cups powdered sugar, sifted
1 egg white

¼ teaspoon salt
1 teaspoon vanilla

1.   Combine powdered sugar with hot water, mixing until smooth.
2.   Add egg white, salt, and vanilla. Beat until consistency for spreading.
Note: For chocolate icing, add 2½ ounces melted chocolate.

MINT JELLY ICING

1 eight-ounce glass mint jelly   1 egg white

1.   In top of double boiler, put jelly and egg white.
2.   Cook, beating constantly, until mixture forms peaks.
Note: Good on chocolate cake.

SEA FOAM ICING I

2 cups brown sugar, firmly
  packed
⅓ cup water
2 egg whites

2 teaspoons dark refined corn
  syrup
¼ teaspoon salt

1. In top of double boiler, mix all ingredients together. Beat enough to blend.
2. Place over boiling water. Beat with electric mixer or egg beater until icing stands in peaks.

SEA FOAM ICING II

1 cup granulated sugar
1 cup brown sugar, firmly
  packed
1 tablespoon dark refined
  corn syrup

1 cup water
2 egg whites
¼ teaspoon salt
1 teaspoon vanilla OR a tea-
2 teaspoons lemon juice

1. In saucepan, stir the sugars, corn syrup, and water together until dissolved.
2. Boil sugar mixture, without stirring, until mixture forms soft ball when dropped into a cup of cold water.
3. Whip egg whites and salt until stiff.
4. Pour syrup over egg whites in a thin stream, whipping constantly.
5. Add vanilla or lemon juice. Remove from heat and whip until icing forms peaks.

Fillings

HEAVENLY ANGEL FOOD CAKE FILLING

6 tablespoons granulated
  sugar
6 tablespoons cocoa

⅛ teaspoon salt
1 pint whipping cream
1 teaspoon vanilla

1. Sift sugar, cocoa, and salt together several times.
2. Add sifted dry ingredients to whipping cream and mix together slightly. Add vanilla.
3. Put into refrigerator for 10 hours or overnight.
4. Remove from refrigerator, and whip the cream mixture until it is thick and fluffy.
5. Split baked and cooled angel food cake in two.
6. Spread filling between the two layers and over the top of cake.
7. Serve immediately.

CUSTARD FILLING

⅔ cup granulated sugar
2½ tablespoons cornstarch
¼ teaspoon salt

2 cups milk or coffee cream,
  scalded
3 egg yolks, beaten
1 teaspoon vanilla

1. Sift sugar, cornstarch, and salt together.
2. In top of double boiler, scald milk or cream. Add dry ingredients to milk a little at a time, until mixture is smooth and thick.
3. Add a little of cooked mixture to beaten egg yolks. Return to hot mixture. Cook, stirring constantly, until mixture thickens. Cool. Add vanilla.

VARIATIONS

1. 1 cup blanched almonds, finely chopped, may be added to custard.
2. 1 cup blanched almonds, finely chopped, one cup miniature marshmallows or equivalent, and 2 tablespoons of sherry, may be added to custard.
3. 2 bananas, thinly sliced, may be added to custard.
4. ⅔ cup crushed or chopped pineapple, drained, may be added to custard.

5. 2 ounces melted chocolate, may be added to custard.
6. ⅔ cup thick apricot pulp and 2 tablespoons lemon juice may be added to custard.

QUICK CHOCOLATE CREAM FILLING

1 package chocolate pudding (not instant type)	1½ cups milk ½ teaspoon vanilla

1. Make pudding as directed on pudding package, using amount of milk designated above.
2. When done, add vanilla.
3. Refrigerate until cold.

CHOCOLATE CUSTARD FILLING

¾ cup milk, scalded	4 tablespoons all-purpose flour
1 ounce chocolate	¼ teaspoon salt
1 tablespoon butter	1 egg, beaten
½ cup granulated sugar	1 teaspoon vanilla

1. To scalded milk add chocolate and butter.
2. Mix dry ingredients together thoroughly and add to milk mixture.
3. Add beaten egg and cook, stirring constantly for 5 minutes. Cook 5 minutes longer, stirring occasionally. Add vanilla.
4. Refrigerate until cold.

LEMON CUSTARD CAKE FILLING

1⅓ cups granulated sugar	1¼ cups water
4 tablespoons cornstarch	1 teaspoon lemon rind, grated
4 egg yolks, unbeaten	1 tablespoon butter or margarine
4 tablespoons lemon juice	

1. Mix sugar and cornstarch together thoroughly.
2. In saucepan combine sugar mixture with egg yolks, lemon juice, and water.
3. Bring to boil, stirring constantly. Cook 1 minute, then remove from heat.
4. Stir in lemon rind and butter or margarine. Cool before putting between cake layers.

RAISIN-NUT FILLING

½ cup granulated sugar
4 tablespoons all-purpose
flour, sifted
1 cup milk
1 egg, beaten

⅛ teaspoon salt
½ cup raisins, chopped
⅓ cup nut meats, chopped
1 teaspoon vanilla
powdered sugar

1. In saucepan, combine sugar and flour. Mix. Add milk and egg.
2. Cook over low heat, stirring constantly, until mixture is thickened.
3. When thick, add salt, raisins, nut meats, and vanilla.
4. Beat for 2 minutes. Cool.
5. Spread cooled filling between layers of cake. Cover top of cake with powdered sugar.

CHOCOLATE GLAZE

For éclairs, doughnuts, cookies, and cream puffs.

1 ounce chocolate, melted
1 tablespoon butter
1 cup powdered sugar, sifted

⅛ teaspoon salt
2 tablespoons hot water
1 teaspoon vanilla

1. Melt chocolate and butter together over simmering water.
2. Add sugar, salt, and hot water. Beat until smooth.
3. Stir in vanilla.
4. Spoon glaze over baked product.

NOTES

COOKIES

Suggestions for Successful Cookie Baking ... 179
Ingredient Definitions ... 179
Tips for Handling Ingredients ... 180
Mixing Tips ... 180
Pan Preparation ... 180
Baking Problems and Solutions ... 181
Removing from Pan and Cooling ... 181
Tips for Freezing Cookies ... 181

DROP COOKIES

Drop Cookie Tips ... 182
Applesauce Cookies ... 182
Bread Crumb Cookies ... 183
Carrot Cookies ... 184
Candy Bar Cookies ... 184
Coconut Macaroons ... 185
Butterscotch-Date Cookies ... 186
Fruit Compote Cookies ... 186
Nutty-Date Macaroons ... 187
Chocolate Drop Cookies ... 188
El's Coconut Cookies ... 188
Pecan Kisses ... 189
Drop Ginger Cookies ... 190
Lace Cookies ... 190
Lacy Wafers ... 191
Drop Hermits ... 192
Molasses Chocolate Bit Cookies ... 192
Peanut Drop Cookies ... 193
Easy Oatmeal Cookies ... 194
Oatmeal Cookies ... 194
Peanut Cluster Cookies ... 195
Toll Oats Cookies ... 196
Peanut-Raisin Cookies ... 196
Pecan Supremes ... 197
Sour Cream Cookies ... 198

Drop Sugar Cookies   198
Mother's Raisin Cookies   199
Orange Cookies   200
Pineapple Nut Cookies   201
Spiced Drop Cookies   202
Crispy Rice Cereal Cookies   202
Pumpkin Cookies   203

REFRIGERATOR COOKIES

Refrigerator Cookie Tips   204
Dutch Almond Cookies   204
Date Pinwheels   205
Butterscotch Crisps   206
Chocolate and Vanilla Pinwheels   206
Refrigerator Date Cookies   207
Refrigerator Hermits   208
Black Walnut Refrigerator Cookies   209
Refrigerator Ginger Cookies   210
Refrigerator Vanilla Wafers   210

ROLLED OR MOLDED COOKIES

Rolled or Molded Cookie Tips   211
Basic Butter Cookies   212
Cottage Cheese Sandwich Cookies   212
Kifflings   213
Cherry Crunchies   214
Date Filled Cookies   215
Cinnamon Sugar Balls   216
Paul's Spiced Molasses Nuggets   216
Peanut Butter Cookies   217
Swedish Nut Crescents   218
Classic Sugar Cookies   218
Grandmother's Sugar Cookies   219
Quick Change Cookies   220
Swedish Spritz   221

BARS AND SQUARES

Tips for Bars and Squares   221
Blonde Brownies   222
Chocolate Bit Brownies   222

Best Basic Brownie 223
Cocoa Brownies 224
Cissie's Fudge Squares 224
Mocha Squares 225
Gum Drop Bars 226
Meringue Cookie Squares 227
Frosted Raisin Squares 228
Rocky Mountain Toffee Bars 228
Mince Meat Bars 230
Chocolate Marble Bars 231

UNCOOKED COOKIES

Changeable Chocolate Treats 232
Chewy Chocolate Bars 232
Chocolate Walnut Treats 233
Date Flake Nuggets 233
Date-Cereal Surprises 234
English Toffee Squares 234
Fry Pan Cookies 235
Puffed Wheat Cereal Bars 236
Rum Balls 236
Walnut Bourbon Balls 237

Spaces for notes, Pages 229, 237, 238

Glaze, page 184; Frosting, page 200; Meringue, page 227

Fillings, pages 205, 215, 234; Icings, pages 226, 230

SUGGESTIONS FOR SUCCESSFUL COOKIE BAKING

Homemade cookies bring warm affection from your loved ones.

INGREDIENT DEFINITIONS

Use double-acting baking powder when following these high altitude recipes. If substitutions are necessary, see "Ingredient Substitutions" on pages 22-23.

Use high grade emulsifier-type or hydrogenated-type shortenings (all vegetable or combination vegetable and meat fat oils), if possible. Do not substitute melted fats or vegetable or salad oils for these shortenings. For extra flavor, half butter and half shortening may be used where shortening is designated.

Butter, emulsified or hydrogenated shortenings, and margarine may be interchanged cupful for cupful.

Use high quality margarine when margarine is specified. In some recipes, the flavor will be jeopardized if margarine is substituted for butter.

Use whole sweet milk when milk is denoted. Use unsweetened canned milk when recipe calls for evaporated milk.

Use pure vanilla extract for best flavor.

TIPS FOR HANDLING INGREDIENTS

Dredge candied fruits, nuts, raisins, and so on, in 2 tablespoons of flour taken from amount called for in recipe. This is to prevent pieces from sticking together, or all going to the bottom of the batter.

Use scissors dipped in hot water when cutting up dates, gum drops, marshmallows, raisins, figs, and so forth.

Melt chocolate in double-boiler or equivalent, over simmering, not boiling, water.

MIXING TIPS

For creaming shortening with sugar use medium speed on electric mixer. *Do not undercream shortening and sugar.* For adding dry ingredients, use low speed. For blending extracts, melted chocolate, rolled oats, coconut, and the like, use low speed. For beating egg whites, use high speed. For beating egg yolks, use medium speed. For beating whole eggs, use medium speed. *We do not recommend* using the electric mixer for stirring in nuts, chocolate bits, and fruits.

PAN PREPARATION

To grease pans, spread lightly with *unsalted* fat. Salted butter burns readily and vegetable or salad oils sometimes are detrimental to the dough.

To flour pans, sprinkle greased pan lightly with flour or gently shake flour sifter over greased surface. Use cocoa to "flour" brownie pans.

If you do not have a cookie sheet, inverted baking pans will do.

BAKING PROBLEMS AND SOLUTIONS

If cookies are too brown on top: (a) heat may be unevenly distributed in oven; (b) cookie sheet may be placed too high in oven.

If cookies are too brown on bottom; (a) heat distribution may be uneven in the oven; (b) pan may be set on too low a rack; (c) pan with too deep sides is being used; (d) pan is too wide or long for the oven. (A pan at least 2 inches narrower and shorter than the oven is best.)

If cookies burn around edges of pan: (a) the oven is too hot; (b) pans may be too large; (c) the oven may be too full, cutting off proper heat circulation.

If cookies brown more on one side than other: (a) the pan may be set nearer one side of oven than the other; (b) the baffle or oven burner may not be level. It is helpful to turn cookie sheet around from front to back halfway through baking period.

REMOVING FROM PAN AND COOLING

Use pancake turner or spatula to remove cookies from pan.

Cool cookies on wire rack or kitchen counter covered with unoiled paper.

Do not stack or overlap cookies until completely cool.

Store soft cookies in jar with loose-fitting cover and crisp cookies in jar with tight-fitting cover.

TIPS FOR FREEZING COOKIES

All kinds of cookies freeze well. They may be frozen either before or after baking. Freezing rolls of dough saves on freezer space, but baking the cookies before freezing saves time.

Home economists write that it is best to *quick* freeze *baked* cookies on cookie sheet, then remove immediately, wrap in moisture-vaporproof (film, foil, or freezer paper) wrapper; or package in plastic bags or rigid containers, and return to freezer. More often than not we simply place the baked and thoroughly cooled cookies in metal tins or even heavy boxes lined with foil; or stack carefully in plastic bags without quick freezing first. It seems to be a matter of how much time you have and how long you plan to store the cookies.

Frozen cookies defrost in a few minutes and are ready to serve. (Our children eat them frozen sometimes.)

Freeze *unbaked* cookies in long rolls, wrapped in moisture-vaporproof wrapping. To use, slice off from partially thawed roll as many as needed. Bake as usual. Be sure to carefully re-wrap unused portion and return immediately to freezer.

Drop Cookies

DROP COOKIE TIPS

Drop batter from a teaspoon onto prepared cookie sheet. Use finger or another teaspoon to push dough off spoon. Most of the stiffer-dough drop cookies may be placed 1 inch to 1½ inches apart on cookie sheet. It is specifically stated in the individual recipe if there is an exception.

APPLESAUCE COOKIES

Here is a hearty, moist cookie that is the perfect after-school snack.

Oven temperature: preheat to 375°F.
Baking time: 10 to 12 minutes

Yield: 4 dozen cookies
Pan: greased cookie sheet

¾ cup shortening
1 cup brown sugar, firmly packed
1 egg, unbeaten
½ cup applesauce
2¼ cups all-purpose flour, sifted

½ teaspoon salt
½ teaspoon baking soda
¾ teaspoon cinnamon
¼ teaspoon ground cloves
1 cup raisins
½ cup nut meats, chopped

1. Cream shortening with brown sugar until light and fluffy.

2. Beat in egg.
3. Blend in applesauce.
4. Sift flour once before measuring. Mix and sift flour, salt, soda, cinnamon, and cloves together.
5. Add dry ingredients to creamed mixture a little at a time, mixing thoroughly after each addition.
6. Stir in raisins and nuts.
7. Drop by teaspoonful onto greased cookie sheet.
8. Bake at 375°F. for 10 to 12 minutes.

BREAD CRUMB COOKIES

Capture your cookie-eating audience with this departure from the usual.

Oven temperature: preheat to 375°F.
Baking time: about 12 minutes

Yield: 7 dozen cookies
Pan: greased cookie sheet

1 cup shortening
2 cups granulated sugar
2 eggs, beaten
1 teaspoon baking soda
1 cup boiling water
2 cups all-purpose flour, sifted

½ teaspoon salt
½ teaspoon cinnamon
½ teaspoon nutmeg
3 cups dried bread crumbs
nut meats, raisins, candied fruit or coconut, if desired

1. Cream shortening with sugar until light and fluffy.
2. Beat in eggs.
3. Dissolve soda in boiling water.
4. Sift flour once before measuring. Mix and sift flour, salt, cinnamon, and nutmeg together.
5. Add dry ingredients alternately with water, mixing thoroughly after each addition.
6. Blend in bread crumbs.
7. Stir in nuts, raisins, candied fruit, or coconut, if desired.
8. Drop by teaspoonful onto greased cookie sheet.
9. Bake at 375°F. for about 12 minutes, or until lightly browned.

CARROT COOKIES

Try frosting these for a flavor treat.

Oven temperature: preheat to 350°F.
Baking time: about 20 minutes

Yield: 4 to 5 dozen cookies
Pan: ungreased cookie sheet

¾ cup butter or margarine
1 cup granulated sugar
1 cup carrots, cooked and mashed
1 egg, beaten
½ teaspoon vanilla

2 cups all-purpose flour, sifted
½ teaspoon salt
2 teaspoons double-acting baking powder
grated rind of 1 orange

1. Cream butter or margarine with sugar until light and fluffy.
2. Add mashed carrots, egg, and vanilla. Beat well.
3. Sift flour once before measuring. Mix and sift flour, salt, and baking powder together.
4. Add dry ingredients a little at a time, mixing thoroughly after each addition.
5. Add the grated orange rind. Stir well.
6. Drop by teaspoonful onto ungreased cookie sheet.
7. Bake at 350°F. for about 20 minutes.
8. Glaze immediately.

GLAZE

juice of ½ lemon
juice of ½ orange

1 cup powdered sugar, sifted

1. Combine juices.
2. Gradually add powdered sugar until mixture is consistency for spreading.
3. Spread thinly on warm cookies.

CANDY BAR COOKIES

Our boys request these regularly. Mother finds herself with hand in the cookie jar, too.

Oven temperature: preheat to 375°F.
Baking time: 12 minutes

Yield: 5 to 6 dozen cookies
Pan: ungreased cookie sheet

½ cup butter, margarine, or shortening
¾ cup granulated sugar
1 egg, unbeaten
½ teaspoon vanilla

1½ cups all-purpose flour, sifted
½ teaspoon salt
½ teaspoon baking soda
2 candy bars (nougat rolled in nuts and chocolate covered)

1. Cream butter or shortening with sugar until light and fluffy.
2. Beat in egg. Add vanilla.
3. Sift flour once before measuring. Mix and sift flour, salt, and soda together.
4. Add dry ingredients to first mixture a little at a time, mixing thoroughly after each addition.
5. Cut candy bars in small pieces and stir into dough.
6. Chill until manageable.
7. Drop by scant teaspoonful onto ungreased cookie sheet.
8. Bake at 375°F. for 12 minutes.

COCONUT MACAROONS

You can't believe how good these are until you try them.

Oven temperature: preheat to 325°F.
Baking time: 15 to 20 minutes

Yield: 3 dozen cookies
Pan: greased cookie sheet

2 egg whites
1 cup granulated sugar
1 tablespoon cornstarch

1 cup shredded coconut
¾ cup walnut meats, ground

1. Beat egg whites until stiff, not dry.
2. Fold in sugar and cornstarch.
3. Heat in double boiler until mixture begins to thicken. Remove from heat.
4. Add coconut and ground walnuts to mixture.
5. Drop by teaspoonful onto greased cookie sheet.
6. Bake at 325°F. until golden brown, 15 to 20 minutes.
7. Cool and remove from cookie sheet.

BUTTERSCOTCH-DATE COOKIES

The icing dresses them up and the ingredients make them good enough for a coffee klatch or afternoon tea.

Oven temperature: preheat to 375°F.
Baking time: about 15 minutes

Yield: 3 to 4 dozen cookies
Pan: greased cookie sheet

¼ cup butter
¾ cup brown sugar, firmly packed
1 egg, unbeaten
½ teaspoon vanilla
½ cup sour cream
½ teaspoon baking soda

1¼ cups all-purpose flour, sifted
¼ teaspoon salt
¼ teaspoon double-acting baking powder
1 cup dates, chopped
1 cup nut meats, chopped

1. Cream butter and brown sugar until light and fluffy.
2. Beat in egg. Add vanilla.
3. Dissolve soda in sour cream.
4. Sift flour once before measuring. Mix and sift flour, salt, and baking powder together.
5. Add dry ingredients alternately with sour cream, mixing thoroughly after each addition.
6. Stir in dates and nuts.
7. Drop by teaspoonful onto greased cookie sheet.
8. Bake at 375°F. for about 15 minutes.

ICING

¼ cup butter
1 cup powdered sugar, sifted

hot water
½ teaspoon vanilla

1. Heat butter over low heat until light brown.
2. Add powdered sugar and enough hot water to make frosting spread well. Blend in vanilla.
3. Spread on cooled cookies.

FRUIT COMPOTE COOKIES

A new taste discovery made with fruit cocktail.

Oven temperature: preheat to 350°F.
Baking time: 15 minutes

Yield: 5 dozen large cookies
Pan: greased cookie sheet

1 cup butter or margarine
1½ cups brown sugar,
  firmly packed
½ cup granulated sugar
3 eggs, well beaten
4 cups all-purpose flour,
  sifted
1 teaspoon double-acting
  baking powder

1 teaspoon baking soda
¼ teaspoon salt
1 teaspoon allspice
1 teaspoon cinnamon
1 teaspoon ground cloves
1 cup nut meats, chopped
2 cups canned fruit cocktail
  (very well drained)

1. Cream butter or margarine with sugars until light and fluffy.
2. Beat in eggs.
3. Sift flour once before measuring. Mix and sift flour, baking powder, soda, salt, allspice, cinnamon, and cloves together.
4. Add dry ingredients to creamed mixture a little at a time, mixing thoroughly after each addition.
5. Stir in nut meats and fruit cocktail (well drained).
6. Drop by teaspoonful onto greased cookie sheet.
7. Bake at 350°F. for 15 minutes.

NUTTY-DATE MACAROONS

You'll want two for tea.

Oven temperature: preheat to
  325°F.
Baking time: 25 minutes

Yield: 3 dozen cookies
Pan: lightly greased cookie
  sheet

½ cup granulated sugar
¼ cup water
1 cup pecan meats, finely
  chopped

¾ cup dates, chopped
4 egg whites, beaten until
  stiff, not dry

1. Boil sugar, water, and pecans for 5 minutes.
2. Drain nuts. Save liquid. Mash nuts.
3. Add liquid and dates to mashed nuts.
4. Gently fold in stiffly beaten egg whites.
5. Drop by teaspoonful onto lightly greased cookie sheet.
6. Bake at 325°F. for 25 minutes.
7. Cool. Remove from cookie sheet.

CHOCOLATE DROP COOKIES

Versatile because its texture makes it a tasty little cake when iced, or a nice, moist cookie if it is not.

Oven temperature: preheat to
   350°F.
Baking time: 12 to 15 minutes

Yield: 4 dozen cookies
Pan: greased cookie sheet

½ cup shortening or butter
2 ounces chocolate
1 cup brown sugar, firmly
   packed
1 egg, unbeaten
1 teaspoon vanilla
½ teaspoon baking soda
½ cup milk

1¾ cups all-purpose flour,
   sifted
½ teaspoon salt
½ teaspoon double-acting
   baking powder
½ cup nut meats, chopped
   if desired

1. Melt butter or shortening and chocolate over simmering water.
2. Mix shortening and chocolate together thoroughly with brown sugar.
3. Beat in egg. Add vanilla.
4. Dissolve soda in milk.
5. Sift flour once before measuring. Mix and sift flour, salt, and baking powder together.
6. Add dry ingredients alternately with milk, mixing thoroughly after each addition.
7. Stir in nut meats.
8. Drop by teaspoonful onto greased cookie sheet.
9. Bake at 350°F. for 12 to 15 minutes.
10. Frost with any chocolate icing, if you wish.

EL'S COCONUT COOKIES

These are excellent for children's birthday parties, Christmas and special occasions. They include everything kiddies love!

Oven temperature: preheat to
   375°F.
Baking time: 10 minutes

Yield: 4 dozen cookies
Pan: ungreased cookie sheet

1 cup butter
1 cup brown sugar,
firmly packed
1 cup granulated sugar
2 eggs, unbeaten
1½ cups all-purpose flour
sifted
1 teaspoon baking soda

1 teaspoon salt
3 cups quick-cooking
rolled oats
1½ cups coconut, shredded
¾ cup dates, finely chopped
½ cup raisins
1 cup nut meats, chopped
1 cup small gum drops

1. Cream butter with sugars until light and fluffy.
2. Beat in eggs and blend well.
3. Sift flour once before measuring. Mix and sift flour, baking soda, and salt together.
4. Add dry ingredients to creamed mixture a little at a time, mixing thoroughly after each addition.
5. Stir in rolled oats, coconut, dates, raisins, nuts, and gum drops.
6. Drop by teaspoonful onto ungreased cookie sheet.
7. Bake at 375°F. for 10 minutes.

PECAN KISSES

Party puffs that will bring praise to the hostess, gastronomic pleasure to the guest.

Oven temperature: preheat to
350°F.
Baking time: 10 to 12 minutes

Yield: 9 dozen cookies
Pan: well greased cookie sheet

3 egg whites
1 pound brown sugar
3 tablespoons all-purpose
flour, sifted

½ teaspoon salt
4 cups pecan meats, chopped

1. Beat egg whites until foamy.
2. Add brown sugar and continue to beat until mixture stands in high, firm, but moist peaks.
3. Sift flour once before measuring. Mix flour and salt together, then add slowly to egg white mixture.
4. Stir in pecans.
5. Drop by small teaspoonful onto well greased cookie sheet.
6. Bake at 350°F. for 10 to 12 minutes.

DROP GINGER COOKIES

A big recipe so that a busy mother may have enough extra cookies to freeze.

Oven temperature: preheat to 375°F.
Baking time: 12 to 15 minutes

Yield: 6 to 7 dozen cookies
Pan: ungreased cookie sheet

1 cup butter, *OR*
½ cup butter and ½ cup shortening
1½ cups brown sugar, firmly packed
½ cup molasses
3 eggs, unbeaten
1½ teaspoons baking soda

1½ cups boiling water
5 cups all-purpose flour, sifted
½ teaspoon salt
4 teaspoons double-acting baking powder
1 tablespoon ginger
1 tablespoon cinnamon

1. Cream butter with brown sugar until light and fluffy.
2. Blend in molasses.
3. Beat in eggs.
4. Dissolve soda in boiling water.
5. Sift flour once before measuring. Mix and sift flour, salt, baking powder, ginger, and cinnamon together.
6. Add dry ingredients alternately with water, mixing thorougly after each addition.
7. Drop by teaspoonful onto ungreased cookie sheet.
8. Top may be decorated with a nut or chopped nuts.
9. Bake at 375°F. for 12 to 15 minutes.

LACE COOKIES

The hostess who serves these delicate crunchies will receive glorious compliments.

Oven temperature: preheat to 350°F.
Baking time: 8 to 10 minutes

Yield: 3 dozen cookies
Pan: greased and floured cookie sheet

1 cup butter or margarine	½ teaspoon salt
1 cup granulated sugar	1 teaspoon double-acting
2 eggs, unbeaten	baking powder
2 cups quick-cooking	
rolled oats	

1. Cream butter or margarine with sugar until light and fluffy.
2. Beat in eggs.
3. Mix rolled oats, salt, and baking powder together.
4. Add oats to creamed mixture. Blend well.
5. Drop small teaspoonful onto greased and floured cookie sheet. Space 2 inches apart.
6. Bake at 350°F. for 8 to 10 minutes. Cookies will puff up, then flatten out. Remove from cookie sheet while slightly warm.
Note: If cookies are not lightly browned, move to upper rack of oven for additional browning.

LACY WAFERS

An old family recipe provides these toothsome morsels that will guarantee your guests will be back for more.

Oven temperature: preheat to	Yield: 2 dozen cookies
325°F.	Pan: well greased cookie sheet
Baking time: 5 minutes	

2 tablespoons butter	1 teaspoon vanilla
1 cup brown sugar,	4 tablespoons all-purpose
firmly packed	flour, sifted
1 egg, unbeaten	1 cup nut meats, chopped

1. Cream butter with brown sugar until light and fluffy.
2. Beat in egg. Add vanilla.
3. Sift flour once before measuring. Measure flour then mix with nuts.
4. Blend flour and nuts with creamed mixture.
5. Drop by teaspoonful onto well greased cookie sheet, spacing 2 inches apart.
6. Bake at 325°F. for 5 minutes.
7. Remove from cookie sheet while still warm.

DROP HERMITS

This will be a mainstay in your recipe file ... and your cookie jar.

Oven temperature: preheat to 350°F.
Baking time: 12 to 15 minutes

Yield: 5 to 6 dozen cookies
Pan: ungreased cookie sheet

1 cup less 1 tablespoon shortening
1½ cups brown sugar, firmly packed
3 eggs, unbeaten
1 teaspoon baking soda
1 tablespoon hot water

1½ cups all-purpose flour, sifted
½ teaspoon salt
½ teaspoon allspice
½ teaspoon ground cloves
1 teaspoon cinnamon
1 cup raisins
1 cup nut meats, chopped

1. Cream shortening with brown sugar until light and fluffy.
2. Beat in eggs.
3. Dissolve soda in water and add to creamed mixture.
4. Sift flour once before measuring. Mix and sift flour, salt, allspice, cloves, and cinnamon together.
5. Add dry ingredients to creamed mixture a little at a time, mixing thoroughly after each addition. Add a little more flour if dough is not stiff enough to hold shape when dropped from teaspoon.
6. Stir in raisins and nuts.
7. Drop by teaspoonful onto ungreased cookie sheet.
8. Bake at 350°F. for 12 to 15 minutes.

MOLASSES CHOCOLATE BIT COOKIES

Hungry kiddies take to these cookies, the cookies take to cold milk. Together, the after-school snack problem is solved.

Oven temperature: preheat to 375°F.
Baking time: 10 to 12 minutes

Yield: 5 dozen cookies
Pan: ungreased cookie sheet

¾ cup shortening
¾ cup granulated sugar
1 egg, unbeaten
½ cup molasses
2½ cups all-purpose flour,
    sifted
1½ teaspoons baking soda

½ teaspoon salt
½ teaspoon cinnamon
½ teaspoon ginger
1 six-ounce package
    chocolate bits
½ cup nut meats, chopped

1. Cream shortening with sugar until light and fluffy.
2. Beat in egg and molasses.
3. Sift flour once before measuring. Mix and sift flour, soda, salt, cinnamon, and ginger together.
4. Add dry ingredients to creamed mixture a little at a time, mixing thoroughly after each addition.
5. Stir in chocolate bits and nuts.
6. Drop by teaspoonful onto ungreased cookie sheet.
7. Bake at 375°F. for 10 to 12 minutes.

PEANUT DROP COOKIES

Tasty and packed with protein.

Oven temperature: preheat to
    425°F.
Baking time: 8 minutes

Yield: 4 dozen cookies
Pan: ungreased cookie sheet

½ cup butter or margarine
1 cup granulated sugar
2 eggs, unbeaten
½ teaspoon vanilla
2 cups all-purpose flour,
    sifted

½ teaspoon salt
2 teaspoons double-acting
    baking powder
¼ cup table cream
1½ cups peanuts, chopped

1. Cream butter or margarine with sugar until light and fluffy.
2. Beat in eggs. Add vanilla.
3. Sift flour once before measuring. Mix and sift flour, salt, and baking powder together.
4. Add dry ingredients alternately with cream, mixing thoroughly after each addition.
5. Stir in peanuts.
6. Drop by teaspoonful onto ungreased cookie sheet.
7. Bake at 425°F. for 8 minutes.

EASY OATMEAL COOKIES

These cookies require little time or patience to make, but fill the cookie jar with wholesome pick-ups.

Oven temperature: preheat to 400°F.
Baking time: about 12 minutes

Yield: about 6 dozen cookies
Pan: ungreased cookie sheet

1 cup shortening
1 cup granulated sugar
2 eggs, unbeaten
2 cups all-purpose flour, sifted
½ teaspoon salt
1 teaspoon baking soda

1 teaspoon cinnamon
1 teaspoon nutmeg
6 tablespoons milk
2 cups quick-cooking rolled oats
1 cup raisins
1 cup nut meats, chopped

1. Cream shortening with sugar until light and fluffy.
2. Beat in eggs.
3. Sift flour once before measuring. Mix and sift flour, soda, salt, cinnamon, and nutmeg together.
4. Add dry ingredients alternately with milk, mixing thoroughly after each addition.
5. Stir in rolled oats, raisins, and nuts.
6. Drop by teaspoonful onto ungreased cookie sheet.
7. Bake at 400°F. for about 12 minutes.

OATMEAL COOKIES

Raisin juice for extra flavor; oats for wonderful, healthful chewiness.

Oven temperature: preheat to 425°F.
Baking time: about 12 minutes

Yield: 5 dozen cookies
Pan: ungreased cookie sheet

1 cup raisins cooked in ½ cup water
1 cup butter or shortening
1 cup granulated sugar
2 eggs, unbeaten
1 teaspoon baking soda
2 cups all-purpose flour, sifted

½ teaspoon salt
1 teaspoon cinnamon
1 teaspoon ground cloves
1 cup quick-cooking rolled oats
1 cup nut meats, chopped

1. Cook raisins in ½ cup water and set aside to cool.
2. Cream butter or shortening with sugar until light and fluffy.
3. Beat in eggs.
4. Dissolve soda in 4 tablespoons of juice from raisins and add to creamed mixture.
5. Sift flour once before measuring. Mix and sift flour, salt, cinnamon, and cloves together.
6. Add dry ingredients to creamed mixture a little at a time, mixing thoroughly after each addition.
7. Stir in rolled oats, nuts, and raisins drained of juice.
8. Drop by teaspoonful onto ungreased cookie sheet.
9. Bake at 425°F. for about 12 minutes.

PEANUT CLUSTER COOKIES

Mashed potatoes add moisture.

Oven temperature: preheat to 375°F.
Baking time: 15 minutes

Yield: 4 to 5 dozen cookies
Pan: greased cookie sheet

½ cup butter or margarine
1 cup granulated sugar
1 egg, beaten
½ cup potatoes, cooked and mashed
2 cups all-purpose flour, sifted

½ teaspoon baking soda
2 teaspoons double-acting baking powder
¼ cup cocoa
½ cup milk
½ cup salted peanuts

1. Cream butter or margarine with sugar until light and fluffy.
2. Beat in egg.
3. Add mashed potatoes. Beat well.
4. Sift flour once before measuring. Mix and sift flour, soda, baking powder, and cocoa together.
5. Add dry ingredients alternately with milk, mixing thoroughly after each addition. Stir in peanuts.
6. Drop by teaspoonful onto greased cookie sheet.
7. Bake at 375°F. for 15 minutes.

TOLL OATS COOKIES

This is the recipe most used in our households as the supply has yet to meet the demand, and the children request it over and over again. Double it. You'll be glad you did.

Oven temperature: preheat to 375°F.
Baking time: 12 minutes

Yield: 3½ dozen cookies
Pan: ungreased cookie sheet

½ cup shortening or margarine
½ cup granulated sugar
½ cup brown sugar, firmly packed
1 egg, unbeaten
½ teaspoon vanilla
1 tablespoon water

¾ cup all-purpose flour, sifted
½ teaspoon salt
½ teaspoon baking soda
1½ cups quick-cooking rolled oats
1 six-ounce package chocolate bits
½ cup nut meats, if desired

1. Cream together very well shortening or margarine, sugars, egg, vanilla, and water.
2. Sift flour once before measuring. Mix and sift flour, salt, and soda together.
3. Add dry ingredients to creamed mixture a little at a time, mixing thoroughly after each addition.
4. Stir in rolled oats, chocolate bits, and nuts.
5. Drop by teaspoonful onto ungreased cookie sheet.
6. Bake at 375°F. for 12 minutes.
Note: When doubling recipe use large, 12-ounce package of chocolate chips.

PEANUT-RAISIN COOKIES

Double-flavored gems that are nutritious as well as delicious.

Oven temperature: preheat to 375°F.
Baking time: 8 minutes

Yield: 3½ dozen cookies
Pan: ungreased cookie sheet

½ cup shortening
½ cup granulated sugar
1 egg, unbeaten
1 teaspoon vanilla
1 cup all-purpose flour, sifted

¼ teaspoon salt
¼ teaspoon baking soda
½ cup raisins
¼ cup salted peanuts

1. Cream shortening with sugar until light and fluffy.
2. Beat in egg. Add vanilla.
3. Sift flour once before measuring. Mix and sift flour, salt, and soda together.
4. Add dry ingredients to creamed mixture a little at a time, mixing thoroughly after each addition.
5. Stir in nuts and raisins.
6. Drop by teaspoonful onto ungreased cookie sheet.
7. Bake at 375°F. for 8 minutes.

PECAN SUPREMES

Divine, heavenly, marvelous, superb . . . these are the words you will hear about these parchment-thin wafers.

Oven temperature: preheat to 350°F.
Baking time: 5 minutes

Yield: 4½ dozen cookies
Pan: very well greased and floured cookie sheet

6 tablespoons butter, melted
2 cups brown sugar, firmly packed
2 eggs, beaten
2 teaspoons vanilla

10 tablespoons all-purpose flour, sifted
½ teaspoon salt
2 cups pecan or walnut meats, chopped

1. Melt butter, add brown sugar, and mix very well.
2. Beat in eggs and vanilla.
3. Sift flour once before measuring. Mix and sift flour and salt together.
4. Add dry ingredients to sugar mixture a little at a time, mixing thoroughly after each addition.
5. Stir in nuts.
6. Drop by scant ½ teaspoonful onto very well greased and floured cookie sheet spacing 2½ inches apart.
7. Bake at 350°F. for 5 minutes. Let cool 5 minutes before removing from cookie sheet.

SOUR CREAM COOKIES

A subtly flavored, cake-like cookies that does well as a little dessert when served warm from the oven.

Oven temperature: preheat to 400°F.
Baking time: about 6 minutes

Yield: 5 dozen cookies
Pan: ungreased cookie sheet

½ cup shortening
1 cup minus 1 tablespoon granulated sugar
1 egg, unbeaten
1 teaspoon vanilla

½ teaspoon baking soda
½ cup plus 2 tablespoons sour cream
2 cups all-purpose flour, sifted
½ teaspoon salt

1. Cream shortening with sugar until light and fluffy.
2. Beat in egg. Add vanilla.
3. Dissolve soda in sour cream.
4. Sift flour once before measuring. Mix and sift flour and salt together.
5. Add flour alternately with sour cream, mixing thoroughly after each addition.
6. Drop by teaspoonful onto ungreased cookie sheet.
7. Bake at 400°F. for 6 minutes Do not over-bake, as cookies should be soft and cake-like.
8. Sprinkle with granulated sugar, nutmeg, or nuts immediately upon removal from oven.

VARIATIONS

1. Add 1 cup shredded coconut after step 5.
2. Add 1 teaspoon cinnamon, ¼ teaspoon nutmeg, ¼ teaspoon ground cloves in step 3.
3. Add 1 cup raisins, 1 cup walnut meats, or 1 cup chopped dates to batter before baking.

DROP SUGAR COOKIES

No trouble at all to make. Easily varied with raisins, nuts, or sugars.

Oven temperature: preheat to 350°F.
Baking time: 12 to 15 minutes

Yield: 4 dozen cookies
Pan: greased cookie sheet

½ cup shortening
¾ cup granulated sugar
2 eggs, unbeaten
1 teaspoon vanilla
2½ cups all-purpose flour, sifted

½ teaspoon salt
3 teaspoons double-acting baking powder
½ cup milk

1. Cream shortening with sugar until light and fluffy.
2. Beat in eggs. Add vanilla.
3. Sift flour once before measuring. Mix and sift flour, salt, and baking powder together.
4. Add dry ingredients alternately with milk, mixing thoroughly after each addition.
5. Drop by teaspoonful onto greased cookie sheet.
6. Sprinkle with sugar, or decorate with nuts or raisins as desired.
7. Bake at 350°F. for 12 to 15 minutes.

MOTHER'S RAISIN COOKIES

Chewy wafers with a rich flavor.

Oven temperature: preheat to 400°F.
Baking time: 8 to 10 minutes

Yield: 4 to 5 dozen cookies
Pan: greased cookie sheet

½ cup shortening
¾ cup granulated sugar
1 egg, unbeaten
½ teaspoon lemon extract
1¾ cups all-purpose flour, sifted

¾ teaspoon baking soda
¾ teaspoon cream of tartar
¼ teaspoon salt
1 teaspoon milk
½ cup raisins, chopped or ground

1. Cream shortening with sugar until light and fluffy.
2. Beat in egg. Add lemon extract.
3. Sift flour once before measuring. Mix and sift flour, soda, cream of tartar, and salt together.
4. Add dry ingredients alternately with milk, mixing thoroughly after each addition.
5. Stir in raisins.
6. Drop by teaspoonful onto greased cookie sheet.
7. Bake at 400°F. for 8 to 10 minutes.

ORANGE COOKIES

We think these are divine. They are light, different, and delicate in texture.

Oven temperature: preheat to
   350°F.
Baking time: 10 minutes

Yield: 5 to 6 dozen cookies
Pan: greased cookie sheet

¾ cup shortening
1¼ cups granulated sugar
2 eggs, well beaten
3 cups all-purpose flour,
   sifted
2½ teaspoons double-acting
   baking powder

1 teaspoon baking soda
½ teaspoon salt
1 cup milk
½ cup orange juice
grated rind of one orange
1 teaspoon vanilla

1. Cream shortening with sugar until light and fluffy.
2. Beat in eggs.
3. Sift flour once before measuring. Mix and sift flour, baking powder, soda, and salt together. Add dry ingredients alternately with milk, mixing thoroughly after each addition.
4. Add orange juice, grated orange rind, and vanilla. Mix very well.
5. Drop by teaspoonful onto greased cookie sheet.
6. Bake at 350°F. for 10 minutes. Cool and frost.

FROSTING

grated rind and juice of
   one orange
grated rind and juice
   of one lemon

2 tablespoons butter, softened
2 cups powdered sugar, sifted

1. Combine juices, rinds, and butter.
2. Add enough powdered sugar to make the frosting the right consistency for spreading.
3. Frost cooled cookies.

PINEAPPLE NUT COOKIES

Perfect accompaniment to custard, ice cream, pudding, and gelatin dessert,

Oven temperature: preheat to 375°F.
Baking time: 12 minutes

Yield: 3 dozen cookies
Pan: greased cookie sheet

½ cup butter or shortening OR ¼ cup butter and ¼ cup shortening
½ cup granulated sugar
½ cup brown sugar, firmly packed
1 egg, beaten
½ teaspoon vanilla

1 cup crushed pineapple (9-ounce can)
2 cups all-purpose flour, sifted
¼ teaspoon baking soda
½ teaspoon salt
½ teaspoon double-acting baking powder
½ cup nut meats, chopped

1. Cream butter or shortening with sugars until light and fluffy.
2. Add beaten egg and vanilla.
3. Drain pineapple well, then add to creamed mixture.
4. Sift flour once before measuring. Mix and sift flour, soda, salt, and baking powder together.
5. Add dry ingredients to creamed mixture a little at a time, mixing thoroughly after each addition.
6. Stir in nuts.
7. Drop by teaspoonful onto greased cookie sheet.
8. Bake at 375°F. for 12 minutes, or until lightly browned.

SPICED DROP COOKIES

Good travelers in lunch box or picnic basket.

Oven temperature: preheat to
  350°F.
Baking time: 10 to 15 minutes

Yield: 6 dozen cookies
Pan: greased cookie sheet

½ cup shortening, melted
1 cup brown sugar,
  firmly packed
½ cup granulated sugar
2 eggs, unbeaten
1 tablespoon hot water
1 teaspoon baking soda

3 cups all-purpose flour,
  sifted
½ teapsoon salt
1 teaspoon nutmeg
1 teaspoon cinnamon
½ teaspoon ground cloves
½ cup raisins
½ cup nut meats, chopped

1. Melt shortening and combine thoroughly with sugars.
2. Beat in eggs.
3. Dissolve soda in hot water and add to sugar mixture.
4. Sift flour once before measuring. Mix and sift flour, salt, nutmeg, cinnamon, and cloves together.
5. Add dry ingredients to sugar mixture a little at a time, mixing thoroughly after each addition.
6. Stir in raisins and nuts.
7. Drop by teaspoonful onto greased cookie sheet.
8. Bake at 350°F. for 10 to 15 minutes.

CRISPY RICE CEREAL COOKIES

A nutritious sweet treat for after school when your children arrive home "starved."

Oven temperature: preheat to
  375°F.
Baking time: about 12 minutes

Yield: 7 dozen cookies
Pan: ungreased cookie sheet

1 cup shortening
1 cup granulated sugar
1 cup brown sugar,
  firmly packed
2 eggs, unbeaten
1 teaspoon vanilla
2 cups all-purpose flour
½ teaspoon salt

1 teaspoon baking soda
½ teaspoon double-acting
  baking powder
2 cups crisp rice cereal
2 cups quick-cooking
  rolled oats
1 cup coconut

1. Cream shortening with sugars until light and fluffy.
2. Beat in eggs. Add vanilla.
3. Sift flour once before measuring. Mix and sift flour, salt, soda, and baking powder together.
4. Add dry ingredients to creamed mixture a little at a time, mixing thoroughly after each addition.
5. Stir in crisp rice cereal, rolled oats, and coconut.
6. Drop by teaspoonful onto ungreased cookie sheet, then press with fork.
7. Bake at 375°F. for about 12 minutes.

PUMPKIN COOKIES

In the fall when appetites are sharpened, these satisfying gems disappear by the handfuls.

Oven temperature: preheat to 350°F.
Baking time: about 10 minutes

Yield: 6 dozen cookies
Pan: greased cookie sheet

½ cup shortening
1½ cups brown sugar, firmly packed
2 eggs, unbeaten
1 teaspoon vanilla
1 teaspoon lemon extract, *OR*
1½ teaspoons lemon rind, grated
1½ cups cooked pumpkin
3 cups all-purpose flour, sifted

½ teaspoon salt
4 teaspoons double-acting baking powder
½ teaspoon ginger
½ teaspoon nutmeg
½ teaspoon allspice
1 teaspoon cinnamon
1 cup nut meats, chopped
1 package cut up candied fruits, if desired

1. Cream shortening with brown sugar until light and fluffy.
2. Add beaten eggs, vanilla, lemon extract or lemon rind, and pumpkin.
3. Sift flour once before measuring. Mix and sift flour, salt, baking powder, ginger, nutmeg, allspice, and cinnamon together.
4. Add dry ingredients to creamed mixture a little at a time, mixing thoroughly after each addition.
5. Stir in nuts and fruit.
6. Drop by teaspoonful onto greased cookie sheet.
7. Bake at 350°F. for about 10 minutes.

Refrigerator Cookies

REFRIGERATOR COOKIE TIPS

Roll dough into equally divided rolls about 2 inches in diameter. Cover rolls with waxed paper and chill in refrigerator until firm (approximately 4 hours) or overnight. With sharp knife, cut rolls into slices 1/8 to 1/4 inch thick. Bake as directed.

Dough may be kept 10 days to 2 weeks, or frozen for future use. (Wrap in freezer paper or seal in plastic bag.)

DUTCH ALMOND COOKIES

A unique refrigerator cookie highly praised by young and old.

Oven temperature: preheat to 400°F.
Baking time: 12 to 15 minutes

Yield: 10 to 12 dozen cookies
Pan: ungreased cookie sheet

2 cups butter, *OR* 1 cup butter and 1 cup shortening
2 cups granulated sugar
½ teaspoon baking soda
⅓ cup sour cream

4 cups all-purpose flour, sifted
½ teaspoon salt
½ teaspoon ground cloves
½ teaspoon nutmeg
1 cup almonds, sliced

1. Cream butter with sugar until light and fluffy.
2. Dissolve soda in sour cream.
3. Sift flour once before measuring. Mix and sift flour, salt, cloves, and nutmeg together.
4. Add dry ingredients alternately with sour cream, mixing thoroughly after each addition.
5. Stir in almonds.
6. Form dough into rolls 2 inches in diameter. Wrap in waxed paper and chill until firm.
7. Cut into slices 1/4 inch thick.
8. Bake at 400°F. for 12 to 15 minutes.

DATE PINWHEELS

These have the look of extra-effort that your guests appreciate.

Oven temperature: preheat to
  350°F.
Baking time: about 15 minutes

Yield: 5 dozen pinwheel slices
Pan: greased cookie sheet

½ cup shortening
1 cup brown sugar,
  firmly packed
2 eggs, beaten
½ teaspoon vanilla

1¾. cups all-purpose flour,
  sifted
¼ teaspoon salt
¼ teaspoon baking soda

FILLING

½ cup granulated sugar
½ cup water

1¼ cups dates, chopped
2 cups nut meats, chopped

1. Cream shortening with brown sugar until light and fluffy.
2. Beat in eggs. Add vanilla.
3. Sift flour once before measuring. Mix and sift flour, salt, and soda together.
4. Add dry ingredients a little at a time to creamed mixture, mixing thoroughly after each addition.
5. Chill dough in refrigerator at least one hour. Meanwhile prepare filling.
6. Cook sugar, water and dates until slightly thickened. Add nuts and cook about 5 minutes longer. Remove from heat and cool.
7. Divide dough into two parts.
8. Roll out on floured surface first half of dough to 1/4 inch thick. Spread with half of filling, then roll up like jelly roll. Repeat with second half of dough and filling.
9. Chill in refrigerator until firm. Slice 1/4 inch thick and place on greased cookie sheet.
10. Bake at 350°F. for about 15 minutes, or until lightly browned, and remove from cookie sheet soon after baking to avoid sticking.

BUTTERSCOTCH CRISPS

These are basic, easy-to-make refrigerator cookies that you may bake as you need them.

Oven temperature: preheat to 375°F.
Baking time: 10 minutes

Yield: 8 dozen cookies
Pan: ungreased cookie sheet

1 cup butter, margarine, shortening OR ½ cup butter and ½ cup shortening
1½ cups brown sugar, firmly packed
2 eggs, unbeaten
½ teaspoon vanilla

3½ cups all-purpose flour sifted
½ teaspoon salt
3 teaspoons double-acting baking powder
½ cup nut meats, chopped, if desired

1. Cream shortening with brown sugar until light and fluffy.
2. Beat in eggs. Add vanilla.
3. Sift flour once before measuring. Mix and sift flour, salt, and baking powder together.
4. Add dry ingredients to creamed mixture a little at a time, mixing thoroughly after each addition. Stir in nuts.
5. Form dough into rolls 2 inches in diameter. Wrap in waxed paper and chill until firm.
6. Cut into slices 1/8 inch thick, place on ungreased cookie sheet.
7. Bake at 375°F. for 10 minutes, or until lightly browned.

CHOCOLATE AND VANILLA PINWHEELS

Tried and true are these. You can never go wrong including them at coffees and teas.

Oven temperature: preheat to 375°F.
Baking time: about 10 minutes

Yield: 4 to 5 dozen cookies
Pan: ungreased cookie sheet

½ cup butter
½ cup granulated sugar
1 egg yolk
1½ cups all-purpose flour, sifted

½ teaspoon salt
½ teaspoon double-acting baking powder
3 tablespoons milk
2 ounces chooclate, melted

1. Cream butter with sugar until light and fluffy.
2. Beat in egg yolk.
3. Sift flour once before measuring. Mix and sift flour, salt, and baking powder together.
4. Add dry ingredients alternately with milk, mixing thoroughly after each addition.
5. Divide dough in half. To one half add melted chocolate and mix well. Leave other half as is.
6. Chill dough until firm, then roll each half 1/8 inch thick. Put chocolate rolled out dough on top of vanilla rolled out dough, and roll up together like jelly roll.
7. Slice 1/4 inch thick and place on ungreased cookie sheet.
8. Bake at 375°F. for about 10 minutes, or until lightly browned.

REFRIGERATOR DATE COOKIES

An ever-useful cookie dough that may be kept in the refrigerator or frozen for that rainy day.

Oven temperature: preheat to
 410°F.
Baking time: 10 minutes

Yield: 6 to 8 dozen cookies
Pan: well greased cookie sheet

1 cup shortening
2 cups brown sugar,
 firmly packed
2 eggs, beaten
1 teaspoon vanilla
few drops maple flavoring

3½ cups all-purpose flour,
 sifted
1 teaspoon baking soda
1 teaspoon cream of tartar
2 tablespoons cream or milk
1 cup nut meats, chopped
1 cup dates, chopped

1. Cream shortening with brown sugar until light and fluffy.
2. Beat in eggs. Add vanilla and maple flavoring. Blend in milk or cream.
3. Sift flour once before measuring. Mix and sift flour with baking soda and cream of tartar.
4. Add dry ingredients to creamed mixture a little at a time, mixing thoroughly after each addition.
5. Stir in nuts and dates.
6. Form dough into rolls 2 inches in diameter. Wrap in waxed paper and chill overnight.
7. Slice 1/8 inch thick and place on well greased cookie sheet.
8. Bake at 410°F. for 10 minutes, or until delicately brown.

REFRIGERATOR HERMITS

Early New England cookbooks rarely omitted this old standby.

Oven temperature: preheat to 375°F.
Baking time: 12 to 15 minutes

Yield: 10 to 12 dozen cookies
Pan: ungreased cookie sheet

1 cup shortening, butter or margarine OR ½ cup butter and ½ cup shortening
2 cups brown sugar, firmly packed
3 eggs, unbeaten
5 cups all-purpose flour, sifted
½ teaspoon salt

½ teaspoon baking soda
1 teaspoon cinnamon
1 teaspoon nutmeg
½ teaspoon ground cloves
½ teaspoon mace, if desired
3 tablespoons milk
1 cup raisins, chopped
1 cup nut meats, chopped

1. Cream shortening with brown sugar until light and fluffy.
2. Beat in eggs.
3. Sift flour once before measuring. Mix and sift flour, salt, soda, cinnamon, nutmeg, cloves, and mace together.
4. Add dry ingredients alternately with milk, mixing thoroughly after each addition. Stir in raisins and nuts.
5. Form dough into rolls 2 inches in diameter. Wrap in waxed paper and chill until firm.
6. Cut in 1/8 to 1/4 inch thick slices and place on ungreased cookie sheet.
7. Bake at 375°F. for 12 to 15 minutes.
Note: This dough may be kept for at least two weeks in refrigerator, or it may be frozen.

BLACK WALNUT REFRIGERATOR COOKIES

This recipe is an old-timer of ours.

Oven temperature: preheat to
375°-400°F.
Baking time: about 12 minutes

Yield: 10 dozen cookies
Pan: ungreased cookie sheet

1¼ cups butter OR ¾ cup
butter and ½ cup
shortening
1¾ cups brown sugar,
firmly packed
2 eggs, unbeaten
2 teaspoons mapeline
extract
4 cups all-purpose flour,
sifted

½ teaspoon salt
1 teaspoon baking soda
1 teaspoon cream of tartar
1 cup black walnut meats,
chopped
½ cup walnut meats,
chopped

1. Cream butter with brown sugar until light and fluffy.
2. Beat in eggs. Add mapeline extract.
3. Sift flour once before measuring. Mix and sift flour, salt, soda, and cream of tartar together.
4. Add dry ingredients to creamed mixture a little at a time, mixing thoroughly after each addition.
5. Stir in nuts.
6. Form dough into rolls 2 inches in diameter. Wrap in waxed paper and chill until firm.
7. Cut into slices 1/4 inch thick, place on ungreased cookie sheet.
8. Bake at 375°-400°F. for about 12 minutes, or until lightly browned.

REFRIGERATOR GINGER COOKIES

Small fry will find these especially suited to their tastes.

Oven temperature: preheat to
400°F.
Baking time: 10 minutes

Yield: 5 dozen cookies
Pan: greased cookie sheet

½ cup butter or margarine
½ cup granulated sugar
1 egg, unbeaten
½ cup light molasses
2¾ cups all-purpose flour,
sifted

½ teaspoon salt
1 teaspoon baking soda
1 teaspoon cinnamon
1 teaspoon ground ginger

1.   Cream butter or margarine with sugar until light and fluffy.
2.   Beat in egg. Stir in molasses.
3.   Sift flour once before measuring. Mix and sift flour, salt, soda, cinnamon, and ginger together.
4.   Add dry ingredients to creamed mixture a little at a time, mixing thoroughly after each addition.
5.   Divide dough in half. Shape each half into a roll about 2 inches in diameter. Wrap in waxed paper. Chill in refrigerator for 4 hours or overnight.
6.   Slice 1/8 inch thick with a sharp knife. Place on greased cookie sheet.
7.   Bake at 400°F. for 10 minutes.

REFRIGERATOR VANILLA WAFERS

Excellent for our large families. We love the taste of this butter-scotchy, crisp cookie.

Oven temperature: preheat to
375°F.
Baking time: 12 to 15 minutes

Yield: 10 to 12 dozen
Pan: ungreased cookie sheet

2 cups margarine	1 teaspoon baking soda
1 cup granulated sugar	3 tablespoons water
1 cup brown sugar, firmly packed	5 cups all-purpose flour, sifted
2 eggs, unbeaten	½ teaspoon salt
1 teaspoon vanilla	1 cup nut meats, chopped

1. Cream margarine with sugars until light and fluffy.
2. Beat in eggs. Add vanilla.
3. Dissolve soda in water. Add to creamed mixture.
4. Sift flour once before measuring. Mix and sift flour and salt together.
5. Add dry ingredients to creamed mixture a little at a time, mixing thoroughly after each addition.
6. Stir in nuts.
7. Form dough into three rolls 2 inches in diameter. Wrap in waxed paper and chill at least 3 hours.
8. Cut into slices 1/4 inch thick. Place on ungreased cookie sheet.
9. Bake at 375°F. for 12 to 15 minutes, or until lightly browned.

Rolled or Molded Cookies

ROLLED OR MOLDED COOKIE TIPS

If dough is too thin (sticky) to roll or mold, add a very small amount of sifted flour until it becomes manageable. If dough is too thick, add a small amount of milk or water (about 1 table-spoon to begin with). Rolling out of dough is usually done on a lightly floured surface. Roll out 1/8 to 1/4 inch thick. Sometimes flouring the rolling pin prevents sticking.

Lightly flouring cookie cutters and cookie press will help keep dough from sticking.

BASIC BUTTER COOKIE

Perennially popular, this favorite dresses up well for the tea table, as well as serving family needs.

Oven temperature: preheat to 350°F.
Baking time: 10 minutes

Yield: 3 dozen cookies
Pan: ungreased cookie sheet

¾ cup butter
1 cup powdered sugar, sifted
2 egg yolks, or 1 whole egg
1 teaspoon vanilla
2 cups all-purpose flour, sifted

½ teaspoon salt
½ teaspoon baking soda
½ teaspoon cream of tartar
granulated sugar, nuts, or candied fruit

1.   Cream butter with powdered sugar until light and fluffy.
2.   Beat in egg yolks, or whole egg. Add vanilla.
3.   Sift flour once before measuring. Mix and sift flour, salt, soda, and cream of tartar together.
4.   Add dry ingredients to creamed mixture a little at a time, mixing thoroughly after each addition.
5.   Make dough into small balls and flatten with fork on ungreased cookie sheet.
6.   Sprinkle with sugar, nuts, or candied fruit.
7.   Bake at 350°F. for 15 minutes.
Note: Lemon or almond extract may be substituted for vanilla. Dough may be put through cookie press.

COTTAGE CHEESE SANDWICH COOKIES

Irresistible, so don't try your will power when these are on the cookie plate.

Oven temperature: preheat to 350°F.
Baking time: 15 to 20 minutes

Yield: 4 dozen cookies
Pan: ungreased cookie sheet

2 cups cottage cheese
¾ cup butter or margarine
2 cups all-purpose flour, sifted

½ teaspoon salt
1 cup thick preserves (strawberry, cherry, peach, or grape)
powdered sugar

1. Put cottage cheese through sieve.
2. Cream butter or margarine and cottage cheese together.
3. Sift flour once before measuring. Mix and sift flour and salt together.
4. Add dry ingredients to creamed mixture a little at a time, mixing thoroughly after each addition.
5. Roll out dough on floured surface to 1/4 inch thick. Cut in rounds 2 inches in diameter. Place half of cookies on ungreased cookie sheet 1/2 inch apart.
6. Put approximately ½ teaspoon preserves in center of each cookie. Cover with remaining cookies. Seal edges with fingers or fork.
7. Bake at 350°F. for 15 to 20 minutes, or until lightly browned.
8. Sprinkle with powdered sugar while still warm.
Note: These are more party-like and colorful if hole is cut out in center of top cookie.

KIFFLINGS

From Sweden come these gems that melt in your mouth. May be shaped many interesting ways.

Oven temperature: preheat to 350°F.
Baking time: 20 minutes

Yield: about 9 dozen cookies
Pan: ungreased cookie sheet

1½ cups butter
6 tablespoons granulated sugar
2 teaspoons vanilla
½ teaspoon salt

3¾ cups all-purpose flour sifted
7 tablespoons almonds, unblanched and ground
powdered sugar

1. Cream butter with sugar until light and fluffy. Add vanilla.
2. Sift flour once before measuring. Mix and sift flour and salt together.
3. Add dry ingredients to first mixture a little at a time, mixing thoroughly after each addition. Stir in nuts.
4. Shape dough in balls, or bracelets, or cut in rounds. Place on ungreased cookie sheet.
5. Bake at 350°F. for 20 minutes.
6. While still hot roll in powdered sugar.

CHERRY CRUNCHIES

Pecans, dates, and cherries add to the flavor of these cookies.

Oven temperature: preheat to 375°F.
Baking time: 10 to 12 minutes

Yield: 4 to 6 dozen cookies
Pan: greased cookie sheet

¾ cup butter or shortening
½ cup granulated sugar
½ cup brown sugar firmly packed
2 eggs, unbeaten
1 teaspoon vanilla
2 tablespoons milk or light cream
2¼ cups all-purpose flour, sifted
½ teaspoon salt

½ teaspoon baking soda
1 teaspoon double-acting baking powder
1 cup pecan meats, chopped
1 cup dates, chopped
⅓ cup maraschino cherries, chopped
2½ cups cornflakes, crushed
maraschino cherries, sliced

1. Cream butter or shortening with sugars until light and fluffy.
2. Beat in eggs. Add vanilla and milk or cream. Beat well.
3. Sift flour once before measuring. Mix and sift flour, salt, soda, and baking powder together.
4. Add dry ingredients to creamed mixture a little at a time, mixing thoroughly after each addition.
5. Add the pecans, dates, and cherries. Mix very well.
6. Form dough into balls using about 1 level tablespoonful of dough for each.
7. Roll each ball in crushed cornflakes. Place on greased cookie sheet and top each with a slice of maraschino cherry.
8. Bake at 375°F. for 10 to 12 minutes.

DATE FILLED COOKIES

Our minister's wife was nice enough to share this good recipe with us.

Oven temperature: preheat to 350°F.
Baking time: 25 minutes

Yield: 40 filled cookies
Pan: greased cookie sheet

1 cup butter *OR*
½ cup butter and ½ cup shortening
1 cup granulated sugar
2 eggs, unbeaten

3 cups all-purpose flour, sifted
½ teaspoon salt
1 teaspoon baking soda
2 teaspoons cream of tartar

FILLING

½ pound dates, finely chopped
1 cup water

½ cup granulated sugar
1 tablespoon lemon juice
½ cup nut meats, chopped

1. Cream butter with sugar until light and fluffy.
2. Beat in eggs.
3. Sift flour once before measuring. Mix and sift flour, salt, soda, and cream of tartar together.
4. Add dry ingredients to creamed mixture a little at a time, mixing thoroughly after each addition.
5. Cook dates with water until soft. Add sugar. Continue cooking.
6. When thick add lemon juice and nuts.
7. Roll out dough on floured surface 1/4 to 1/8 inch thick. Cut in rounds 2 inches in diameter. Place half of cookies on greased cookie sheet 1/2 inch apart.
8. Put approximately 1 teaspoonful of filling in center of each cookie. Cover with remaining cookies. Seal edges with fingers or fork.
9. Bake at 350°F. for 25 minutes.

215

CINNAMON SUGAR BALLS

Little tots can manage these very well.

Oven temperature: preheat to
400°F.
Baking time: 10 minutes

Yield: 5 to 6 dozen cookies
Pan: ungreased cookie sheet

1 cup shortening
1½ cups plus 2 tablespoons
granulated sugar
2 eggs, unbeaten
½ teaspoon vanilla

2¾ cups all-purpose flour,
sifted
½ teaspoon salt
½ teaspoon baking soda
2 teaspoons cream of tartar
2 tablespoons cinnamon

1. Cream shortening with 1½ cups sugar until light and fluffy.
2. Beat in eggs. Add vanilla.
3. Sift flour once before measuring. Mix and sift flour, salt, soda, and cream of tartar together.
4. Add dry ingredients to creamed mixture a little at a time, mixing thoroughly after each addition.
5. Chill dough until firm, then roll into balls size of small walnut.
6. Mix remaining 2 tablespoons sugar and cinnamon together. Roll balls in this mixture and place about 2 inches apart on ungreased cookie sheet.
7. Bake at 400°F. for 10 minutes.

PAUL'S SPICED MOLASSES NUGGETS

One son prefers this to all other cookies.

Oven temperature: preheat to
350°F.
Baking time: 15 minutes

Yield: 3½ dozen cookies
Pan: ungreased cookie sheet

½ cup butter or shortening,
melted
¼ cup granulated sugar
⅓ cup molasses
1½ cups all-purpose flour,
sifted

1 teaspoon cinnamon
¼ teaspoon salt
½ teaspoon ginger
powdered sugar
½ cup nut meats, chopped

1. Mix melted butter or shortening with sugar.
2. Add molasses and blend well.
3. Sift flour once before measuring. Mix and sift flour, cinnamon, salt, and ginger together.
4. Add dry ingredients to molasses mixture a little at a time, mixing thoroughly after each addition.
5. Stir in nut meats.
6. Roll dough into 3/4 inch balls and place 1 inch apart on ungreased cookie sheet.
7. Bake at 350°F. for 15 minutes.
8. Remove from cookie sheets. Roll in powdered sugar while still warm.
9. Store in tightly closed jar or box.

PEANUT BUTTER COOKIES

The peanut butter fans at our houses love these wholesome goodies.

Oven temperature: preheat to 375°F.

Baking time: 10 to 12 minutes

Yield: 4 dozen cookies

Pan: ungreased cookie sheet

½ cup peanut butter
½ cup shortening
½ cup granulated sugar
½ cup brown sugar, firmly packed
1 egg, unbeaten

1 teaspoon vanilla
1¼ cups all-purpose flour, sifted
½ teaspoon salt
1 teaspoon baking soda

1. Cream peanut butter and shortening with sugars until light and fluffy.
2. Beat in egg. Add vanilla.
3. Sift flour once before measuring. Mix and sift flour, salt, and soda together.
4. Add dry ingredients to creamed mixture a little at a time, mixing thoroughly after each addition.
5. Roll dough into balls 1 inch in diameter, placing balls 2 inches apart on ungreased cookie sheet. Take fork and flatten balls with the tines parallel to the cookie. Press vertically, then horizontally to form crisscross.
6. Bake at 375°F. for 10 to 12 minutes.

SWEDISH NUT CRESCENTS

One cook we know called these "Love Cookies" because everyone who ever tasted them loved them so much.

Oven temperature: preheat to 350°F.
Baking time: 15 minutes

Yield: 4 to 5 dozen cookies
Pan: ungreased cookie sheet

1 cup shortening (half butter improves the taste)
1½ cups powdered sugar, sifted
1 tablespoon water
1 tablespoon vanilla

2 cups all-purpose flour, sifted
½ teaspoon salt
1¼ cups unblanched almonds, ground
powdered sugar

1. Cream shortening with 1 cup sugar until light and fluffy.
2. Add water and vanilla.
3. Sift flour once before measuring. Mix and sift flour and salt together.
4. Add dry ingredients to creamed mixture a little at a time, mixing thoroughly after each addition.
5. Blend in ground almonds.
6. Shape dough into balls or crescents using 1 level tablespoon of dough for each cookie. Place on ungreased cookie sheet.
7. Bake at 350°F. for 15 minutes, or until lightly browned.
8. Roll in remaining ½ cup powdered sugar while still warm.

CLASSIC SUGAR COOKIES

Simple but flavorful.

Oven temperature: preheat to 425°F.
Baking time: 5 to 6 minutes

Yield: 6 dozen cookies
Pan: greased cookie sheet

½ cup butter or margarine
1 cup granulated sugar
2 eggs, well beaten
1 teaspoon lemon juice
grated rind of 1 lemon
2 tablespoons coffee cream

2½ to 3 cups all-purpose flour, sifted
2 teaspoons double-acting baking powder
1 teaspoon salt
¼ teaspoon nutmeg
¼ teaspoon cinnamon

1.   Cream butter or margarine with sugar until light and fluffy.
2.   Add eggs, lemon juice, lemon rind, and cream. Beat very well.
3.   Sift flour once before measuring. Mix and sift flour, baking powder, salt, nutmeg, and cinnamon together several times.
4.   Add dry ingredients to the creamed mixture a little at a time, mixing thoroughly after each addition. Batter should be smooth and somewhat dry.
5.   Roll out dough to 1/8 inch thick. Cut cookies with cookie cutter. Sprinkle tops generously with granulated sugar.
6.   Bake on greased cookie sheet at 425°F. for 5 to 6 minutes.

GRANDMOTHER'S SUGAR COOKIES

This recipe came West with grandmother in a covered wagon.

Oven temperature: preheat to 425°F.
Baking time: 5 to 6 minutes

Yield: 4 dozen cookies
Pan: ungreased cookie sheet

½ cup plus 1 tablespoon shortening
1 cup granulated sugar
1 egg, unbeaten
1 teaspoon vanilla
1 teaspoon baking soda

½ cup buttermilk
3 cups all-purpose flour, sifted
1 teaspoon double-acting baking powder
½ teaspoon salt

1.   Cream shortening with sugar until light and fluffy.
2.   Beat in egg. Add vanilla.
3.   Dissolve soda in buttermilk.
4.   Sift flour once before measuring. Mix and sift flour, baking powder, and salt together.
5.   Add dry ingredients alternately with buttermilk, mixing thoroughly after each addition.
6.   Roll out dough to 1/8 inch thick on lightly floured surface. Cut any desired size or shape.
7.   Sprinkle with granulated sugar. (Colored sugars are nice at Christmas time.) Place on ungreased cookie sheet.
8.   Bake at 450°F. for 10 to 12 minutes.

QUICK CHANGE COOKIES

Start your holiday baking with this generous-sized recipe that can be rolled into cut-outs, or refrigerated and sliced.

Oven temperature: preheat to
   350°F.
Baking time: 15 minutes

Yield: 6 dozen cookies
Pan: ungreased cookie sheet

2 cups butter
2 cups powdered sugar,
   sifted
1 egg, unbeaten

1 teaspoon vanilla
4 cups all-purpose flour,
   sifted
1 teaspoon salt

   (See below for ingredients to be used for variations.)

1.   Cream butter with powdered sugar until light and fluffy.
2.   Beat in egg. Add vanilla.
3.   Sift flour once before measuring. Mix and sift flour and salt together.
4.   Add dry ingredients to creamed mixture a little at a time, mixing thoroughly after each addition. Set dough in refrigerator to chill for 15 minutes.

VARIATIONS

1.   Roll out 1/4 inch thick on floured surface. Cut any desired shape or size. Sprinkle with colored sugars, cinnamon-sugar mix or colored decorations; *OR* ice with frosting or glaze.
2.   Roll out 1/4 inch thick on floured surface. Cut into squares, rounds, or triangles. Place one teaspoonful of jelly, mincemeat, cooked filling, or a few chocolate bits in the center of one cookie. Top with another cookie and press around edges with fingers or floured fork. Brush with cream if desired.
3.   Divide dough into rolls 1½ inches in diameter. Roll dough in finely chopped nuts, colored sugars, or crushed cereal flakes. Slice 1/4 inch thick and bake.
4.   Roll out dough 1/4 inch thick. Cut in rounds. Press center with thumb. In indentation place jelly, nut halves, candied fruit, or maraschino cherry.
5.   Place on ungreased cookie sheet. Bake any variation at 350°F. for 15 minutes. Filled cookies will take longer.

SWEDISH SPRITZ

*Always delectable; we bake over 500 in holiday shapes and dec-
orate them at Christmastide.*

Oven temperature: preheat to
   400°F.
Baking time: 10 to 12 minutes

Yield: 5 dozen cookies
Pan: ungreased cookie sheet

1 cup butter
¾ cup granulated sugar
1 egg, unbeaten
1 teaspoon almond extract

2¼ cups all-purpose flour,
   sifted
½ teaspoon double-acting
   baking powder
⅛ teaspoon salt

1. Cream butter with sugar until light and fluffy.
2. Add egg. Beat well.
3. Blend in almond extract.
4. Sift flour once before measuring. Mix and sift flour, baking
powder, and salt together.
5. Add dry ingredients to creamed mixture a little at a time,
mixing thoroughly after each addition.
6. Fill cookie press and form cookies in desired shapes on ungreased cookie sheet. (A pastry tube may be substituted.)
7. Bake at 400°F. for 10 to 12 minutes. Decorate if desired.
Note: These are only good made with butter.

Bars and Squares

TIPS FOR BARS AND SQUARES

Use correct pan size because it affects some of the best qualities
of bars and squares, such as the moist fudginess of brownies.

BLONDE BROWNIES

For those who prefer blondes.

Oven temperature: preheat to 350°F.

Baking time: 25 to 30 minutes

Yield: 2 to 3 dozen brownies

Pan: 9"x9"x2" square pan, greased and floured

¼ cup butter, margarine, or shortening, melted
1 cup brown sugar, firmly packed
1 egg, beaten
1 teaspoon vanilla

1 cup all-purpose flour, sifted
¼ teaspoon salt
1 teaspoon double-acting baking powder
¾ cup nut meats, chopped

1. Melt shortening in pan that may double as mixing bowl.
2. Add brown sugar, beaten egg, and vanilla to melted shortening.
3. Sift flour once before measuring. Mix and sift flour, salt, and baking powder together.
4. Add dry ingredients to sugar mixture a little at a time, mixing thoroughly after each addition.
5. Stir in nuts.
6. Spread batter in greased and floured 9"x9"x2" pan.
7. Bake at 350°F. for 25 to 30 minutes.
8. Cut into squares when cool.
Note: May be iced with icing of choice, or sprinkled with powdered sugar.

CHOCOLATE BIT BROWNIES

A modern twist to an old favorite.

Oven temperature: preheat to 350°F.

Baking time: 35 minutes

Yield: approximately 2½ dozen bars

Pan: 8"x8"x2" square pan, greased and floured

1 six-ounce package chocolate bits
½ cup butter
1 ounce chocolate, melted
1 cup granulated sugar

3 eggs, beaten
1 teaspoon vanilla
1 cup cake flour, sifted
¼ teaspoon salt
½ cup walnut or pecan meats

1. Melt chocolate bits, butter, and chocolate over simmering water. Remove from heat.
2. Gradually add sugar, then add beaten eggs and vanilla.
3. Sift flour once before measuring. Mix and sift flour and salt together.
4. Add dry ingredients to chocolate mixture, mixing thoroughly.
5. Stir in nuts.
6. Spread batter in greased and floured 8"x8"x2" pan.
7. Bake at 350°F. for 35 minutes.
8. When cool, cut into desired size bars.

BEST BASIC BROWNIE

Who could live without brownies? They are quickly made for family or company. They travel well. They are a marvelous patio dessert.

Oven temperature: preheat to 350°F.
Baking time: 25 to 30 minutes

Yield: approximately 32 bars
Pan: 8"x8"x2" square pan, or 9"x9"x2" square pan, greased and floured

2 ounces chocolate, melted
½ cup butter or margarine
1 cup granulated sugar
2 eggs, beaten
1 teaspoon vanilla

½ cup plus 2 tablespoons all-purpose flour, sifted
¼ teaspoon salt
½ to 1 cup walnut or pecan meats, chopped

1. Melt chocolate and butter or margarine over simmering water. Remove from heat.
2. Gradually add sugar, then add beaten eggs and vanilla.
3. Sift flour once before measuring. Mix and sift flour and salt together.
4. Add dry ingredients to chocolate mixture a little at a time, mixing thoroughly after each addition.
5. Stir in nuts.
6. Pour into greased and floured 8"x8"x2" or 9"x9"x2" pan.
7. Bake at 350°F. for 25 minutes, 8-inch pan; 30 minutes, 9-inch pan.
8. When cool, cut into desired size bar.
Note: Brownies are very good iced with chocolate frosting, or dusted with powdered sugar.

COCOA BROWNIES

Another candidate for high honors at teas and little dinners or in lunch boxes.

Oven temperature: preheat to 400°F.
Baking time: about 20 minutes

Yield: approximately 2 to 3 dozen bars
Pan: 8"x8"x2" square pan, greased and floured

½ cup butter or shortening
1 cup granulated sugar
3 tablespoons cocoa
hot water
2 eggs, beaten
1 teaspoon vanilla

1 cup all-purpose flour, sifted
½ teaspoon salt
¼ cup milk
1 cup nut meats, chopped

1. Cream butter or shortening with sugar until light and fluffy.
2. Dissolve cocoa in a little hot water and add to creamed mixture.
3. Beat in eggs. Add vanilla.
4. Sift flour once before measuring. Mix and sift flour and salt together.
5. Add dry ingredients alternately with milk, mixing thoroughly after each addition.
6. Stir in nuts.
7. Spread batter in greased and floured 8"x8"x2" pan.
8. Bake at 400°F. for about 20 minutes.
9. When cool, cut into desired size bars and sprinkle with powdered sugar.

CISSIE'S FUDGE SQUARES

These are so good we usually make a double batch because they freeze beautifully. They are delicious served topped with a scoop of vanilla ice cream.

Oven temperature: preheat to 350°F.
Baking time: 20 to 30 minutes

Yield: 16 squares
Pan: 8"x8"x2" square pan, greased and floured

1 ounce chocolate, melted
½ cup butter or margarine
1 cup granulated sugar
2 eggs, separated (beat whites until stiff, not dry)
4 tablespoons milk
1 teaspoon vanilla

1 cup all-purpose flour, sifted
½ teaspoon salt
½ teaspoon double-acting baking powder
½ cup nut meats, chopped, if desired

1. Melt chocolate over simmering water.
2. Cream butter or margarine with sugar until light and fluffy.
3. Beat in egg yolks, melted chocolate, milk, and vanilla.
4. Mix and sift flour with salt and baking powder.
5. Add dry ingredients to chocolate mixture a little at a time, mixing thoroughly after each addition. Stir in nuts.
6. With pliable rubber scraper or whisk, gently fold in stiffly beaten egg whites.
7. Spread batter in greased and floured 8"x8"x2" pan.
8. Bake on top rack of oven at 350°F. for 20 to 30 minutes.
9. Cool before cutting into squares.

MOCHA SQUARES

Definitely party fare. Richly iced and rolled in ground nuts.

Oven temperature: preheat to 350°F.
Baking time: about 30 minutes

Yield: approximately 3 dozen squares
Pan: 9"x9"x2" square pan, greased and floured

1 cup less 1 tablespoon granulated sugar
5 eggs, beaten well
1 teaspoon vinegar

1 cup all-purpose flour, sifted
¼ teaspoon salt
½ teaspoon double-acting baking powder

1. Add sugar to eggs. Beat well.
2. Add vinegar.
3. Sift flour once before measuring. Mix and sift flour, salt, and baking powder together.
4. Add dry ingredients to sugar mixture a little at a time, mixing thoroughly after each addition.
5. Spread batter in greased and floured 9"x9"x2" pan.
6. Bake at 350°F. for about 30 minutes. Cool.
7. Cut into 2-inch squares and ice all sides.

2 tablespoons butter	2 cups salted peanuts, finely
1⅔ cups powdered sugar,	ground
sifted	2 tablespoons evaporated milk

1. Cream butter and sugar well.
2. Add milk little at a time until mixture is consistency for spreading.
3. Grind salted nuts and roll iced cakes in the nuts.

GUM DROP BARS

These are the chewy, rich, sweet, special-occasion bars from which childhood memories are made.

Oven temperature: preheat to 350°F.
Baking time: 35 minutes

Yield: 4 dozen 1"x2" bars
Pan: 13"x9"x2" oblong pan, greased and floured

3 eggs, beaten	½ teaspoon salt
2 cups brown sugar,	1 teaspoon cinnamon
firmly packed	1 cup spice gumdrops,
¼ cup evaporated milk	omitting licorice
2 cups all-purpose flour,	½ cup nut meats, chopped
sifted	

1. Beat eggs until light.
2. Add brown sugar and evaporated milk.
3. Sift flour once before measuring. Reserve 1 tablespoon to dredge gumdrops and nuts. Mix and sift remaining flour, salt, and cinnamon.
4. Add dry ingredients to sugar mixture a little at a time, mixing thoroughly after each addition.
5. Cut gumdrops into pieces, add nuts, and dredge with reserved flour. Stir into dough.
6. Spread dough in greased and floured 13"x9"x2" pan.
7. Bake at 350°F. for 35 minutes.
8. Ice with powdered sugar frosting and cut into bars.

MERINGUE COOKIE SQUARES

Meringue-topped delicacy that will bring you compliments for having the unusual.

Oven temperature: preheat to 325°F.
Baking time: 30 minutes

Yield: approximately 24 squares
Pan: 8"x8"x2" square pan, greased and floured

½ cup butter
1 cup granulated sugar
2 eggs, beaten
½ teaspoon vanilla

1½ cups all-purpose flour, sifted
½ teaspoon salt
1 teaspoon double-acting baking powder

1. Cream butter with sugar until light and fluffy.
2. Beat in eggs. Add vanilla.
3. Sift flour once before measuring. Mix and sift flour, salt, and baking powder together.
4. Add dry ingredients to creamed mixture a little at a time, mixing thoroughly after each addition.
5. Spread batter 1/2 inch thick in greased and floured 8"x8"x2" pan. Cover with meringue.

MERINGUE

½ teaspoon vanilla
1 egg white, beaten until stiff, not dry
1 cup brown sugar, firmly packed

½ cup nut meats, finely chopped

1. Add vanilla to stiffly beaten egg white.
2. Fold in brown sugar.
3. Spread over batter and top with nuts.
4. Bake at 325°F. for 30 minutes.

FROSTED RAISIN SQUARES

Suit the fancy of raisin fans.

Oven temperature: preheat to
   350°F.
Baking time: 25 to 30 minutes

Yield: 6 dozen squares
Pan: two 13"x9"x2" oblong
   pans, greased and floured

1 cup shortening
1½ cups granulated sugar
2 eggs, beaten
2½ cups all-purpose flour,
   sifted
½ teaspoon salt
1 teaspoon baking soda

½ teaspoon ground cloves
¼ teaspoon ginger
1 teaspoon cinnamon
1 cup raisins
1 cup water
½ cup nut meats, chopped

1.   Cream shortening with sugar until light and fluffy.
2.   Beat in eggs.
3.   Sift flour once before measuring. Mix and sift flour, salt, soda, cloves, ginger, and cinnamon together.
4.   Bring raisins and water to boil. Cool and save juice.
5.   Add dry ingredients alternately with 1 cup raisin juice, mixing thoroughly after each addition.
6.   Stir in raisins and nuts.
7.   Spread batter in greased and floured 13"x9"x2" pans.
8.   Bake at 350°F. for 25 to 30 minutes.
9.   Frost with powdered sugar icing. Cut into squares when cool.

ROCKY MOUNTAIN TOFFEE BARS

As easy as A B C . . . and as good as any French pastry.

Oven temperature: preheat to
   350°F.
Baking time: 15 to 20 minutes

Yield: 2½ dozen bars
Pan: greased cookie sheet

1 cup butter or margarine
1 cup brown sugar,
   firmly packed
1 egg yolk
1 teaspoon vanilla

2 cups all-purpose flour,
   sifted
½ teaspoon salt
1 six-ounce package
   chocolate bits, melted
ground nuts for topping

1. Cream butter or margarine with brown sugar until fluffy.
2. Beat in egg yolk. Add vanilla.
3. Sift flour once before measuring. Mix and sift flour and salt together.
4. Add dry ingredients to creamed mixture a little at a time, mixing thoroughly after each addition.
5. Spread batter on greased cookie sheet to depth of 1/4 inch.
6. Bake at 350°F. for 15 to 20 minutes.
7. Melt chocolate bits over simmering water.
8. Remove baked toffee mixture from oven. Spread top with melted chocolate bits. Sprinkle with ground nuts.
9. When cooled, cut in desired size squares.

NOTES

MINCE MEAT BARS

Welcome a new neighbor with a batch of these nifty, frosted bars. They'll say a memorable greeting.

Oven temperature: preheat to
  350°F.
Baking time: about 25 minutes

Yield: 2½ dozen bars
Pan: 9"x9"x2" square pan,
  greased and floured

½ cup shortening
¾ cup granulated sugar
¼ cup honey
2 eggs, unbeaten
1 teaspoon vanilla
1½ cups all-purpose flour,
  sifted

½ teaspoon salt
1 teaspoon double-acting
  baking powder
1 teaspoon cinnamon
1 eight-ounce package dry
  mince meat

1. Cream shortening with sugar until light and fluffy.
2. Blend in honey.
3. Beat in eggs. Add vanilla.
4. Sift flour once before measuring. Mix and sift flour, salt, baking powder, and cinnamon together.
5. Add dry ingredients a little at a time to creamed mixture, mixing thoroughly after each addition.
6. Stir in mince meat.
7. Spread batter into greased and floured 9"x9"x2" pan.
8. Bake at 350°F. for about 25 minutes.
9. When cool, frost with the following icing.

BUTTER ICING

⅓ cup butter, softened
3 cups powdered sugar,
  sifted

3 tablespoons cream
¼ teaspoon salt

1. Cream all ingredients together until light and fluffy.
2. Spread over top of baked, cooled batter. Then cut into squares.

CHOCOLATE MARBLE BARS

Interestingly different, two-flavored bar or light dessert.

Oven temperature: preheat to 350°F.

Baking time: 25 to 30 minutes

Yield: 4 dozen bars

Pan: 13"x9"x2" oblong pan, greased and floured

⅔ cup shortening
1¼ cups granulated sugar
1 cup brown sugar, firmly packed
3 eggs, unbeaten
2 ounces chocolate, melted
⅓ cup hot water

2 cups all-purpose flour, sifted
½ teaspoon salt
1 teaspoon double-acting baking powder
2 tablespoons milk
1 teaspoon vanilla
1 cup coconut

1. Cream shortening with ½ cup granulated sugar and brown sugar until light and fluffy.
2. Beat in eggs.
3. Melt chocolate over simmering water with water and ¾ cup granulated sugar. Set aside to be used later.
4. Sift flour once before measuring. Mix and sift flour, salt, and baking powder together.
5. Add milk and vanilla to creamed mixture. Add dry ingredients a little at a time, mixing thoroughly after each addition.
6. Blend in coconut.
7. Spread batter in greased and floured 13"x9"x2" pan. Pour chocolate mixture in a thin stream over batter in a close diagonal pattern. Cut through batter with knife to give marbled effect.
8. Bake at 350°F. for 25 to 30 minutes.
9. Cool. Cut in desired size bars.

Uncooked Cookies

CHANGEABLE CHOCOLATE TREATS

Why not be prepared? These no-bake cookies are better made up way ahead of their use.

Yield: about 5 dozen

1 six-ounce package
   chocolate bits, melted
3 tablespoons light refined
   corn syrup
3 cups powdered sugar, sifted
½ teaspoon salt
½ teaspoon vanilla

2 teaspoons instant coffee
⅓ cup hot water
1¾ cups vanilla wafers,
   finely crushed
1 cup walnut or pecan meats,
   finely chopped
powdered sugar

1. Melt chocolate bits over simmering water.
2. Add corn syrup, powdered sugar, salt, and vanilla.
3. Dissolve instant coffee in hot water and mix thoroughly with chocolate mixture.
4. Stir in crushed vanilla wafers and nuts.
5. Form dough into 1-inch balls and roll in powdered sugar.

Note: ⅓ cup orange juice may be substituted for coffee and water. Store in tight container to mellow.

CHEWY CHOCOLATE BARS

No cooking necessary for these delicious novelties.

Yield: 1½ dozen squares

Pan: 8″x8″x2″ square pan,
   greased

¼ cup butter or margarine
2 cups miniature
   marshmallows
¼ teaspoon vanilla
3 cups crisp rice cereal

1 six-ounce package
   chocolate bits
¼ teaspoon salt
½ cup nut meats,
   finely chopped

232

1. In top of double boiler, melt butter or margarine and marshmallows over low heat. Add vanilla.
2. In separate bowl combine cereal, chocolate bits, salt, and nuts.
Pour melted mixture over this and mix thoroughly.
3. Press dough into greased 8"x8"x2" pan.
4. Cool, then cut into desired size squares.

CHOCOLATE WALNUT TREATS

No oven to heat on a warm day when you need something sweet.

Yield: 2 dozen

1 six-ounce package
  chocolate bits, melted
½ cup graham cracker
  crumbs

1 cup walnut meats, coarsely
  chopped

1. Melt chocolate bits over simmering water.
2. Stir in graham cracker crumbs and nut meats.
3. Drop by teaspoonful onto waxed paper.

DATE-FLAKE NUGGETS

Nobody will guess you didn't bake these go-for-more tidbits.

Yield: 2½ dozen

2 cups bran flakes, wheat
  flakes or corn flakes
¾ cup dates,
  refrigerated
½ cup pecan meats, chopped

2 tablespoons honey
1 tablespoon butter
½ teaspoon salt
2 teaspoons lemon juice
powdered sugar
pecan halves

1. Grind cereal, dates, and ½ cup pecans together.
2. Add honey, butter, lemon juice, and salt to ground mixture. Blend thoroughly.
3. Shape dough in 1-inch balls and roll in powdered sugar. Top with pecan halves.

DATE-CEREAL SURPRISES

These are made differently from most other cookies, with a delicious result.

Yield: 4 to 5 dozen

1½ cups granulated sugar
1 cup butter or margarine
½ teaspoon salt
2 cups dates, chopped
2 eggs, beaten
½ teaspoon vanilla

2 tablespoons milk
2 cups crisp rice cereal
1 cup nut meats, chopped
powdered sugar, or grated
coconut

1. Cook sugar, butter or margarine, salt, and dates over low heat until mixture boils. Remove from heat.
2. In mixing bowl beat eggs, vanilla, and milk together. Add to date mixture and cook for 2 minutes more.
3. Pour cooked mixture into mixing bowl. Slowly stir in rice cereal and nuts.
4. Cool. Form dough into balls and roll in powdered sugar or grated coconut.

ENGLISH TOFFEE SQUARES

Richly divine, but speedily devised.

Yield: 2 dozen squares

Pan: 9"x9"x2" square pan,
well greased

CRUST

½ pound vanilla wafers,
finely crushed

1 cup pecan or walnut meats,
chopped

FILLING

½ cup butter
1 cup granulated sugar
3 eggs, separated (beat
whites until stiff, not dry)

½ teaspoon salt
½ teaspoon vanilla
1½ ounces chocolate, melted

1. Combine finely crushed vanilla wafers and nut meats.
2. Reserve ¾ cup of mixture. Press remaining mixture into well greased 9″x9″x2″ pan.
3. Cream butter with sugar and salt, until light and fluffy.
4. Beat egg yolks. Add egg yolks and vanilla to creamed mixture.
5. Blend in chocolate melted over simmering water.
6. Fold in stiffly beaten egg whites.
7. Spread over crust. Sprinkle top with remaining crumb mixture.
8. Chill in refrigerator for several hours or overnight.
9. Cut into desired size squares.

FRY PAN COOKIES

These cookies will never tell how little time it took you to make them.

Yield: 4 to 5 dozen cookies

2 tablespoons butter
2 eggs, beaten
1 cup granulated sugar
1 cup dates, cut up
½ teaspoon salt

1 teaspoon vanilla
1 cup nut meats, chopped
2 cups crisp rice cereal
powdered sugar or coconut

1. Melt butter in frying pan.
2. Add beaten eggs, sugar, and dates. Cook, stirring constantly, until thickness of pudding.
3. Remove from heat and add salt, vanilla, nuts, and rice cereal.
4. Form dough into balls and roll in powdered sugar or coconut.

PUFFED WHEAT CEREAL BARS

No fuss, no muss to make, but they pack a punch of vitamins.

Yield: 4 dozen bars

Pan: 9"x12"x1½" oblong pan
greased

⅓ cup butter
½ cup molasses
1 cup brown sugar,
firmly packed
2 tablespoons cocoa

½ teaspoon salt
1 teaspoon vanilla
8 cups puffed wheat cereal
(other puffed cereals may
be substituted)

1. Melt butter in pan.
2. Add molasses, brown sugar, cocoa, salt, and vanilla.
3. Remove syrup from heat when it begins to bubble.
4. Add puffed cereal and mix thoroughly.
5. Press dough into greased 9"x12"x1½" pan.
6. Cool, then cut into squares.

RUM BALLS

A sophisticated confection that needs no baking.

Yield: about 2 dozen balls

1 cup vanilla wafers, crushed
1 cup powdered sugar, sifted
1½ cup pecan meats, finely
chopped
2 tablespoons cocoa

2 tablespoons light refined
corn syrup
¼ cup rum
½ cup granulated sugar

1. Combine crushed vanilla wafers, powdered sugar, 1 cup
pecans, and cocoa.
2. Add corn syrup and rum, mixing thoroughly.
3. Shape mixture into 1-inch balls. Roll in granulated sugar and
remaining ½ cup pecans.

WALNUT BOURBON BALLS

Mother gives these to her friends at Christmas time.

Yield: 3½ dozen balls

2½ cups vanilla wafers,
   finely crushed
1 cup powdered sugar, sifted
2 tablespoons cocoa
1 cup walnut meats, finely
   chopped

¼ teaspoon salt
3 tablespoons light refined
   corn syrup
¼ cup bourbon
powdered sugar

1. Combine in mixing bowl vanilla wafers, powdered sugar, cocoa, nuts, and salt.
2. Add syrup and bourbon. Mix thoroughly.
3. Roll into 1-inch balls. Roll in powdered sugar.

NOTES

NOTES

PIES

Suggestions for Successful Pie Baking   240
Ingredient Definitions   240
Mixing Tips   241
Tips for Rolling Out Pie Crusts   242
Baking Problems and Solutions   244
General Baking Tips   245
Suggestions for Successful Meringues   245
Timetable for Pie Baking   246
Tips for Freezing Pie Crusts   246
Tips for Freezing Pies   247

PIE CRUSTS

Basic Pie Crust   248
Basic Pie Crust II   248
Quick Pie Crust   249
Hot Water Pie Crust   250
French Pastry Pie Crust   250
Cheese Pie Crust   251
Crumb Crusts   252

MERINGUES

Meringue Pie Shell   254
Meringue Topping   254

BERRY OR FRUIT PIES

Berry Pie   255
Darrell's Favorite Apple Pie   256
Apple Pie with Cheese Crust   257
Quick Canned Cherry Pie   258
Fresh Cherry Pie   258
Gooseberry Pie   259
Frozen Cherry Pie   260
Concord Grape Pie   260
Mincemeat   261
Crumble Peach Pie   262
Fresh Strawberry Pie   262
Fruit Tarts   263

CREAM OR CUSTARD PIES

Marvelous Chocolate Pie   264
Angelfood Pie   265
Chocolate Pie   266
Butterscotch Sour Cream Pie   266
Hazel's Coconut Custard Pie   267
Chocolate Cream Meringue Pie   268
Custard Pie   268
Old Fashioned Pumpkin Pie   269
Lemon Angel Pie   270
Debby's Pecan Pie   270
Lemon Meringue Pie   271
Jerry's Favorite Pumpkin Pie   272
Pineapple Cream Pie   272
Raisin Cream Pie   273
Puff Crust Cream Pie   274
Rocky Mountain Dream Pie   275
Pennsylvania Crumb Pie   276
Rhubarb Cream Pie   276

CHIFFON AND UNCOOKED FILLINGS

Chocolate Chiffon Pie   277
Black Bottom Pie   278
Butterscotch Chiffon Pie   278
Margie's Frenchmint Pie   279
Coffee Eggnog Chiffon Pie   280
Lemonade Chiffon Pie   280
Nesselrode Chiffon Pie   281
Lime Chiffon Pie   282
Florida Lime Pie   282
Pumpkin Chiffon Pie   283
Mincemeat Chiffon Pie   284
Strawberry Chiffon Pie   285

Space for notes, Page 286

SUGGESTIONS FOR SUCCESSFUL PIE BAKING

The success or failure of a pie depends on its crust.

INGREDIENT DEFINITIONS

All-purpose flour is best for pie crust. It is a blend of hard and soft wheat flours which gives it more and tougher gluten than cake flour. The elastic and porous qualities of gluten make flakier pie crusts.

Emulsified or hydrogenated shortenings, or new-type or regular lards are best for pie crusts. They have *quick blending* qualities that make good pastry. Modern method recipes that call for salad or vegetable oil have proved satisfactory. *Do not substitute butter or margarine* in pastry recipes unless recipe so provides. Use butter as it comes from refrigerator unless otherwise specified.

Liquid in pie crust is generally water, although milk is sometimes used. When cold water is called for it means to use tap water from the cold faucet. Boiling water means the water should be boiling hot. Use milk as it comes from the refrigerator.

MIXING TIPS

Always sift flour before measuring. Too much flour makes pie crust tough.

Too much shortening makes dough dry and crumbly.

To cut the shortening into the flour, use pastry blender or two table knives. Knives should be held one in each hand as a knife and fork are held when cutting meat. Criss cross the blades in center of bowl filled with flour and shortening, then with each hand pull blades to outer edge of bowl. Repeat this cutting motion until the shortening and flour are the consistency of grain. The grainy consistency should be achieved with the pastry blender, too.

The amount of liquid used in pie crust is *most important.* Too little makes the dough crumble and split when rolled. Too much makes dough tough and soggy. The latter is the greater problem. Dough with a tendency to crumble a little is not as easily rolled, nor does it have a professional look, but it will be deliciously tender and flaky when baked. Soggy dough is very manageable, but results in the ill-famed "lunch wagon" pie.

Liquid is to bind together the flour and shortening, but *loosely* bind, both in amount of liquid and method of mixing it into dough. Dough should not be wet or slippery. When blending liquids into flour and shortening, start by sprinkling a few drops at a time over dough. Mix quickly with fork using light strokes as you would toss a salad. *Do not beat or stir.* Dough will look

241

crumbly, so as soon as liquid has been added to dry ingredients, *stop* handling it. On a warm day, dough may need refrigerating for about 20 minutes before you roll it out.

TIPS FOR ROLLING OUT PIE CRUST

Quickly and lightly form dough into a ball with cupped hands. *One of the secrets of flaky crust is in this step. Do not roll or pack dough* in palms of hands, making the ingredients warm and sticky.

Divide dough into two parts, making one a little larger than the other. The larger is for the bottom crust.

On lightly floured surface, between 12-inch squares of waxed paper, or on pastry canvas, place the dough to be rolled out. Sprinkle top with a very little bit of flour. This prevents rolling pin sticking to dough during rolling procedure. A stockinette covered rolling pin may be used.

Roll from center toward outer edge, lifting rolling pin just before edge is reached to prevent splitting and cracking of dough. Do this several times following the pattern of spokes in a wheel. This will form a circle. The circle should measure 11 to 12 inches in diameter and the dough should be 1/8 inch thick. This will fit an 8 or 9-inch pie plate.

Before preparing to put pastry in pan, check to see that it is not stuck to rolling-out surface. If it has adhered to surface, run spatula or table knife between surface and dough to loosen.

Fold pastry circle in half and place pastry in *ungreased* pie plate (aluminum or oven glass is best) with fold along center line. Gently unfold by putting spatula between layers and flipping from center to side.

If there are small breaks or holes in dough, repair them by gently pressing the edges of breaks together, or using extra dough for patches. Trim edges if uneven, leaving as much edge as possible.

For *unbaked pie shell in which the filling is to be placed and baked,* do *not* prick bottom of crust and be certain there are no breaks in crust.

Make *filling* as directed and put in crust-lined pie plate. Roll out top crust using same method used for bottom crust. It will be a bit smaller than bottom crust. As before, fold round of dough in half in preparation for covering filling and place with fold along center line. An alternate method is to gently roll dough around rolling pin and unroll over filled pie.

Even edges of top crust by trimming with scissors. Fold edge of bottom crust over edge of top crust and pinch or press together. Fork tines may be used to press two together. *Prick top* crust with toothpick, *or cut small slits with sharp knife* to allow the steam to escape while cooking. If you wish a design, the perforations made with the toothpick may be made in an outline of the fruit used in the pie, or any other attractive placement of slits and perforations. If you are feeling ambitious, add a little red food coloring to a few dough remnants and a little green food coloring to others. Press out. With knife, cut red dough into shape of apple, cherry, or berry. Cut leaves and stem for fruit out of green dough. Place on top of unbaked pie. Crust lovers like leftover dough crumbled over top of unbaked pie.

In case berry or fruit pies cook over, protect oven by placing sheet of aluminum foil on rack below the one on which pie is placed. A pie tape placed around rim of pie plate will help to prevent pies from running over.

Glazes for top crusts may be brushed on with pastry brush before baking.

Egg White Glaze: Slightly beat egg white. Brush on top of crust and sprinkle with granulated sugar if you wish.

Evaporated Milk Glaze: Brush top crust with undiluted evaporated milk. Sprinkle with granulated sugar if you wish.

Butter Glaze: Dot top crust with bits of butter, or melt butter and brush over surface of crust with pastry brush.

Cheese Glaze: Grate 1½ cups American cheese. Add milk to make smooth paste. Spread on after baking, then place under broiler to brown.

Cream or Milk Glaze: Brush either of these over top crust. The more you brush on, the browner the crust will be. Sprinkle with granulated sugar if you wish.

For baked pie shell, roll out dough and place it on pie plate as you would for unbaked pie shell. Even edges. Fold overhang under and form desired design along edge. To keep crust from slipping down toward bottom of pie plate, firmly press dough over outside edge of pie plate. With fork tines, prick bottom of crust deeply and closely. Prick sides once every inch all the way around. Chill about 1/2 hour. Bake 12 to 15 minutes or until lightly browned. *Cool* before filling.

To shape turnovers: Roll out all of dough to ⅛ inch thick on lightly floured surface or pastry canvas. Cut circles 3½ to 4½ inches in diameter or 4½-inch squares from dough. Fill with jam, applesauce, mincemeat, fruit, or other fillings. Fold dough in half over filling. Press and seal edges together. Slit or prick top and brush with desired glaze if you wish.

To shape tarts: (a) Roll out all of dough to ⅛ inch thick on lightly floured surface or pastry canvas. Cut 5-inch squares from dough. Place squares inside of ungreased muffin cups, letting corners stand up. Press dough firmly to bottom or edges; *or* (b) turn muffin pan bottom side up. Roll out all of dough. Cut dough in circles 5 inches in diameter for 2½-inch muffin pans and 5½ inches in diameter for 3-inch muffin pans. Fit dough over inverted muffin cups. Pinch in tucks to make dough fit snugly. Prick pastry with fork tines. Bake for 10 to 15 minutes. Cool, then carefully slip crust from muffin pan. Fill with pie filling.

Deep dish pies: For individual deep dish pies, use baking dishes or casseroles approximately 4½"x2"; *or* square, oblong, or round casseroles or baking dishes with 1½ to 2-quart capacity. Deep dish pies have no bottom crust. The filling can be made by doubling any berry or fruit filling recipe. Make pastry for two-crust pie. Roll out as you would pie dough to 3/8 inch thick. The dough should be the shape and size of casserole you are using, plus an extra 1 inch for overhang. Fit rolled crust loosely over top of filling. Press overhang firmly to edge of baking dish. If you wish, a 3/4 inch strip long enough to go around baking dish may be cut from rolled out dough. After top crust is placed over filling and firmly pressed to edge of dish, the 3/4 inch strip may be placed around outer edge to seal pie.

BAKING PROBLEMS AND SOLUTIONS

Pie burned around edges: (a) oven was too hot; (b) pan used may have granite pan or black metal, which causes scorching.

Pie not brown enough to top: (a) oven temperature too low; (b) pan not placed high enough in oven.

Pie not done enough on bottom: (a) filling too thin, soaking bottom pastry; (b) oven temperature too low.

Pie has soggy crust: (a) ingredients were mishandled, or recipe was not followed correctly; (b) heat was not high enough during first part of baking; (c) unduly shiny pans reflected heat from pan; (d) too much liquid put in filling.

GENERAL BAKING TIPS

Never grease a pie plate.

To avoid spilling custard and pumpkin pies when putting into oven, partially fill pie shell, then set it on oven rack and pour in remaining filling.

Size and type of fruit make difference in baking time.

To *prevent pie shell baking problems,* prick shell on sides and bottom as directed. Check after 5 minutes of baking, and prick any blisters that have appeared. Be certain that crust is securely fastened to edge of pie plate. Chilling crust before baking helps very much.

Always refrigerate custard, cream, and gelatin pies. It is best to refrigerate other pies that have been cut into.

Freshen pies by warming a few minutes in oven preheated to 325°F.

Use floured cookie cutters for cut-outs to decorate pie tops.

If you do not care to make your own crust, use a packaged pastry mix with any of the recipes for fillings in this section.

To prevent cream filling from curdling, add a little of hot mixture slowly to beaten egg yolks. Return the egg yolks combined with hot mixture to saucepan containing cooked mixture.

SUGGESTIONS FOR SUCCESSFUL MERINGUES

Be sure filling is cool before covering with meringue.

Never add more than 2 tablespoons sugar for each egg white, as too much sugar causes unwanted weeping or beading when meringue is baked.

Success depends upon gradual addition of sugar.

Always "seal" meringue to edges of pie crust to prevent shrinking during baking.

Cool slowly, away from drafts. One cook turns oven off, opens oven door when baking time is over, and leaves pie to cool.

TIMETABLE FOR PIE BAKING

Type of Pie	Oven Temperature	Baking Time
Double Crust Fruit Pies	preheat to 450°F.	450°F. for 10 minutes, 350°F. for 30 to 40 minutes more
Double Crust Pies with Cooked Filling	preheat to 450°F.	30 to 35 minutes
Custard, and Pumpkin Pies	preheat to 450°F.	450°F. for 10 minutes, 350°F. for 35 minutes more
Pie Shells	preheat to 450°F.	12 to 15 minutes
Deep Dish Pies	preheat to 450°F.	450°F. for 10 minutes, 350°F. for 30 to 40 minutes more
Turnovers with cooked filling uncooked filling	preheat to 450°F. preheat to 350°F.	15 minutes 30 minutes
Meringue	preheat to 350°F.	12 to 15 minutes

TIPS FOR FREEZING PIE CRUSTS

Pie crusts may be frozen baked or unbaked.

If you choose to freeze them *unbaked*, leave the shells in the pie plates. Place unwrapped on cookie sheet *directly* on freezer shelf, to quick-freeze. Immediately remove, then wrap at once in moisture-vaporproof freezer wrap. They may be successfully stacked if a cushion of crumpled waxed paper is placed between each individually wrapped pie shell. (They are too fragile to stack without padding between them.) To use unbaked frozen pie shell, unwrap and place in oven for 5 minutes at 450°F. Remove, prick bottom and sides of shell, and return to oven for

15 minutes more. Unbaked pie shells may be thawed in freezer wrapper first for about 45 minutes, then baked for 12 to 15 minutes at 450°F.

If you choose to freeze *baked* pie shells, cool them to room temperature. Quick-freeze them before wrapping, as with unbaked pie shells. Wrap, and store stacked with waxed paper padding between each one. To use baked frozen pie shell, unwrap, and bake at 375°F. for 8 to 10 minutes, or until thawed.

TIPS FOR FREEZING PIES

Many pies will taste as good having been frozen as the day they were made. What could be handier?

If wrapped carefully and frozen, pies will keep for 2 to 4 months in the freezer.

Fresh fruit or berry pies are best frozen unbaked. Prepare the pie as usual, omitting the slits or the pricking of top crust. Use aluminum foil pie plate or other plate in which you intend to bake the pie. Wrap it in moisture-vaporproof wrapping (film, foil, or freezer wrap) and seal. Label it and note any special instructions. Use the frozen pie within 2 months for maximum flavor quality. When ready to use, unwrap, and place frozen in a 450°F. oven for 15 to 20 minutes. Remove, cut gashes or designs in top crust, or prick. *Reduce* oven temperature to 350°F. and bake 20 to 40 minutes more, or until done. Frozen fruit or berry pies may also be thawed before baking, but are tastiest when baked frozen and are less likely to have a soggy crust.

Chiffon pies freeze handsomely. Prepare them as usual. After the pie has set, cover it with another inverted pie plate to prevent crushing and to allow stacking other pies on top of it in the freezer. Wrap it as berry pies, seal, label, and note any special instruction. Plan to use within 4 months. When you are ready to use a chiffon pie, remove from freezer, unwrap, and thaw for 1 to 2 hours at room temperature, then place it in refrigerator until ready to serve. While pie is frozen or just before it is served, top with whipped cream if desired. (We have found that whipped cream topping placed on chiffon pies before freezing works fine, too.)

Use pumpkin pie within 6 weeks for best results.

Meringue topping may be spread on top of frozen fillings (not chiffon), and baked at 325°F. for 15 minutes.

Pie Crusts

BASIC PIE CRUST I

Follow the directions carefully and you will find this is THE perfect pie crust.

Yield: two 8 or 9-inch pie shells, or one 8 or 9-inch two crust pie

Pan: 8 or 9-inch pie plate

2 cups all-purpose flour, sifted

1 teaspoon   salt

⅔ cup shortening (hydrogenated, emulsified, or lard)

¼ cup cold water

1.   Read "Suggestions for Successful Pie Baking" on page 240.
2.   Sift flour once before measuring. Mix and sift flour and salt together.
3.   With two table knives or pastry blender, cut shortening into flour until consistency of small grain.
4.   Sprinkle few drops of water over flour mixture. Quickly blend by tossing dough with light strokes of fork. Add remainder of water and repeat blending with fork.
5.   With loosely cupped hands, gently form dough into two balls
6.   On lightly floured surface or pastry canvas, roll out dough to 1/8 inch thick in shape of circle 11 or 12 inches in diameter.

BASIC PIE CRUST II

Yield: one 8 or 9-inch pie shell

Pan: 8 or 9-inch pie plate

1 cup all-purpose flour, sifted

¼ cup shortening (hydrogenated, emulsified, or lard)

¼ cup butter

½ teaspoon salt

¼ cup milk

1.   Read "Suggestions for Successful Pie Baking" on page 240.
2.   Sift flour once before measuring. Mix and sift flour and salt together.

248

3. With two table knives or pastry blender, cut shortening and butter into flour until consistency of small grain.
4. Sprinkle few drops of milk over flour mixture. Quickly blend by tossing dough with light strokes of fork. Add remainder of milk and repeat blending with fork.
5. With loosely cupped hands gently form dough into ball.
6. On lightly floured surface or pastry canvas, roll out dough 1/8 inch thick in shape of circle 11 or 12 inches in diameter.

QUICK PIE CRUST

Salad oil hastens the mixing process.

Yield: 1 recipe pie crust makes one 2 crust pie, or 2 pie shells: 1/2 recipe makes 1 pie shell

Pan: 8 or 9-inch pie plate

1 RECIPE PIE CRUST:

2¼ cups all-purpose flour, sifted
1 teaspoon salt
½ cup plus 1 tablespoon salad oil
⅓ cup cold milk

½ RECIPE PIE CRUST:

1 cup plus 2 tablespoons all-purpose flour, sifted
½ teaspoon salt
5 tablespoons salad oil
3 tablespoons cold milk

1. Sift flour once before measuring. Mix and sift flour and salt together.
2. Measure salad oil and milk in same cup, leaving them unmixed.
3. Place dry ingredients in mixing bowl. Pour liquid over them all at once. Toss lightly with fork until completely combined.
4. Place dough between sheets of waxed paper. Roll out 1/8 inch thick in shape of circle 11 or 12 inches in diameter.
5. Remove top sheet of waxed paper. Pick up remaining waxed paper with dough and place it on pie plate with paper side up. Peel off paper. Mend any breaks or tears by gently pressing with fingers.

HOT WATER PIE CRUST

Yield: two 8 or 9-inch pie
    shells, or one 8 or 9-inch
    two crust pie

Pan: 8 or 9-inch pie plate

2 cups all-purpose flour,
    sifted
¾ cup shortening (hydrogen-
    ated, emulsified, or lard)

1 teaspoon salt
¼ cup boiling water
1 tablespoon milk

1.   Read "Suggestions for Successful Pie Baking" on page 240.
2.   Sift flour once before measuring. Mix and sift flour and salt together.
3.   Place shortening in mixing bowl. Add boiling water and milk. Whip with fork until smooth and thick.
4.   Stir dry ingredients into shortening mixture.
5.   Form dough into two balls.
6.   On lightly floured surface or pastry canvas, roll out dough 1/8 inch thick in shape of circle 11 or 12 inches in diameter.

FRENCH PASTRY PIE CRUST

May be stored in the refrigerator and used as needed.

Yield: four 8 or 9-inch pie
    shells, or two 8 or 9-inch
    two-crust pies

Pan: 8 or 9-inch pie plate

4 cups all-purpose flour,
    sifted
½ teaspoon salt
½ teaspoon double-acting
    baking powder

2 cups shortening (hydrogen-
    ated, emulsified, or lard)
1 egg, beaten
½ cup water
1 teaspoon vinegar *OR*
    juice of ½ lemon

1.   Read "Suggestions for Successful Pie Baking" on page 240.
2.   Sift flour once before measuring. Mix and sift flour, salt, and baking powder together.
3.   With two table knives or pastry blender, cut shortening into dry ingredients until consistency of small grain.

4.   Mix together the beaten egg, cold water, and vinegar or lemon juice.
5.   Sprinkle few drops of liquid over flour mixture. Quickly blend by tossing dough with light strokes of fork. Add remaining liquid and repeat blending with fork.
6.   To store in refrigerator, place dough in foil or plastic bag.
7.   When ready to use, gently form dough into balls.
8.   On lightly floured surface or pastry canvas, roll out dough 1/8 inch thick in shape of circle 11 or 12 inches in diameter.

CHEESE PIE CRUST

Versatile, because this dough may be rolled and cut wafer size for cocktail parties or luncheons.

Oven temperature: preheat to 425°F.

Baking time: about 15 minutes

Yield: one 9-inch pie shell, or about 2 dozen wafers

Pan: 9-inch pie plate, or ungreased cookie sheet

1 cup all-purpose flour, sifted
½ cup butter
1 teaspoon salt

1 cup New York sharp cheese, grated

1.   Sift flour once before measuring. Mix and sift flour and salt together.
2.   With two table knives or pastry blender, cut butter into flour until consistency of small grain. Add grated cheese that has been gently packed into measuring cup. Mix well.
3.   Shape dough into ball. Chill a few minutes if too sticky to roll out.
4.   On lightly floured board or pastry canvas, roll out dough 1/8 inch thick in shape of circle 11 or 12 inches in diameter (for pie shell); or roll out and cut with cookie cutter to desired shape and size (for wafers).
5.   Place dough in 9-inch pie plate, or place wafers on cookie sheet.
6.   Bake at 425°F. for about 15 minutes.
Note: One-half pecan on each wafer makes a wonderful addition to cocktail wafers.

CRUMB CRUSTS

Instructions: To make crumbs: (a) Place in deep bowl and mash with potato masher. (b) Break product for crumbs into blender. Blend using medium speed, and inverting blender glass occasionally to reverse crumbs and unblended crumbs. (c) Roll out with rolling pin on bread board.

Mix crumbs with sugar and softened butter, or melt butter in pie plate and stir in sugar and crumbs. Reserve 2 or 3 tablespoons crumbs to sprinkle on top of pie (optional). Press crumbs with back of spoon or fork tines into bottom and sides of 8 or 9-inch pie plate, forming slight rim.

These crusts may either be refrigerated before filling, or baked at 375°F. for 10 minutes and cooled before filling.

Pie Crust	Crumbs	Butter or Margarine	Sugar	Other Ingredients	Instructions
Graham Cracker Crust	about 16 crackers or 1⅓ cups crumbs	¼ cup, soft	⅓ cup, granulated	(optional) 1 ounce chocolate, grated	Line pan; chill, or bake at 375°F. for 15 minutes
Cookie Crust: (vanilla wafer, chocolate wafer, or gingersnap)	about 20 to 24 wafers, or 1⅓ cups crumbs	6 tablespoons, soft	none	none	Line pan; chill, or bake at 375°F. for 15 minutes

Zwieback Crust	1¼ cups zwieback crumbs	½ cup, melted	⅓ cup, powdered	(optional) ¼ cup unblanched almonds, ground	Bake at 375°F. for 10 minutes (it is best baked)
Cereal Crust (corn flakes, wheat flakes, or crisp rice cereal)	about 3 cups cereal or 1⅓ cups crushed	¼ cup	¼ cup, granulated	(optional) 1 ounce chocolate, grated	Line pan; chill, or bake at 375°F. for 15 minutes
Nut-Crumb Crust	1 cup crumbs plus ½ cup nut meats, ground	⅓ cup, soft	¼ cup, granulated	none	Line pan: chill, or bake at 375°F. for 5 minutes
Nut Crust (pecan, peanut, walnut, brazil nuts, or blanched almonds)	1 cup	none	2 tablespoons, granulated	(optional) 2 ounces chocolate, grated	Do not form rim on crust. Bake at 400°F. for 8 minutes

Meringues

MERINGUE TOPPING

Oven temperature: preheat to
   325°F.
Baking time: about 15 minutes

Yield: meringue for 8 or
   9-inch pie

3-EGG MERINGUE:

3 egg whites
⅛ teaspoon salt
¼ teaspoon cream of tartar
6 tablespoons granulated
   sugar
½ teaspoon vanilla, if
   desired

2-EGG MERINGUE:

2 egg whites
⅛ teaspoon salt
¼ teaspoon cream of tartar
4 tablespoons granulated
   sugar
¼ teaspoon vanilla, if
   desired

1.   Have egg whites at room temperature.
2.   Place eggs, salt, and cream of tartar in mixing bowl. Beat until frothy.
3.   Gradually add sugar and vanilla, beating constantly, until glossy, stiff peaks are formed that do not curl over when beater is removed.
4.   Top filling with meringue, being careful to "seal" the edges to the pie crust to avoid shrinking during baking.
5.   Bake at 325°F. for about 15 minutes, or until golden brown.

MERINGUE PIE SHELL

Don't be intimidated! This isn't nearly as hard to make as you might think.

Oven temperature: preheat to
   275°F.
Baking time: 1 hour

Yield: 6 to 8 servings
Pan: 9-inch pie plate or
   casserole, greased

4 egg whites
1 cup granulated sugar
⅛ teaspoon salt

½ teaspoon cream of tartar
1 teaspoon white vinegar
1 teaspoon vanilla

254

1. Beat egg whites until *very* stiff, but not dry.
2. Sift sugar, salt, and cream of tartar together.
3. Very gradually add sugar alternately with few drops of vinegar and vanilla, beating constantly.
4. With a spatula or pliable rubber scraper, spread meringue evenly over bottom and sides of greased 9-inch pie plate or casserole. Do not have meringue above rim of baking dish.
5. Bake at 275°F. for 1 hour, or until light brown and crisp to touch.
6. Cool away from draft.
7. Fill with fresh fruit, custard and fruit, or sherbert. Top with whipped cream.

Berry or Fruit Pies

BERRY PIE

One of life's feasting pleasures. Use fresh or fresh frozen blueberries, blackberries, raspberries, or loganberries.

Oven temperature: preheat to 450°F.
Baking time: about 40 minutes

Yield: 6 to 8 servings
Pan: 8 or 9-inch pie plate

1 recipe pie crust
4 cups berries, fresh or fresh-frozen
1 cup granulated sugar
4 tablespoons all-purpose flour

2 tablespoons quick-cooking tapioca
½ teaspoon cinnamon
1 tablespoon lemon juice
1 tablespoon butter

1. Place unbaked pie crust in 9-inch pie plate.
2. Wash, pick over, and remove stems or hulls from fresh berries. Let drain until quite dry.
3. Combine sugar, flour, tapioca, and cinnamon together.
4. Place berries in bowl. Sprinkle with lemon juice. Combine flour mixture with berries, being careful not to mash fruit.
5. Put berries in pie shell. Dot with butter.
6. Cover with top crust. Seal edges. To allow steam to escape during cooking, prick crust or cut design desired.
7. Bake at 450°F. for 10 minutes. *REDUCE* temperature to 350°F. and bake for 30 minutes more, or until done.

DARRELL'S FAVORITE APPLE PIE

A pièce de résistance. Worth trying.

Oven temperature: preheat to 450°F.
Baking time: about 50 minutes

Yield: 6 to 8 servings
Pan: 9-inch pie plate

1 recipe pie crust
6 medium sized apples, peeled, cored, and thinly sliced
1½ tablespoons lemon juice
⅓ cup brown sugar, firmly packed
⅓ cup granulated sugar

1½ tablespoons cornstarch OR
3 tablespoons all-purpose flour
⅛ teaspoon salt
¾ teaspoon cinnamon
¼ teaspoon nutmeg
1½ tablespoons butter
1 cup cheese, grated, if desired

1. Place unbaked pie crust in 9-inch pie plate.
2. Arrange apple slices in pie shell. Sprinkle lemon juice over apples.
3. Combine sugars, salt, cornstarch or flour, cinnamon, and nutmeg. Sprinkle over apples.
4. Dot apples with butter.
5. Cover with top crust. Seal edges. To allow steam to escape during cooking, prick crust or cut design desired.
6. Bake at 450°F. for 10 minutes. *REDUCE* temperature to 350°F. and bake for 30 to 40 minutes more, or until done.
Note: The grated cheese may be sprinkled over top crust when pie is done. Place under broiler until cheese is melted and lightly browned.
   Some cooks prefer to sprinkle pie crust top lightly with mixture of cinnamon and sugar, or brush it lightly with milk, before it is baked.

APPLE PIE WITH CHEESE CRUST

The cheese crust gives this American favorite a new flavor twist.

Oven temperature: preheat to
450°F.
Baking time: about 50 minutes

Yield: 6 to 8 servings
Pan: 9-inch pie plate

CRUST

1¾ cups all-purpose flour,
sifted
½ cup shortening (hydrogenated, emulsified, or lard)

1 teaspoon salt
2 tablespoons Port wine
cheese, crumbled
¼ cup ice water

1. Read "Suggestions for Successful Pie Baking" on page 240.
2. Sift flour once before measuring. Mix and sift flour and salt together.
3. With two table knives or pastry blender, cut shortening and cheese into flour until consistency of small grain.
4. Sprinkle few drops of ice water over flour mixture. Quickly blend by tossing dough with light strokes of fork. Add remainder of water and repeat blending with fork.
5. With loosely cupped hands, gently form dough into two balls.
6. On lightly floured surface or pastry canvas, roll out each ball of dough 1/8 inch thick in shape or circle 11 or 12 inches in diameter.

FILLING

6 medium sized apples,
peeled, cored, and thinly
sliced
juice of ½ lemon

⅞ cup granulated sugar
½ teaspoon cinnamon
¼ teaspoon nutmeg
grated rind of 1 lemon

1. Place bottom crust in 9-inch pie plate.
2. Arrange apple slices in pie shell. Sprinkle lemon juice over apples.
3. Combine sugar, cinnamon, nutmeg, and grated lemon rind. Sprinkle over apples.
4. Cover with top crust. Seal edges. To allow steam to escape during cooking, prick crust or cut design desired.
5. Bake at 450°F. for 10 minutes. *REDUCE* temperature to 350°F. and bake for 30 to 40 minutes more or until done. Serve warm.

QUICK CANNED CHERRY PIE

One clever hostess makes this her specialty. Guests never go to her house expecting any other dessert.

Oven temperature: preheat to
425°F.
Baking time: about 45 minutes

Yield: 4 to 6 servings, 8-inch
pie; 6 to 8 serving, 9-inch
pie
Pan: 8 or 9-inch pie plate

9-INCH PIE:

1 recipe pie crust
1½ cups granulated sugar
4 tablespoons cornstarch
½ teaspoon salt
3½ cups canned cherries
(two No. 2 cans), drained
¾ cup cherry juice
¼ teaspoon almond extract
2 teaspoons lemon rind, grated
5 to 6 drops red food coloring,
if desired
2 tablespoons butter

8-INCH PIE:

1 recipe pie crust
¾ cup granulated sugar
2 tablespoons cornstarch
¼ teaspoon salt
2 cups canned cherries
(No. 2 can), drained
½ cup cherry juice
⅛ teaspoon almond extract
1 teaspoon lemon rind, grated
3 to 4 drops red food coloring,
if desired
1 tablespoon butter

1. Place unbaked pie crust in 8 or 9-inch pie plate.
2. Combine sugar, cornstarch, and salt.
3. In mixing bowl, put drained cherries, juice, almond flavoring, lemon rind, and food coloring. Stir well.
4. Combine sugar mixture with cherries. Let set few minutes.
5. Put cherries in pie shell. Dot with butter.
6. Cover with top crust. Seal edges. To allow steam to escape during cooking, prick crust or cut design desired.
7. Bake at 425°F. for about 45 minutes, or until done.

FRESH CHERRY PIE

As American as the Fourth of July.

Oven temperature: preheat to
450°F.
Baking time: about 45 minutes

Yield: 6 to 8 servings
Pan: 9-inch pie plate

1 recipe pie crust
5 cups fresh pie cherries,
  pitted
1 tablespoon lemon juice
¼ teaspoon almond extract
few drops red food coloring,
  if desired
1½ cups granulated sugar

7 tablespoons all-purpose
  flour, *OR*
5 tablespoons cornstarch, *OR*
4 tablespoons quick-cooking
  tapioca
¼ teaspoon salt
2 tablespoons butter

1. Place unbaked pie crust in 9-inch pie plate.
2. Wash and pit cherries. Place in bowl and sprinkle with lemon juice, almond extract, and food coloring.
3. Combine sugar; flour, cornstarch, or tapioca; and salt. Pour over cherries and mix, being careful not to mash fruit.
4. Put cherries in pie shell. Dot with butter.
5. Cover with top crust. Seal edges. To allow steam to escape during cooking, prick crust or cut design desired.
6. Bake at 450°F. for 10 minutes. *REDUCE* temperature to 350°F. and bake for about 35 minutes more, or until done.

GOOSEBERRY PIE

This favored recipe comes from a long-time friend.

Oven temperature: preheat to
  325°F.
Baking time: about 15 minutes

Yield: 6 to 8 servings
Pan: 8 or 9-inch pie plate

8 or 9-inch pie shell, baked
2 cups gooseberries, cooked
  or canned
1 cup granulated sugar

½ cup juice
¼ cup flour
¼ teaspoon salt
meringue for topping

1. Mix cooked or canned gooseberries, sugar, juice, flour, and salt together. Cook until thickened. Cool.
2. Pour into baked and cooled pie shell.
3. Top with meringue, being careful to "seal" the edges to the pie crust to avoid shrinking during baking.
4. Bake at 325°F. for about 15 minutes.

FROZEN CHERRY PIE

Don't be undecided about dessert. Bake a cherry pie. Everybody loves it.

Oven temperature: preheat to
   400°F.
Baking time: 25 to 30 minutes

Yield: 6 to 8 servings
Pan: 9-inch pie plate

1 recipe pie crust
2½ cups frozen cherries,
   thawed
¾ cup granulated sugar
2 tablespoons cornstarch
¼ teaspoon salt

⅔ cup cherry juice
1 tablespoon lemon juice
⅛ teaspoon almond extract
1 tablespoon butter
3 to 4 drops red food coloring

1.   Place unbaked pie crust in 9-inch pie plate.
2.   Drain thawed cherries. Save juice.
3.   In sauce pan, combine sugar, cornstarch, and salt. Stir in ⅔ cup cherry juice. Cook, stirring constantly, until thickened and clear.
4.   Add cherries to cooked mixture. Remove from heat and add lemon juice, almond extract, butter, and food coloring.
5.   Put cherries in pie shell.
6.   Cover with top crust. Seal edges. To allow steam to escape during cooking, prick crust or cut design desired.
7.   Bake at 400°F. for 25 to 30 minutes.

CONCORD GRAPE PIE

Infrequently served, but should not be forgotten.

Oven temperature: preheat to
   450°F.
Baking time: 30 to 35 minutes

Yield: 6 to 8 servings
Pan: 9-inch pie plate

1 recipe pie crust
4 cups Concord grapes
1 tablespoon lemon juice
1 tablespoon lemon or orange
   rind, grated

¾ cup granulated sugar
¼ teaspoon salt
1 tablespoon quick-cooking
   tapioca

1. Place unbaked pie crust in 9-inch pie plate.
2. Wash and stem grapes. Slip the pulp out of skins. Save skins.
3. Cook the pulp until seeds loosen. Press through colander or sieve.
4. In mixing bowl, put pulp, skins, lemon juice, and lemon or orange rind.
5. Combine sugar, salt, and tapioca together. Pour over grapes. Mix lightly. Let stand for about 10 minutes.
6. Put grape mixture in pie shell.
7. Cover with top crust. Seal edges. To allow steam to escape during cooking, prick crust or cut design desired.
8. Bake at 450°F. for 10 minutes. *REDUCE* temperature to 350°F. and bake for 20 to 25 minutes more, or until done.

MINCEMEAT

Recall the warmth of a kitchen filled with cooking aromas on a cold winter day?

Yield: about 2 gallons

3 pounds lean beef, chopped
1½ pounds beef suet, chopped
or grind above together
8 pounds apples, peeled, cored, and thinly sliced
2½ pounds granulated sugar
2 quarts fruit cider
3 pounds seedless raisins
2½ pounds currants
1½ pounds citron, chopped
⅓ pound preserved orange peel, chopped

¼ pound preserved lemon peel, chopped
juice and rind of 1 lemon
2 pounds nut meats, chopped
2 teaspoons allspice
1 teaspoon ginger
2 teaspoons ground cloves
1 tablespoon cinnamon
1 teaspoon ground pepper
2 teaspoons nutmeg
1 teaspoon salt
2 cups brandy or rum, if desired

1. Place all ingredients, except rum or brandy, in very large cooking pan. Cook, stirring occasionally, for 2 to 4 hours.
2. Cool. Add brandy or rum. Seal in jars to ripen for 3 to 4 weeks before using. May also be stored in stone crock, uncovered. If uncovered, stir every few days.
Note: Use about 2 cups for an 8 or 9-inch pie.

CRUMBLE PEACH PIE

A fitting climax to any dinner.

Oven temperature: preheat to
   450°F.
Baking time: about 40 minutes

Yield: 6 to 8 servings
Pan: 9-inch pie plate

½ recipe pie crust
1½ cups granulated sugar
1 cup all-purpose flour, sifted
½ teaspoon cinnamon

4 cups fresh peaches, peeled
   and sliced
2 tablespoons lemon juice
½ cup butter or margarine

1.   Place unbaked pie crust in 9-inch pie plate.
2.   Combine 1 cup sugar, ¼ cup sifted flour, and cinnamon together.
3.   Place peach slices in bowl. Sprinkle with lemon juice. Combine flour mixture with peaches being careful not to mash fruit.
4.   Put peaches in pie shell.
5.   Cream butter or margarine with remaining ½ cup sugar and ¾ cup flour until crumbly.
6.   Spread crumbled mixture over peach filling.
7.   Bake at 450°F. for 10 minutes. *REDUCE* temperature to 350°F. and bake for 30 minutes more, or until done. Serve warm.

FRESH STRAWBERRY PIE

A "must" in strawberry season.

Yield: 6 to 8 servings

Pan: 9-inch pie plate

9-inch graham cracker crust,
   baked and cooled
2 pints fresh strawberries or
   fresh-frozen whole strawberries

1 cup granulated sugar
3 tablespoons cornstarch
2 tablespoons lemon juice
½ pint whipping cream,
   whipped

1.   Wash, pick over, and remove stems or hulls from fresh berries.
2.   In saucepan, with fork or pastry blender, crush 1 pint prepared berries.

3. Stir in sugar; cornstarch, and lemon juice.
4. Cook over medium heat, stirring constantly, until mixture is thickened and clear. Cool.
5. Halve remaining pint berries. Add to cooled mixture.
6. Pour into baked and cooled crust. Refrigerate for 4 hours, or until well chilled.
7. Top with whipped cream.

TOPPING VARIATION

1 pint commercial sour cream   ½ teaspoon vanilla
¼ cup granulated sugar

1. Blend sour cream, sugar, and vanilla.
2. Spread on strawberries.
3. Bake at 350°F. for 5 minutes.
4. Refrigerate for 4 hours or until well chilled.

FRUIT TARTS

Tarts are forever tempting. Especially nice for buffet parties or picnics.

Oven temperature: preheat to 425°F.   Yield: approximately 8 tarts
Baking time: about 25 minutes   Pan: 3"x1½" muffin pan, well greased or buttered

CRUST

2 cups all-purpose flour, sifted   2 tablespoons granulated
½ teaspoon salt   sugar
1 cup butter, softened   grated rind of 1 lemon
2 egg yolks

1. Sift flour once before measuring. Sift flour and salt together.
2. Place dry ingredients in bowl or on pastry canvas. Make a well in center. Put butter, egg yolks, sugar, and lemon rind in well.
3. With hands, quickly work all the ingredients into a smooth paste. Add a little ice water to moisten dough if necessary.
4. Lightly press dough into well greased or buttered muffin pan cups. Refrigerate for 1/2 hour.

3 cups sugared fruit, fresh or fresh-frozen whole cinnamon	nutmeg 1 egg yolk 3 tablespoons heavy cream

1. Fill unbaked tarts with fruit. Sprinkle with cinnamon and nutmeg.
2. Bake for 10 minutes.
3. Beat egg yolk and cream together. Spoon over partially baked tarts. Return tarts to oven and bake 15 to 20 minutes more.
Note: The dough may be placed in well greased or buttered 9"x9"x2" square pan. Arrange fruit on crust and bake as for tarts. Cut into individual servings.

Cream or Custard Pies

MARVELOUS CHOCOLATE PIE

Chill well, then "frost" with whipping cream.

Yield: 4 to 6 servings   Pan: 8-inch pie plate

8-inch pie shell, baked
1 six-ounce package chocolate bits
3 tablespoons milk or cream
3 tablespoons granulated sugar

3 eggs, separated (beat whites until stiff, not dry)
1 teaspoon vanilla
½ pint whipping cream, whipped

1. In top of double boiler, melt together the chocolate bits, milk or cream, and sugar. Stir well to blend thoroughly. Cool.
2. Add egg yolks one at a time, beating well after each addition.
3. Add vanilla.
4. With pliable rubber scraper or wire whisk, gently fold stiffly beaten egg whites into chocolate mixture.
5. Pour into baked and cooled pie shell. Chill well before serving. Top with whipped cream.

ANGELFOOD PIE

A recipe adapted from a famous restaurant owner's file.

Oven temperature: preheat to
   450°F.
Baking time: 40 to 45 minutes

Yield: 12 to 16 servings
Pan: two 9-inch pie plates,
   floured

CRUST

3 cups all-purp... f...
   sifted
2 teaspoons sal...

1½ cups shortening (hydrogenated, emulsified, or lard)
½ cup minus 1 tablespoon
   ice water

1.   Sift flour on... measuring. Sift flour and salt together.
2.   Add shorten... two table knives or pastry blender, cut
shortening into fl... mixture is crumbly. Do *not* overmix.
3.   Add water, a... nful at a time. Quickly blend by tossing
dough with light ... of fork. Use just enough to hold mixture
together.
4.   Place pastry ... re of waxed paper, gather up corners,
and press lightly t... a ball. Refrigerate for 10 minutes.
5.   Roll out sligh... cker than usual pie crust.
6.   Dust two 9-in... e plates with flour. Do not grease. Line
with pastry. Prick ... of pastry with fork.
7.   Bake at 450°F... 5 minutes. *REDUCE* temperature to
350°F. and bake ab... 0 minutes more. Cool.

FILLING

1 cup egg whites (ab... 8 to
   10)
1 cup granulated su...
¼ teaspoon salt

1 teaspoon vanilla
½ teaspoon almond extract
whipped cream and chopped
   nuts for topping

1.   Beat egg whites until they form soft peaks. Add sugar, salt,
vanilla, and almond extract a little at a time, beating continually
until egg whites are very stiff.
2.   Spread into baked and cooled pie shells.
3.   Bake at 290°F. for 25 to 30 minutes. Cool, then chill thoroughly.
4.   Top with whipped cream. Sprinkle chopped nuts over all.

CHOCOLATE PIE

A good summer pie.

Yield: 6 to 8 servings Pan: 9-inch pie plate

9-inch pie shell, baked
3 to 4 ounces chocolate,
  melted
1 cup plus 1 tablespoon
  granulated sugar
2 eggs, beaten
1 teaspoon vanilla

1 tablespoon plus 1 teaspoon
  butter
2 tablespoons cornstarch
1½ cups milk
whipping cream for topping,
  if desired

1. Melt chocolate over simmering water. Cool.
2. In double boiler, place sugar, eggs, vanilla, butter, corn-starch, and milk. Cook, stirring constantly, until thickened.
3. Add melted chocolate. Beat until smooth. Cool.
4. Pour into baked and cooled pie shell.
5. Top with whipped cream if desired. Semi-sweet chocolate grated over the top of the whipped cream is delicious.

BUTTERSCOTCH SOUR CREAM PIE

A different dessert that is very rich.

Oven temperature: preheat to
  425°F.
Baking time: about 40 minutes

Yield: 4 to 6 servings
Pan: 8-inch pie plate

½ recipe pie crust
1 cup brown sugar,
  firmly packed
2 tablespoons all-purpose
  flour
⅛ teaspoon salt

2 eggs, separated
  (reserve whites)
1 cup commercial sour cream
1 teaspoon vanilla
4 tablespoons granulated
  sugar (for meringue)

1. Place unbaked pie crust in 8-inch pie plate.
2. Mix brown sugar, flour, and salt together.
3. Beat egg yolks slightly. Gradually beat eggs into brown

266

sugar and flour mixture until smooth.

4. Stir in sour cream, and vanilla.

5. Pour into unbaked pie shell.

6. Bake at 425°F. for 10 minutes. *REDUCE* temperature to 350°F. and bake 10 to 12 minutes more. Cool.

7. To make meringue, beat egg whites until stiff, not dry. Gradually add 4 tablespoons granulated sugar.

8. Top filling with meringue, being careful to "seal" the edges to the pie crust to avoid shrinking during baking.

9. Bake at 325°F. for 15 minutes or until golden brown.

HAZEL'S COCONUT CUSTARD PIE

Hazel makes this for us as a special treat. It is also luscious when changed to a banana cream pie.

Oven temperature: preheat to 325°F.
Baking time: about 15 minutes

Yield: 6 to 8 servings
Pan: 9-inch pie plate

9-inch pie shell, baked
⅔ cup granulated sugar
5 tablespoons all-purpose flour, sifted
½ teaspoon salt
2½ cups milk

3 eggs, separated (reserve whites)
1 teaspoon vanilla
¾ cup coconut, shredded
6 tablespoons granulated sugar (for meringue)
¼ teaspoon salt (for meringue)

1. In top of double boiler, place ⅔ cup sugar, flour, and ½ teaspoon salt. Mix well.

2. Add milk and egg yolks. Cook, stirring constantly, until thickened.

3. When mixture is thickened, add shredded coconut and vanilla. Cool.

4. Pour into baked and cooled pie shell.

5. To make meringue, beat egg whites until stiff, not dry. Gradually add 6 tablespoons sugar and ¼ teaspoon salt.

6. Top filling with meringue, being careful to "seal" the edges to the pie crust to avoid shrinking during baking.

7. Bake at 325°F. for about 15 minutes or until golden brown.

Note: For banana cream pie, substitute 1 cup diced bananas for coconut.

CHOCOLATE CREAM MERINGUE PIE

Delicious almost beyond description.

Oven temperature: preheat to
   275°F.
Baking time: 45 minutes

Yield: 6 to 8 servings
Pan: 9-inch pie plate, greased

MERINGUE SHELL

3 egg whites
⅛ teaspoon cream of tartar
¼ teaspoon salt
¾ cup granulated sugar,
   sifted

¾ cup walnut meats, finely
   chopped
1 teaspoon vanilla

1.   Beat egg whites until foamy. Add cream of tartar, salt, and sugar a little at a time, mixing carefully after each addition.
2.   Beat until stiff, not dry.
3.   With pliable rubber scraper or whisk, gently fold in nuts and vanilla.
4.   Spread in greased 9-inch pie plate, building up sides to shape "nest" of shell.
5.   Bake at 275°F. for 45 minutes. Cool.

FILLING

4 ounces sweet chocolate,
   melted
3 tablespoons strong coffee

1 teaspoon vanilla
½ pint whipping cream,
   whipped

1.   Melt chocolate over simmering water. Add coffee and vanilla. Cool.
2.   With pliable rubber scraper or whisk, gently fold whipped cream into chocolate mixture.
3.   Pour into baked and cooled meringue shell.
4.   Chill for 4 hours or more.
Note: Meringue shells may be made in size for individual servings. Shape and place on greased cookie sheet to bake.

CUSTARD PIE

A recipe that goes back 100 years.

Oven temperature: preheat to
   450°F.
Baking time: about 35 minutes

Yield: 6 to 8 servings
Pan: 9-inch pie plate

½ recipe pie crust
2 cups milk, scalded
3 eggs or 6 egg yolks, beaten
½ cup granulated sugar

¼ teaspoon salt
¼ teaspoon nutmeg
½ teaspoon vanilla

1. Place unbaked pie crust in 9-inch pie plate.
2. Scald milk. Cool slightly.
3. To beaten eggs or egg yolks, add sugar, salt, nutmeg, and vanilla. Mix well.
4. Slowly add scalded milk. (Adding too hot or too fast will cook eggs.) Stir thoroughly.
5. Pour into unbaked pie shell.
6. Bake at 450°F. for 10 minutes. *REDUCE* temperature to 350°F. and bake for about 25 minutes more. Pie is done when knife inserted in thickest part of filling comes out clean.
Note: We think this pie is interesting if sprinkled with nutmeg before being put into the oven.

OLD FASHIONED PUMPKIN PIE

Hearty, full-bodied pumpkin custard pie from the farm kitchen.

Oven temperature: preheat to
    450°F.
Baking time :about 45 minutes

Yield: 6 to 8 servings
Pan: 9-inch pie plate

½ recipe pie crust
1 cup pumpkin, cooked
3 eggs, slightly beaten
2 cups milk
1 tablespoon all-purpose flour

¼ cup brown sugar,
    firmly packed
½ cup granulated sugar
½ teaspoon salt
½ teaspoon nutmeg
½ teaspoon cinnamon

1. Place unbaked pie crust in 9-inch pie plate.
2. In mixing bowl, place pumpkin, eggs, and milk. Stir well.
3. Add the flour, sugars, salt, nutmeg, and cinnamon. Mix thoroughly.
4. Pour into unbaked pie shell.
5. Bake at 450°F. for 10 minutes. *REDUCE* temperature to 350°F. and bake for about 35 minutes more. Pie is done when knife inserted in thickest part of filling comes out clean.
Note: 1 cup carrots, cooked and mashed, may be substituted for pumpkin.

269

LEMON ANGEL PIE

Glamorous individual pies.

Oven temperature: preheat to 300°F.
Baking time: about 45 minutes

Yield: 5 to 6 servings
Pan: individual pie plates, buttered

MERINGUE CRUST

4 egg whites
½ teaspoon cream of tartar

1 cup granulated sugar

1. Beat egg whites until foamy.
2. Add cream of tartar.
3. Gradually beat in sugar.
4. Beat until stiff, but not dry.
5. Spread in buttered individual pie plates.
6. Bake at 300°F. for about 45 minutes. Cool.

FILLING

4 egg yolks, beaten
½ cup granulated sugar
3 tablespoons lemon juice

1 tablespoon lemon rind, grated
½ pint whipping cream, whipped

1. Beat egg yolks until thick and lemon-colored. Beat in sugar.
2. Add lemon juice and rind.
3. Place in double boiler. Cook until thickened. Cool.
4. When cool, fold in whipped cream.
5. Pour into baked and cooled meringue crusts.
6. Chill 4 hours or overnight in refrigerator.

DEBBY'S PECAN PIE

Absolutely the best! Takes only minutes to make.

Oven temperature: preheat to 350°F.
Baking time: 50 minutes

Yield: 6 to 8 servings
Pan: 8-inch pie plate

½ recipe pie crust
3 eggs, slightly beaten
½ cup granulated sugar
1 cup dark refined corn syrup

1 cup pecan meats, chopped
½ teaspoon salt
1 teaspoon vanilla

1. Place unbaked pie crust in 8-inch pie plate.
2. To slightly beaten eggs, add sugar, syrup, nuts, salt, and vanilla.
3. Pour into pie shell.
4. Bake at 350°F. for 50 minutes.
This pie is delicious served with whipped cream topping.

LEMON MERINGUE PIE

The consistent choice of many pie-fanciers.

Oven temperature: preheat to 325°F.
Baking time: about 15 minutes

Yield: 6 to 8 servings
Pan: 9-inch pie plate

9-inch pie shell, baked
1½ cups granulated sugar
7 tablespoons cornstarch
¼ teaspoon salt
1½ cups water
3 eggs, separated
 (reserve whites)

grated **rind,** of 1 lemon
2 tablespoons butter
¼ to ⅓ cup lemon juice
6 tablespoons granulated
 sugar (for meringue)

1. In saucepan, combine 1½ cups sugar, cornstarch, salt, and water. Over medium heat bring to boil. Cook, stirring constantly, until thickened (about 5 minutes).
2. Remove from heat. Stir small amount of hot mixture into egg yolks. Return to hot mixture. Bring to boil. Cook for 1 minute more, stirring constantly.
3. Add lemon rind and butter. Stir in lemon juice. Cool to luke-warm.
4. Pour into baked and cooled pie shell. Cool.
5. To make meringue, beat egg whites until stiff, not dry. Gradually add 6 tablespoons sugar to stiffly beaten egg whites.
6. Top filling with meringue, being careful to "seal" the edges to the pie crust to avoid shrinking during baking.
7. Bake at 325°F. for about 15 minutes, or until golden brown.

JERRY'S FAVORITE PUMPKIN PIE

One husband's idea of a perfect food.

Oven temperature: preheat to
   350°F.
Baking time: about 1 hour

Yield: 12 to 16 servings
Pan: two 9-inch pie plates

1 recipe pie crust
3½ cups pumpkin, cooked
   (No. 2½ can)
1 cup brown sugar,
   firmly packed
1 cup granulated sugar
¼ teaspoon ground cloves
2½ teaspoons cinnamon

2½ teaspoons ginger
1 teaspoon salt
4 eggs, beaten
1 cup evaporated milk,
   scalded
½ pint whipping cream,
   scalded

1.   Place unbaked pie crusts in two 9-inch pie plates.
2.   In large bowl, place pumpkin, sugars, cloves, cinnamon, ginger, salt, and beaten eggs. Stir well.
3.   Add scalded evaporated milk and whipping cream. Mix thoroughly.
4.   Pour into two unbaked pie shells.
5.   Bake at 350°F. for about 1 hour. Pie is done when knife inserted in thickest part of filling comes out clean.
Note: Serve with whipped cream to which powdered sugar and rum have been added.

PINEAPPLE CREAM PIE

A mouth-watering creation.

Oven temperature: preheat to
   325°F.
Baking time: about 15 minutes

Yield: 6 to 8 servings
Pan: 9-inch pie plate

9-inch pie or crumb shell,
   baked
2 cups crushed pineapple
   (No. 2 can)
4 tablespoons cornstarch
1 cup granulated sugar
4 teaspoons butter

2 eggs, separated (reserve
   whites)
1 tablespoon lemon juice
½ cup whipping cream,
   whipped
4 tablespoons granulated
   sugar (for meringue)

1. In top of double boiler, place pineapple, cornstarch, and sugar. Cook, stirring constantly, until thickened. Cool.
2. Add butter and egg yolks. (If custard is too hot, it will cook the egg yolks.) Stir in lemon juice.
3. Chill until mixture will form little mounds when dropped from spoon.
4. With pliable rubber scraper or whisk, gently fold in whipped cream.
5. To make meringue, beat egg whites until stiff, not dry. Gradually add 4 tablespoons sugar to stiffly beaten egg whites.
6. Top filling with meringue, being careful to "seal" the edges to pie crust to avoid shrinking during baking.
7. Bake at 325°F. for about 15 minutes, or until golden brown.

RAISIN CREAM PIE

As yummy as anything you'll ever serve.

Oven temperature: preheat to 450°F.
Baking time: about 55 minutes

Yield: 6 to 8 servings
Pan: 8 or 9-inch pie plate

½ recipe pie crust
1 cup raisins
1 tablespoon flour
1 cup commercial sour cream
⅔ cup milk
¼ teaspoon salt
1 tablespoon vinegar

1 teaspoon cinnamon
1 cup granulated sugar
2 eggs, separated (reserve whites)
4 tablespoons granulated sugar (for meringue)

1. Place unbaked pie crust in 8 or 9-inch pie plate.
2. Mix together raisins, flour stirred into sour cream, milk, salt, vinegar, cinnamon, sugar, and beaten egg yolks. Stir well.
3. Pour into pie shell.
4. Bake at 450°F. for 10 minutes. *REDUCE* temperature to 350°F. and bake for 30 minutes more. Cool.
5. To make meringue, beat egg whites until stiff, not dry. Gradually add 4 tablespoons sugar.
6. Top filling with meringue, being careful to "seal" the edges to the pie crust to avoid shrinking during baking.
7. *REDUCE* temperature and bake at 325°F. for 15 minutes, or until golden brown.

PUFF CRUST CREAM PIE

It is so good you'll be glad the recipe is double-size.

Oven temperature: preheat to 400°F.
Baking time: about 30 minutes

Yield: 12 to 16 servings
Pan: two 9-inch pie plates

PUFF CRUST

2 eggs, separated (reserve whites)
2 cups all-purpose flour, sifted
4 tablespoons butter, softened

4 tablespoons granulated sugar
1 teaspoon double-acting baking powder

1. Blend 2 beaten egg yolks, flour, softened butter, sugar, and baking powder together with beater or hands until mixture holds together.
2. Press dough gently into two 9-inch pie plates as for pie crusts.
3. Bake at 400°F. for about 15 minutes, or until golden brown. Cool.

FILLING

6 eggs, separated (reserve whites)
6 tablespoons granulated sugar

4 tablespoons all-purpose flour
¼ teaspoon salt
2 cups milk
2 teaspoons vanilla

1. Combine 6 egg yolks, sugar, flour, and salt together.
2. Heat milk in top of double boiler. Gradually stir in egg mixture. Cook, stirring constantly, until thickened.
3. Add vanilla.
4. Pour into baked and cooled pie shells. Spread with meringue.

MERINGUE

8 egg whites
½ teaspoon cream of tartar

¾ cup granulated sugar
1 teaspoon vanilla

1. To make meringue, beat egg whites until stiff, not dry. Gradually add cream of tartar, sugar, and vanilla.
2. Top fillings with meringue being careful to "seal" the edges to the pie crust to avoid shrinking during baking.
3. *REDUCE* temperature and bake at 325°F. for about 15 minutes.

274

ROCKY MOUNTAIN DREAM PIE

This fine old recipe makes a most luscious lemon custard pie.

Oven temperature: preheat to 325°F.
Baking time: 15 minutes

Yield: 6 to 8 servings
Pan: 9-inch pie plate

MERINGUE

9-inch pie shell, baked
3 eggs, separated (reserve yolks)

5 tablespoons granulated sugar
½ teaspoon vanilla

1. Beat egg whites until stiff, not dry. Gradually add sugar and vanilla.
2. Spread sides and bottom of 9-inch baked and cooled pie shell with meringue.
3. Bake at 325°F. for 15 minutes, or until light golden brown.
4. Fill with custard.

LEMON CUSTARD FILLING

1¼ cups lukewarm water
2½ tablespoons cornstarch
grated rind of ½ lemon
juice of 1 lemon
¾ cup granulated sugar

1 tablespoon butter
3 egg yolks, beaten
½ pint whipping cream, whipped

1. In heavy saucepan or top of double boiler, combine water, cornstarch, lemon rind and juice, sugar, and butter. Cook, stirring constantly, until thickened.
2. Beat egg yolks.
3. Slowly beat some of hot mixture into beaten egg yolks, being careful not to curdle mixture. Return to hot mixture.
4. Cook about 5 minutes more, stirring constantly. Mixture should be quite thick.
5. Remove from heat. Cool.
6. Pour into baked pastry-meringue shell. Refrigerate no longer than 3 hours before serving. (It will become soggy if poured into shell for longer period.)
7. Top pie with whipped cream.

PENNSYLVANIA CRUMB PIE

This recipe is very old and came to the West with the pioneers.

Oven temperature: preheat to
  350°F.
Baking time: 30 minutes

Yield: 6 to 8 servings
Pan: 9-inch pie plate

FILLING

½ recipe pie crust
½ cup granulated sugar
1 egg, beaten
2 teaspoons all-purpose flour

¼ cup molasses
⅞ cup water
½ teaspoon baking soda
½ teaspoon vanilla

1.   Place unbaked pie crust in 9-inch pie plate.
2.   In saucepan, put sugar, egg, flour, molasses, water, and soda.
Bring to boil over medium heat. Remove from heat. Cool.
3.   Add vanilla.

CRUMB MIXTURE

1 cup all-purpose flour, sifted
½ cup granulated sugar

¼ cup shortening (hydrogenated, emulsified, or lard)

1.   Place all ingredients in bowl. Mix together thoroughly with
hands, two table knives, or pastry blender. Mixture should be
crumbly.
2.   Sprinkle small amount of crumb mixture lightly in unbaked
pie shell.
3.   Alternate filling with remaining crumb mixture, ending with
crumbs.
4.   Bake at 350°F. for 30 minutes, or until golden brown.

RHUBARB CREAM PIE

*When rhubarb is on the market, surprise the family with this
delightful pie.*

Oven temperature: preheat to
  450°F.
Baking time: 45 minutes

Yield: 8 to 10 servings
Pan: 9-inch pie plate

1 recipe pie crust
3 cups rhubarb, cut up
1½ cups granulated sugar
3 tablespoons all-purpose
  flour

½ teaspoon nutmeg
1 tablespoon butter
2 eggs, well beaten

part strawberry

1. Place unbaked pie crust in 9-inch pie plate.
2. Place rhubarb in pie shell.
3. Blend sugar, flour, nutmeg, and butter.
4. Add eggs. Beat until smooth.
5. Pour over rhubarb.
6. Top with pie crust or pastry cut in fancy shapes.
7. Bake at 450°F. for 10 minutes. *REDUCE* temperature to 350°F. and bake for 35 minutes more.

Chiffon and Uncooked Fillings

CHOCOLATE CHIFFON PIE

Just as good made the day before serving.

Pan: 9-inch pie plate

Yield: 6 to 8 servings

9-inch pie shell or graham cracker crust, baked
1 envelope unflavored gelatin
¼ cup cold water
3 eggs, separated (beat whites until stiff, not dry)
1 cup granulated sugar

1 cup milk, scalded
2 ounces chocolate, melted
¼ teaspoon salt
1 teaspoon vanilla
whipped cream for topping, if desired

1. Soak gelatin in water for 5 minutes.
2. Melt chocolate over simmering water. Cool.
3. Beat egg yolks lightly. Place in top of double boiler with sugar, scalded milk, melted chocolate, and salt. Cook, stirring constantly, until thickened.
4. Add gelatin to egg and sugar mixture. Cool. Add vanilla.
5. With pliable rubber scraper or whisk, gently fold in stiffly beaten egg whites.
6. Pour into baked pie shell or baked graham cracker crust. Chill.
7. Top with whipped cream if desired.
Note: A few drops of peppermint flavoring may be substituted for vanilla.

BLACK-BOTTOM PIE

So favored, it was brought to this cook in the hospital after the birth of a son.

Yield: 6 to 8 servings
9-inch cookie crumb crust (½ chocolate, ½ ginger wafers), chilled
1 envelope unflavored gelatin
2¼ cups cold milk
¾ cup plus 1 tablespoon granulated sugar
1½ tablespoons cornstarch
½ teaspoon salt
4 egg yolks, beaten

Pan: 9-inch pie plate
2 egg whites (beat until stiff, not dry)
¼ teaspoon fresh cream of tartar
3 tablespoons rum
1½ ounces chocolate, melted
1 teaspoon vanilla
½ pint whipping cream, whipped
1 ounce chocolate, shaved

1. Soak gelatin in ¼ cup cold milk for 5 minutes.
2. In top of double boiler, place ½ cup sugar, cornstarch, ½ teaspoon salt, and 2 cups milk. Cook, stirring constantly, until mixture boils. Cover and cook, stirring occasionally, for about 15 to 20 minutes more.
3. Slowly beat some of cooked mixture into beaten egg yolks. Return to hot mixture. Cook about 5 minutes more, stirring constantly. Divide into 2 parts.
4. Into one half, add softened gelatin. Cool. Add ¼ cup sugar and cream of tartar to stiffly beaten egg whites. With pliable rubber scraper or whisk, gently fold in stiffly beaten egg whites. Add rum. Chill until mixture makes little mounds when dropped from spoon.
5. Melt chocolate over simmering water. Cool. Add chocolate and vanilla to other half of mixture. Pour into chilled cookie crumb crust.
6. Pour cooled gelatin mixture over chilled chocolate mixture. Refrigerate overnight.
7. Add 1 tablespoon sugar and ½ teaspoon salt to whipped cream. Spread on pie. Sprinkle shaved chocolate on top.

BUTTERSCOTCH CHIFFON PIE

Cloud-light and lovely.

Yield: 6 to 8 servings   Pan: 9-inch pie plate

9-inch graham cracker crust,
  baked
1 envelope unflavored gelatin
¼ cup cold water
3 eggs, separated (beat
  whites until stiff, not dry)
1 cup brown sugar,
  firmly packed

1 cup milk, scalded
2 tablespoons butter
¼ teaspoon salt
½ teaspoon vanilla
¼ cup granulated sugar
whipped cream for topping, if
  desired

1. Soak gelatin in water for 5 minutes.
2. Beat egg yolks lightly. Place in top of double boiler with brown sugar, scalded milk, butter, and salt. Cook, stirring constantly, until thickened.
3. Add gelatin to egg and sugar mixture. Cool. Add vanilla.
4. Gradually add granulated sugar to stiffly beaten egg whites. With pliable rubber scraper or whisk, gently fold in egg whites.
5. Pour into baked graham cracker crust. Chill. Top with whipped cream if desired.

MARGIE'S FRENCHMINT PIE

She's given the recipe to so many friends, it's hardly a secret any more!

Yield: 6 to 8 servings

Pan: 9-inch pie plate

9-inch vanilla wafer or
  graham cracker crust,
  baked
½ cup butter, softened
1 cup powdered sugar, sifted

2 ounces chocolate, melted
2 eggs, well beaten
4 or 5 drops oil of peppermint
  OR
¼ teaspoon peppermint
  flavoring

1. Melt chocolate over simmering water. Cool.
2. Cream butter with sugar until light and fluffy.
3. Add eggs one at a time and beat very well after each addition.
4. Add melted chocolate. Beat well. Add peppermint flavoring.
5. Pour into baked and cooled pie shell.
Note: This pie may be served with whipped cream. It is also very good made with chocolate wafer crust.

COFFEE EGGNOG CHIFFON PIE

The height of dessert sophistication.

Yield: 6 to 8 servings

Pan: 9-inch pie plate

9-inch pie shell, baked
2 envelopes unflavored
   gelatin
½ cup cold coffee
2 eggs, separated (beat
   whites until stiff not dry)

½ cup granulated sugar
2 cups hot coffee
⅛ teaspoon salt
1 teaspoon brandy flavoring
½ pint whipping cream, whip
1 ounce chocolate, grated

1. Soak gelatin in cold coffee for 5 minutes.
2. Beat egg yolks lightly. Place in top of double boiler with sugar, hot coffee, and salt. Cook, stirring constantly, until thickened.
3. Add gelatin to egg and sugar mixture. Cool. Add brandy flavoring.
4. With pliable rubber scraper or whisk, gently fold in stiffly beaten egg whites.
5. Pour into baked and cooled pie shell. Chill.
6. Top with whipped cream. Sprinkle grated chocolate over top.

LEMONADE CHIFFON PIE

Frozen lemonade concentrate adds new zip.

Yield: 6 to 8 servings

Pan: 9-inch pie plate

9-inch graham cracker crust,
   baked
1 envelope unflavored gelatin
2 tablespoons cold water
4 eggs, separated (beat
   whites until stiff, not dry)

¾ cup granulated sugar
¼ teaspoon salt
1 six-ounce can frozen
   lemonade concentrate
whipped cream for topping,
   if desired

1. Soak gelatin in water for 5 minutes.
2. Beat egg yolks lightly. Place in top of double boiler with

sugar, salt, and frozen lemonade concentrate. Cook, stirring constantly, until thickened.

3. Add gelatin to sugar and lemonade mixture.

4. Remove from heat. Refrigerate until mixture makes little mounds when dropped from spoon.

5. With pliable rubber scraper or wire whisk, gently fold in stiffly beaten egg whites.

6. Pour into baked graham cracker crust. Serve with whipped cream, if desired.

NESSELRODE CHIFFON PIE

A light dessert for holiday dinners.

Yield: 6 to 8 servings   Pan: 9-inch pie shell

9-inch pie shell, baked
1 envelope unflavored gelatin
⅔ cup granulated sugar
⅛ teaspoon salt
1¼ cups milk
½ pint whipping cream or
    thick cream
3 eggs, separated (beat
    whites until stiff, not dry)

2 teaspoons rum flavoring, OR
3 tablespoons rum, OR
3 tablespoon sherry
¼ cup maraschino cherries,
    drained well and chopped
2 tablespoons seedless
    raisins, chopped fine
2 tablespoons almonds,
    ground

1. In top of double boiler, place gelatin, sugar, salt, milk, and cream.

2. Beat egg yolks lightly. Place in double boiler with milk mixture. Cook, stirring constantly, until thickened. Cool.

3. When cool, add rum or sherry, cherries, raisins, and almonds.

4. Refrigerate until mixture makes little mounds when dropped from spoon.

5. With pliable rubber scraper or whisk, gently fold in stiffly beaten egg whites.

6. Spread into baked and cooked pie shell. Chill for 4 hours or overnight.

Note: Shaved chocolate over the top of the pie is a pleasant addition.

LIME CHIFFON PIE

Wonderful wind-up for ladies' luncheon.

Yield: 6 to 8 servings   Pan: 9-inch pie plate

9-inch pie shell or graham   ½ cup granulated sugar
  cracker crust, baked   ½ teaspoon salt
2 teaspoons unflavored   5 tablespoons lime juice
  gelatin   ½ teaspoon vanilla
5 tablespoons water   whipped cream for topping,
4 eggs, separated (beat   if desired
  whites until stiff, not dry)

1. Soak gelatin in water for 5 minutes.
2. Beat egg yolks lightly. Place in top of double boiler with sugar, salt, and lime juice. Cook, stirring constantly, until thickened
3. Add gelatin to egg and sugar mixture. Cool. Add vanilla.
4. With pliable rubber scraper or whisk, gently fold in stiffly beaten egg whites.
5. Pour into baked pie shell or graham cracker crust. Chill. Top with whipped cream, if desired.

FLORIDA LIME PIE

This delicious pie is served frozen.

Yield: 6 to 8 servings   Pan: 8 or 9-inch pie plate

9-inch graham cracker crust,   ¼ cup fresh lime juice
  chilled   ⅛ teaspoon salt
4 eggs, separated   ¼ teaspoon cream of tartar
⅔ cup sweetened, condensed   4 tablespoons granulated
  milk   sugar

1. Beat egg yolks until thick, lemon-colored, and fluffy.
2. Add sweetened condensed milk. Beat more until doubled in bulk.

3. Blend in, but do not beat, lime juice and salt. Place in refrigerator.
4. Partially beat egg whites. Add cream of tartar and sugar. Continue beating until mixture is stiff, but not dry.
5. Remove egg yolk mixture from refrigerator. With pliable rubber scraper or whisk, gently fold stiffly beaten egg whites into egg and milk mixture.
6. Spread into chilled graham cracker lined 8 or 9-inch pie plate.
7. Place in freezer. Serve frozen.

PUMPKIN CHIFFON PIE

Divine!

Yield: 6 to 8 servings   Pan: 9-inch pie plate

9-inch pie shell or walnut
   shell, baked
1 envelope unflavored gelatin
¼ cup water
3 eggs, separated (beat
   whites until stiff, not dry)
½ cup milk
¾ cup brown sugar,
   firmly packed

½ teaspoon salt
½ teaspoon nutmeg
½ teaspoon cinnamon
1½ cups pumpkin, cooked
¼ cup granulated sugar
whipped cream for topping
nut meats and rum for
   flavoring, if desired

1. Soak gelatin in water for 5 minutes.
2. Beat egg yolks lightly. In top of double boiler, combine milk, brown sugar, salt, nutmeg, and cinnamon. Add gelatin and beaten egg yolks. Cook, stirring constantly, until thickened. Add pumpkin. Continue cooking for about 5 minutes.
3. Remove from heat. Refrigerate until mixture makes little mounds when dropped from spoon.
4. Gradually add ¼ cup granulated sugar to stiffly beaten egg whites.
5. With pliable rubber scraper or wire whisk, gently fold stiffly beaten egg whites into pumpkin mixture.
6. Pour into baked pastry or walnut pie shell. Serve with whipped cream flecked with nut meats and laced with rum.

MINCEMEAT CHIFFON PIE

A modern version of a traditional favorite.

Yield: 6 to 8 servings   Pan: 9-inch pie plate

9-inch pie shell, baked
1 envelope unflavored gelatin
½ cup water
1½ cups prepared mincemeat
⅛ teaspoon lemon juice
¼ cup nut meats, ground
¼ teaspoon nutmeg

¼ cup rum or brandy
   (if desired)
⅓ cup granulated sugar
⅛ teaspoon salt
3 egg whites, beaten until
   stiff, not dry
½ pint whipping cream,
   whipped

1. Soak gelatin in water for 5 minutes.
2. Stir in mincemeat, lemon juice, nuts, nutmeg, and rum or brandy. Refrigerate until mixture makes little mounds when dropped from spoon.
3. Add sugar and salt to stiffly beaten egg whites. With pliable rubber scraper or whisk, gently fold egg whites into chilled mincemeat and gelatin.
4. Fold in whipped cream.
5. Spread into baked 9-inch pie shell. Chill.

STRAWBERRY CHIFFON PIE

Strawberries know no season now that they may be purchased frozen. Lucky strawberry-lovers may now have this pie the year 'round.

Yield: 6 to 8 servings   Pan: 9-inch pie plate

9-inch pie shell or crumb
  crust, baked
1 envelope unflavored gelatin
3 tablespoons water
4 eggs, separated (beat
  whites until stiff, not dry)

1⅓ cups strawberries (fresh
  or fresh-frozen whole),
  mashed
⅔ cup granulated sugar
2 tablespoons lemon juice
¼ teaspoon salt

1.   Soak gelatin in water for 5 minutes.
2.   Beat the egg yolks lightly. Place in top of double boiler with strawberries, ⅓ cup sugar, lemon juice, and salt. Cook, stirring constantly, until thickened.
3.   Add gelatin to strawberry mixture. Cool.
4.   Gradually add ⅓ cup sugar to stiffly beaten egg whites. With pliable rubber scraper or whisk, gently fold egg whites into strawberry mixture.
5.   Pour into baked pie shell or crumb crust. Chill. Top with whipped cream, if desired.

DESSERTS

Baked Alaska   288
Blueberry Dessert   288
Scalloped Apple Pudding   290
Bread Pudding   290
Mother Anderson's Petite Cheese Cakes   291
Brown Betty   292
Baron's Cheesecake with Strawberry Glaze   292
Caramel Dumplings   294
Cherry Pudding   294
Cherry Cobbler   295
Italian Cherry-Chocolate Soufflé   296
Baked Custard   297
Chocolate Bread Pudding   298
Cottage Pudding   298
Cranberry Dessert   299
Cream Puffs or Eclairs   300
Date-Nut Pudding   300
Virginia's Lady Finger Lemon Cake   301
Favorite Fruit Dessert   302
Graham Cracker Pudding   302
Peach Betty   303
Peach Crunch   304
Johnstown Prune Whip   304
Rice Pudding   305

Space for notes, Page 306
Fillings, Pages 289, 293
Topping, Page 289
Glaze, Page 293

BAKED ALASKA

One of life's sweetest confections.

Oven temperature: preheat to
  450°F.
Baking time: about 8 minutes

Yield: 6 servings
Pan: wooden plank or bread
  board covered with heavy
  paper or foil

6 egg whites, beaten until
  stiff, not dry
½ cup powdered sugar, sifted
¼ teaspoon salt

½ teaspoon vanilla
1 8"x6"x1" layer sponge
  cake
1 quart brick ice cream

1.   When egg whites are beaten until almost stiff, add powdered
sugar, salt, and vanilla. Continue beating until egg whites are
stiff, not dry.
2.   Place 1-inch thick layer cake on wooden plank or bread
board covered with heavy paper or foil.
3.   Place brick of ice cream on cake.
4.   Cover the ice cream and cake with meringue, being careful
to "seal" meringue to sides of cake so it will not shrink away during baking.
5.   Bake at 450°F. for about 8 minutes, or until light golden
brown.
6.   Serve immediately.
Note: Individual servings may be made by cutting the cake and
the ice cream into smaller portions and following the directions
given above.

BLUEBERRY DESSERT

*This scrumptious dessert will add a fine finishing touch to a com-
pany menu.*

Oven temperature: preheat to
  400°F.
Baking time: 25 minutes

Yield: 6 to 9 servings
Pan: 9"x9"x2" square pan,
  ungreased

1¼ cups all-purpose flour, sifted

2 tablespoons granulated sugar

½ cup butter

1.   Sift flour once before measuring. Mix and sift flour and sugar together.
2.   With two table knives or pastry blender, cut butter into dry ingredients until consistency of small grain.
3.   Press dough with fingers into bottom of ungreased 9″x9″x2″ pan.
4.   Bake at 400F. for 25 minutes.

FILLING

1½ cups milk
¼ cup granulated sugar
¼ teaspoon salt
1 egg yolk, beaten

3 tablespoons all-purpose flour
1 tablespoon butter
½ teaspoon vanilla

1.   Scald 1 cup of milk with sugar, and salt.
2.   Mix remaining ½ cup milk and egg yolk together. Stir into flour a little at a time.
3.   Add flour mixture to scalded milk. Cook, stirring constantly, until thickened. Add butter. Cool. Add vanilla. Pour into baked crust.

BLUEBERRY TOPPING

6 tablespoons granulated sugar
3 tablespoons cornstarch
⅛ teaspoon salt
1 cup blueberry juice
2 teaspoons butter

4 cups canned blueberries (two No. 2 cans), drained
2 teaspoons lemon juice
½ pint whipping cream, whipped

1.   In saucepan mix sugar, cornstarch, and salt together. Slowly add blueberry juice, then butter. Cook over low heat, stirring constantly, until thick and clear. Add blueberries and lemon juice.
2.   Pour over filled crust. Top with whipped cream.

SCALLOPED APPLE PUDDING

For those who relish a fruit dessert.

Oven temperature: preheat to
    325°F.
Baking time: about 30 minutes

Yield: 6 servings
Pan: 8"x8"x2" square baking
    pan, or 1½-quart casserole,
    buttered

6 large apples, pared, cored,
    and thinly sliced
½ cup water
½ teaspoon nutmeg
1 teaspoon cinnamon

1 teaspoon lemon extract
1 cup granulated sugar
½ cup cake flour, sifted
½ cup butter

1.   Place sliced apples in buttered 8"x8"x2" square pan or 1½-quart casserole.

2.   Mix together water, nutmeg, cinnamon and lemon extract. Pour over apples.

3.   Mix and sift sugar and cake flour together. With fingers, mix dry ingredients with butter to make crumbly texture. Sprinkle on top of apples.

4.   Bake at 325°F. for about 30 minutes.

BREAD PUDDING

Try the variations, too.

Oven temperature: preheat to
    350°F.
Baking time: 40 to 50 minutes

Yield: 6 to 8 servings
Pan: 2-quart casserole,
    buttered

2 cups dry bread cubes, *OR*
4 slices buttered bread,
    cubed
4 cups milk, scalded
¼ cup butter, melted
¼ teaspoon salt

1 cup granulated sugar
¼ teaspoon nutmeg
1 tablespoon cornstarch
4 eggs, beaten
1 teaspoon vanilla
½ cup raisins, if desired

1   Soak bread cubes in scalded milk for 5 minutes.

2. Add butter, salt, sugar, nutmeg, and cornstarch.
3. Slowly add beaten eggs. Add vanilla and raisins. Mix.
4. Pour into buttered 2-quart casserole.
5. Bake at 350°F. for 40 to 50 minutes, or until done.

Variations: For butterscotch bread pudding, use brown sugar in place of granulated sugar. For chocolate bread pudding, add 1 ounce melted chocolate to scalded milk, omit raisins, and add ½ cup chopped nuts.

MOTHER ANDERSON'S PETITE CHEESE CAKES

Originally from Seattle, this recipe has "taken hold" in our families.

Oven temperature: preheat to 350°F.
Baking time: 25 to 30 minutes

Yield: 26 little cakes
Pan: 2½"x1¼" muffin pans, lightly buttered

1 recipe graham cracker crust, unbaked
2 eight-ounce packages cream cheese (at room temperature)
1 cup granulated sugar

2 teaspoons vanilla
3 eggs, unbeaten
1 pint commercial sour cream
3 tablespoons granulated sugar (for topping)
graham cracker crumbs

1. In large mixing bowl place cream cheese, 1 cup sugar, 1 teaspoon vanilla, and 3 eggs. Beat well for 2 minutes with electric mixer at medium speed, or by hand until very well beaten.
2. Line lightly buttered muffin pan cups with graham cracker crust.
3. Pour cheese mixture into crust-lined cups, filling each cup 3/4 full.
4. Bake at 350°F. for 18 to 20 minutes.
5. Remove from oven. Cool for 15 minutes.
6. Stir 3 tablespoons granulated sugar and 1 teaspoon vanilla into sour cream.
7. Spread topping over cakes. Sprinkle lightly with additional graham cracker crumbs.
8. Bake at 350°F. for 7 to 9 minutes more.

Note: A blender makes wonderfully fine cracker crumbs and creamy smooth cheese filling.

BROWN BETTY

A reliable family dessert.

Oven temperature: preheat to
  375°F.
Baking time: 30 to 40 minutes

Yield: 6 servings
Pan: 2-quart casserole,
  buttered

2 cups bread crumbs or
  graham cracker crumbs
3 tablespoons butter, melted
4 medium apples, peeled,
  cored, and thinly sliced
1 tablespoon lemon juice
grated rind of ½ lemon

¼ cup granulated sugar
¼ cup brown sugar,
  firmly packed
¼ teaspoon nutmeg
½ teaspoon cinnamon
¼ teaspoon salt
⅓ cup hot water

1. Brown crumbs and butter in skillet. Place about one-third in bottom of buttered 2-quart casserole.
2. Arrange one half of the sliced apples on top of buttered crumbs.
3. Sprinkle with one half the lemon juice, rind, and sugars.
4. Add second third of buttered crumbs, remaining apples, lemon juice, rind, and sugar. Cover with final third of crumbs.
5. Mix together the nutmeg, cinnamon, salt, and hot water. Pour over all.
6. Bake at 375°F. for 30 to 40 minutes, or until apples are tender. Serve hot with cream or hard sauce.

BARON'S CHEESECAKE WITH STRAWBERRY GLAZE

Two generations have cherished this delightful dessert.

Oven temperature: preheat to
  375°F.
Baking time: about 40 minutes

Yield: 10 to 12 servings
Pan: 9-inch spring-form pan,
  buttered

CRUST

1½ cups zweiback crumbs,
  finely crushed

¼ cup granulated sugar
⅓ cup butter, melted

1. Combine all ingredients. Mix very well.
2. Line bottom and sides of buttered, 9-inch spring-form pan with crumb mixture, pressing crust firmly into place.

FILLING I

3 eight-ounce packages cream cheese (at room temperature)

1¼ cups granulated sugar

3 tablespoons *fresh* lemon juice

4 large eggs, unbeaten

1. Cream cheese with sugar until light and fluffy.
2. Add lemon juice and eggs. Beat thoroughly with mixer or by hand until very smooth.
3. Pour into prepared crust.
4. Bake at 375°F. for 35 minutes, or until set.
5. Cool for 5 minutes. Spread with second layer of filling.

FILLING II

1 pint commercial sour cream

½ cup granulated sugar

1 teaspoon vanilla

1. Blend together sour cream, sugar, and vanilla.
2. Spread over top of cake.
3. *INCREASE* oven temperature to 475°F. Bake for 5 minutes.

STRAWBERRY GLAZE

1 quart strawberries (fresh or whole fresh-frozen)

½ cup granulated sugar

¼ cup water

1 tablespoon cornstarch

1 tablespoon lemon juice

1 teaspoon butter

few drops red food coloring

1. Wash, pick over, and remove stems or hulls from fresh berries.
2. Crush enough prepared strawberries to fill ½ cup. Keep remaining berries whole.
3. In saucepan, combine crushed berries, sugar, water, cornstarch and lemon juice.
4. Cook over medium heat until thickened and clear, about 3 minutes after mixture reaches a boil.
5. Add butter and food coloring. Strain through sieve. Cool.
6. Do not remove pan sides from cake. Arrange whole or halved berries on *cooled* cheesecake.
7. Pour *cooled* sauce over berries. Chill cake in refrigerator 4 hours or overnight. Remove sides of pan just before serving.

Note: A blender makes wonderfully fine crumbs and creamy smooth cheese filling.

CARAMEL DUMPLINGS

Tempting and syrupy.

Oven temperature: preheat to
   350°F.
Baking time: about 20 minutes

Yield: 6 servings
Pan: 2-quart Dutch oven or
   equivalent

2 cups granulated sugar
2½ cups boiling water
3 tablespoons butter
¼ teaspoon salt

1 cup all-purpose flour, sifted
1 teaspoon double-acting
   baking powder
½ cup milk

1. In 9-inch skillet, quickly melt until golden brown, ½ cup sugar.
2. Add boiling water, 1½ tablespoons butter, salt, and 1 cup sugar. Mix together and let boil for 10 minutes. Mixture should be syrupy. Set aside to cool.
3. Cream remaining butter with remaining ½ cup sugar.
4. Sift flour once before measuring. Mix and sift flour and baking powder together.
5. Add dry ingredients to creamed mixture alternately with milk, mixing thoroughly after each addition.
6. Drop by spoonfuls into the cold caramel.
7. Bake at 350°F. about 20 minutes or until dumplings are done.

CHERRY PUDDING

Add this to the menu when you are planning an oven dinner.

Oven temperature: preheat to
   350°F.
Baking time: 30 minutes

Yield: 8 servings
Pan: 9"x9"x2" square pan,
   greased

2 tablespoons shortening
2 cups granulated sugar
2 cups all-purpose flour,
   sifted
2 teaspoons double-acting
   baking powder

½ teaspoon salt
1 cup milk
1 cup hot water
2 cups canned pie cherries
   (No. 2 can), drained

1. Cream shortening with 1 cup sugar.

294

2.   Sift flour once before measuring. Mix and sift flour, baking powder, and salt together.
3.   Add dry ingredients alternately with milk, mixing thoroughly after each addition. Pour batter into greased 9"x9"x2" pan.
4.   Mix remaining cup sugar, hot water and cherries together. Pour over cake batter. During baking, the batter will come to the top and the cherry mixture will make a sauce.
5.   Bake at 350°F. for 30 minutes.
Note: Blueberries may be substituted.

CHERRY COBBLER

From the leaves of an old cookbook.

Oven temperature: preheat to 425°F.
Baking time: 25 to 30 minutes

Yield: 6 to 8 servings
Pan: 8"x8"x2" square pan, greased

2 cups canned red pitted cherries (No. 2 can)
1 tablespoon quick-cooking tapioca
⅓ cup granulated sugar
⅛ teaspoon salt
¾ cup cherry juice
1 tablespoon lemon juice
few drops red food coloring
½ teaspoon almond extract

¾ cup all-purpose flour, sifted
1 teaspoon double-acting baking powder
¼ teaspoon salt
3 tablespoons shortening
¼ cup almonds chopped and toasted to deep-brown color
6 tablespoons milk

1.   Place cherries in greased 8"x8"x2" square baking dish. Sprinkle tapioca over cherries.
2.   Combine sugar, salt, cherry juice, lemon juice, food coloring, and almond extract. Pour over cherries.
3.   Sift flour once before measuring. Mix and sift flour, baking powder, and salt together.
4.   With two table knives or pastry blender cut shortening into flour mixture until consistency of small grain.
5.   Add almonds. Mix well. Add milk. Mix thoroughly with fork.
6.   Drop dough by spoonfuls onto cherry mixture and spread slightly.
7.   Bake at 425°F. for 25 to 30 minutes.

ITALIAN CHERRY-CHOCOLATE SOUFFLÉ

An exotic dessert, very opulent looking.

Oven temperature: preheat to 375°F.
Baking time: about 45 minutes

Yield: 4 to 6 servings
Pan: 1½-quart soufflé dish or casserole, buttered lightly and dusted with granulated sugar

1 jar brandied Bing cherries (1 pound 4 ounces)
1 ounce chocolate, melted
1 ounce dark sweet chocolate, melted
2 tablespoons butter
3 tablespoons all-purpose flour

¾ cup milk, scalded
4 tablespoons granulated sugar
3 tablespoons rum
5 eggs, separated (beat whites until stiff, not dry)
⅛ teaspoon salt
½ pint whipping cream, whipped

1.   Drain cherries. Save juice.
2.   Melt chocolates and ½ cup cherry liqueur over simmering water. Set aside.
3.   In saucepan, melt butter. Blend in flour. Add scalded milk. Cook, stirring constantly, until mixture thickens. Mixture should be smooth. Add sugar, rum, and salt. Stir three or four times. Remove from heat.
4.   Add chocolate mixture. Blend well. Cool at least 1/2 hour in refrigerator or 2 hours at room temperature.
5.   Line prepared bottom of 1½-quart casserole or soufflé dish with drained cherries.
6.   Beat egg yolks until thick and lemon-colored. Add to cooled chocolate mixture.
7.   With pliable rubber scraper or whisk, gently fold stiffly beaten egg whites into chocolate mixture.
8.   Pour over cherries.
9.   Place baking dish in pan of hot water (the water reaching to within 1 inch of top edge of soufflé dish) in oven.
10.   Bake at 375°F. for about 45 minutes. Serve with whipped cream.

BAKED CUSTARD

Young and old enjoy this old-fashioned dessert favorite.

1.   Scald milk gently over medium heat until a film begins to form on top and tiny bubbles appear around edge of pan.
2.   Add milk *gradually* to egg mixture. (The hot milk will cook the eggs if added all at once.)
3.   Set baking dish in a pan on the oven rack, then pour hot water into the pan to within one inch from top of custard cups.
4.   Custard is done when a silver knife inserted in center comes out clean.
5.   To unmold, run thin knife all around custard cup, then invert onto serving plate.

Oven temperature: preheat to 325° F
Baking time: 45 minutes

Yield: 6 servings
Pan: individual custard cups

3 eggs, beaten
¼ cup granulated sugar
¼ teaspoon salt

2 cups milk, scalded
½ teaspoon vanilla
nutmeg

1.   Combine eggs with sugar and salt. Beat to mix.
2.   Slowly add scalded milk and vanilla to mixture. Stir well.
3.   Pour into custard cups. Sprinkle with nutmeg.
4. Bake in pan of hot water at 325° F. for 45 minutes or until mixture is firm and does not adhere to a silver knife when it is inserted in center of custard. Bake individual custards 20 to 30 minutes.
5.   Serve warm, or chill and serve cold.

VARIATIONS

1.   Coconut custard: Add ½ cup coconut to custard mixture.
2.   Maple custard: Omit nutmeg. Chill custard after it is cooled. Top with maple syrup.
3.   Party custard: Use 6 egg yolks and omit all egg whites.
4.   Honey custard: Use ½ cup honey in place of sugar. Omit vanilla and nutmeg. Add a dash of cinnamon.

CHOCOLATE BREAD PUDDING

We do not have to urge the children to "save room" for this simple, nourishing dessert.

Oven temperature: preheat to 375°F.
Baking time: 8 to 10 minutes

Yield: 6 servings
Pan: individual custard cups, well greased

1 cup soft bread crumbs
⅓ cup granulated sugar
1 six-ounce package chocolate bits
1 tablespoon butter
2 cups milk

1 egg, beaten
¼ teaspoon cinnamon
½ teaspoon vanilla
¼ teaspoon nutmeg
¼ teaspoon salt

1. In top of double boiler, place crumbs, sugar, chocolate bits, butter, and 1½ cups milk. Cook until chocolate melts thoroughly.
2. In separate bowl, combine egg, ½ cup milk, cinnamon, vanilla, nutmeg, and salt. Add to chocolate mixture.
3. Cook, stirring constantly, until thickened.
4. Pour into 6 well greased individual custard cups.
5. Bake at 375°F. for 8 to 10 minutes or until quite bubbly.
6. Serve warm, or chill and serve with whipped cream.

COTTAGE PUDDING

Still an effective dessert.

Oven temperature: preheat to 400°F.
Baking time: 25 to 30 minutes

Yield: 6 servings
Pan: 8"x8"x2" square pan, buttered and floured

¼ cup butter or margarine
½ cup granulated sugar
1 egg, unbeaten
½ teaspoon lemon extract
1½ cups all-purpose flour, sifted

2 teaspoons double-acting baking powder
½ teaspoon salt
½ cup milk

1. Cream butter or margarine with sugar until light and fluf
2. Add egg and beat well. Add lemon extract.
3. Sift flour once before measuring. Mix and sift flour, bak
powder, and salt together.
4. Add sifted dry ingredients alternately with milk, mi
thoroughly after each addition.
5. Pour into buttered and floured 8"x8"x2" square pan.
6. Bake at 400°F. for 25 to 30 minutes. Serve warm with
sauce, chocolate sauce, or with sweetened fresh or canned

CRANBERRY DESSERT

Quite a different, easy-to-make "little" dessert.

Oven temperature: preheat to
  350°F.
Baking time: 45 minutes

Yield: 4 to 6 servin
Pan: 8"x8"x2" squ
  greased or butt

1 cup brown sugar,
  firmly packed
½ cup all-purpose flour
1 cup quick-cooking rolled
  oats

½ teaspoon salt
½ cup butter
1¾ cups cranberry sauce,
  jellied or whole
1 tablespoon lemon juice

1. In mixing bowl, put brown sugar, flour, rolled oats, and salt. Blend together.
2. With two table knives or pastry blender, cut butter into dry ingredients until mixture is crumbly.
3. Spread half of crumb mixture evenly over bottom of buttered or greased 8"x8"x2" pan. Spread cranberries over crumbs. Sprinkle lemon juice over berries. Top with remaining crumb mixture.
4. Bake at 350°F. for 45 minutes.
5. Serve with ice cream.

CREAM PUFFS OR ÉCLAIRS

What effect these always achieve, yet they are no trouble to whip up! Freeze some to fill with ice cream later, or freeze them with ice cream filling and take them right to the table.

Oven temperature: preheat to 390°F.
Baking time: 25 minutes

Servings: 24 large puffs, or eclairs, or 5 dozen 1" puffs
Pan: greased and floured cookie sheet

1 cup boiling water
¼ teaspoon salt
½ cup butter

1 cup all-purpose flour, sifted
4 eggs, unbeaten

1. Start water boiling in pan large enough to accommodate all ingredients.
2. When water is boiling, add salt and butter.
3. Sift flour once before measuring. To the boiling mixture, add the flour all at once, stirring constantly until the mixture leaves the sides of the pan.
4. Remove pan from heat. Add unbeaten eggs, one at a time, beating continually.
5. Drop 2-inch rounds of dough on greased and floured cookie sheet, heaping the dough up in the center. Use smaller amount for miniature puffs. Allow 2 inches between the puffs. Elongate the dough for éclairs.
6. Bake at 390°F. for 20 minutes. *REDUCE* temperature to 350°F. Bake 5 minutes more, or until done. Puffs are done when a test puff does not fall when removed from oven.
7. Cool, then cut gash in side of each puff to fill.
Note: Good fillings are whipped cream, ice cream, custard, or flavored cream fillings. Ice éclairs with any chocolate icing.

DATE-NUT PUDDING

Sometimes called a torte.

Oven temperature: preheat to 325°F.
Baking time: 20 to 40 minutes

Yield: about 6 servings
Pan: 8 or 9-inch soufflé dish

3 eggs, separated (beat
  whites until stiff, not dry)
1 cup dates, chopped
½ cup blanched almonds,
  chopped

½ cup walnut meats,
  chopped
1 cup granulated sugar
2 tablespoons all-purpose
  flour
whipping cream for topping

1. Beat egg yolks until thick and lemon-colored.
2. Combine dates, nuts, sugar, flour, and egg yolks.
3. With pliable rubber scraper or whisk, gently fold in stiffly beaten egg whites.
4. Spread mixture into 8 or 9-inch soufflé dish.
5. Bake at 325°F. for 20 minutes, for soufflé-type texture; 35 to 40 minutes for more solid center.
6. Serve hot with whipped cream for pudding. Chill and serve with whipped cream for torte.

VIRGINIA'S LADY FINGER LEMON CAKE

This piquant dessert is very successful.

Oven temperature: preheat to
  350°F.
Baking time: 25 minutes

Yield: approximately
  12 servings
Pan: 10-inch spring-form pan,
  well greased

24 lady fingers
8 eggs, separated (beat
  whites until stiff, not dry)
2½ cups sweetened
  condensed milk (2 cans)

juice of 4 lemons
1 teaspoon vanilla
½ pint whipping cream,
  whipped

1. Line well greased 10-inch spring-form pan with lady fingers split into halves, cut side facing inward.
2. Beat egg yolks well.
3. Add milk, lemon juice, and vanilla.
4. Add stiffly beaten egg whites to yolk mixture. Beat well.
5. Pour into pan lined with lady fingers.
6. Bake at 350°F. for 25 minutes. Remove sides of pan just before serving. Serve with whipped cream topping.

FAVORITE FRUIT DESSERT

What will your choice be? This is good made with peaches, apples, cherries, pineapple, or berries.

Oven temperature: preheat to
 350°F.
Baking time: about 30 minutes

Yield: approximately
 6 servings
Pan: 2-quart casserole or
 baking dish, well greased
 or buttered

2 to 3 cups fruit, fresh or
 canned
2 tablespoons lemon juice
½ cup granulated sugar
¼ cup brown sugar

1 cup all-purpose flour, sifted
½ teaspoon salt
1 teaspoon double-acting
 baking powder
1 egg, unbeaten

1. Place fruit evenly in bottom of well greased or buttered 2-quart casserole or baking dish. Sprinkle lemon juice over fruit.
2. In mixing bowl, put sugars, flour, salt, and baking powder. Add unbeaten egg and mix until crumbly.
3. With spoon, sprinkle crumbly mixture over fruit in casserole. Pour melted butter over top.
4. Bake at 350°F. for about 30 minutes, or until brown.

GRAHAM CRACKER PUDDING

The "youngsters" eight to eighty will find this most enjoyable.

Oven temperature: preheat to
 350°-375°F.
Baking time: 20 to 30 minutes

Yield: approximately
 10 servings
Pan: 9"x5"x3" loaf pan,
 greased

3 eggs, separated
1 cup granulated sugar
1 cup graham crackers,
 crumbled

½ teaspoon double-acting
 baking powder
½ teaspoon salt
½ cup nut meats, chopped
½ teaspoon vanilla

1. Beat egg yolks very well.
2. Combine sugar, crackers, baking powder, salt, and nuts completely. Add dry ingredients to egg yolks.
3. Beat egg whites until very frothy, and add with the vanilla to other mixture.
4. Pour batter into greased 9"x5"x3" loaf pan.
5. Bake at 350°-375°F. for 20 to 30 minutes. Test for doneness as you would cake.
Note: Serve with a vanilla or lemon sauce, or with whipped cream.

PEACH BETTY

Husbands ask for "seconds" when served this.

Oven temperature: preheat to 350°F.
Baking time: 45 minutes

Yields: 6 servings
Pan: 1½-quart baking dish, buttered

3 slices dry bread, torn in small bits
⅓ cup butter, melted
3 cups canned sliced peaches, drained
2 tablespoons lemon juice

½ cup warm water
¼ teaspoon nutmeg
¼ teaspoon cinnamon
¼ teaspoon salt
½ cup brown sugar, firmly packed

1. Mix bread crumbs with melted butter.
2. In 1½-quart buttered baking dish, arrange alternate layers of bread crumbs and peaches. Use crumbs for bottom and top layers.
3. Combine lemon juice, water, nutmeg, cinnamon, salt, and brown sugar. Mix well.
4. Pour liquid ingredients over top.
5. Bake at 350°F. for 45 minutes. Serve plain or with cream, ice cream, lemon, or hard sauce.
Note: If crumbs get too brown, cover dish.

PEACH CRUNCH

Fresh peach desserts are hard to beat. Try this one.

Oven temperature: preheat to
  350°F.
Baking time: about 25 minutes

Yield: approximately
  6 servings
Pan: 9"x9"x2" square pan,
  greased or buttered

4 or 5 ripe peaches, peeled
  and finely sliced
2 tablespoons granulated
  sugar
⅓ cup orange or pineapple
  juice
3 tablespoons butter or
  margarine

⅓ cup brown sugar,
  firmly packed
½ cup all-purpose flour,
  sifted
½ teaspoon cinnamon
½ teaspoon salt
½ cup cornflakes, crushed

1.   Arrange sliced peaches on bottom of greased or buttered 9"x9"x2" square pan. They should make a layer about 3/4 to 1 inch thick.
2.   Combine granulated sugar and fruit juice. Pour over peaches.
3.   Cream butter or margarine with brown sugar.
4.   Sift flour once before measuring. Mix and sift flour, cinnamon, and salt together. Combine crushed cornflakes with flour mixture.
5.   Mix sugar mixture and flour mixture together until crumbly. Spread on top of peaches.
6.   Bake at 350°F. for about 25 minutes.
7.   Serve hot with coffee cream, or cold with ice cream.
Note: For crunchier topping, use more cornflakes.

JOHNSTOWN PRUNE WHIP

An old Colorado recipe that tastes good made anywhere.

Oven temperature: preheat to
  350°F.
Baking time: 20 to 30 minutes

Yield: 4 to 6 servings
Pan: 1½-quart casserole,
  greased

1 teaspoon lemon juice
4 tablespoons powdered
  sugar
2 cups cooked prunes, pitted
  and finely chopped

6 egg whites, beaten until
  stiff, not dry
½ cup chopped nut meats, if
  desired
whipped cream for topping

1. Add lemon juice and 2 tablespoons sugar to chopped prunes.
2. With pliable rubber scraper or whisk, gently fold remaining
sugar into stiffly beaten egg whites.
3. Fold prune mixture and nuts into egg whites.
4. Gently pile into greased 1½-quart casserole.
5. Bake at 350°F. for 20 to 30 minutes, or until "set."
6. Serve cold with whipped cream.

RICE PUDDING

Any cookbook would be incomplete without this.

Oven temperature: preheat to
  325°F.
Baking time: about 2½ hours

Yield: 6 servings
Pan: 2-quart casserole,
  buttered

½ cup rice, washed
4 cups milk
½ teaspoon salt
½ cup granulated sugar
2 eggs, beaten

1 tablespoon butter
¼ teaspoon nutmeg
½ cup raisins
1 teaspoon vanilla
1 teaspoon lemon rind, grated
1 teaspoon lemon juice

1. To washed rice add all remaining ingredients. Mix well
2. Pour into buttered 2-quart casserole.
3. Bake at 325°F. for 1 hour, stirring occasionally.
4. Remove and add nutmeg, raisins, and vanilla.
5. Bake for about 1 or 2 hours longer, or until set.

NOTES

306

DIET BAKING

Low Calorie Apple Sauce Topping   308

Low Calorie-Low Cholesterol Buckwheat Cakes   308

Health Cake   309

Low Cholesterol Baking Powder Biscuits   310

No-Fat Buttermilk Pancakes   310

Low Cholesterol Pie Crust   311

Low Fat-Low Cholesterol White Bread   312

Diet Skillet Cake   313

Low Calorie Dessert Topping   314

Peanut Butter Balls   314

Most bakery breads, sweet rolls, and coffee cakes are high in fat (lard or butter), contain egg yolk, and preservatives, and are made from over-processed flours. For specialized diets, home-made baked products may be made with non-fat milk and low cholesterol vegetable oils, and egg yolks may be omitted.

For those on a specialized diet to lose weight, control choles-terol intake, keep sugar level low, or generally keep a sharp eye on nutrition, here is a collection of recipes that may be of interest. (Also see: High Protein Bread, page 36; Multi Flour Health Bread, page 35; Whole Wheat Bread or Rolls, page 40; and Whole Wheat or Graham Griddle Cakes, page 95.)

LOW CALORIE APPLE SAUCE TOPPING

Serve it warm over diet cakes or puddings.

2 tablespoons butter
¼ cup brown sugar,
   firmly packed

1 teaspoon cinnamon
1 sixteen-ounce can
   applesauce

1. Melt butter in sauce pan.
2. Stir in brown sugar and cinnamon. When completely dis-solved, add applesauce. Blend and heat mixture thoroughly.
Note: 3 tablespoons has 35 calories.

LOW CALORIE-LOW CHOLESTEROL
BUCKWHEAT CAKES

Yield: batter to serve 4 to 6

Pan: heavy griddle, skillet, or electric fry pan, *very* lightly oiled with corn oil; or greaseless type griddle or skillet

¾ cup all-purpose flour,
   sifted
1¼ cups buckwheat flour
½ teaspoon salt

5 teaspoons double-acting baking powder
2 cups non-fat milk
1 tablespoon blackstrap molasses

308

1. Sift flour once before measuring. Mix flour, buckwheat flour, salt, and baking powder together very well.
2. Put dry ingredients in pitcher or mixing bowl that pours. Make a well in center of dry ingredients. Add small amount of non-fat milk and blend quickly. Add remaining milk and molasses, using as few strokes as possible to mix all together.
3. Preheat griddle or skillet *very* lightly greased with corn oil. When a few drops of water sprinkled on hot cooking surface bounce and sputter, the temperature is right (about 400°F. on electric skillet).
4. Pour or spoon batter onto cooking surface in amount for desired size pancakes. When top of pancake is well covered with bubbles beginning to burst, turn pancake. *Turn only once.*
5. Serve immediately.
Note: About 78 calories per pancake.

HEALTH CAKE

Have your cake and eat your vitamins, too.

Oven temperature: preheat to 375°F.	Servings: 10 to 12 servings
Baking time: 45 minutes	Pan: 10″x5″x3″ loaf pan, greased and floured

1 pound seedless raisins	½ teaspoon salt
2 cups brown sugar, firmly packed	1 teaspoon baking soda dissolved in
2 cups hot water	1 tablespoon hot water
1 teaspoon ground cloves	2½ cups whole wheat flour, sifted, OR
1 teaspoon cinnamon	3 cups all-purpose flour, sifted
2 tablespoons butter or margarine	

1. For 5 minutes, boil together the raisins, brown sugar, 2 cups hot water, cloves, cinnamon, butter or margarine, and salt. Cool.
2. Dissolve soda in 1 tablespoon hot water. Add to raisin mixture.
3. Sift flour once before measuring. Mix flour a little at a time with boiled mixture, blending thoroughly after each addition.
4. Pour batter into greased and floured 10″x5″x3″ loaf pan.
5. Bake at 375°F. for 45 minutes.

LOW CHOLESTEROL BAKING POWDER BISCUITS

Oven temperature: preheat to
    450°F.
Baking time: 12 to 15 minutes

Yield: about 12 biscuits
Pan: ungreased cookie sheet

2 cups all-purpose flour,
    sifted
¾ teaspoon salt
4 teaspoons double-acting
    baking powder

¼ cup vegetable shortening
    (hydrogenated or
    emulsified)
⅔ to ¾ cup non-fat milk

1. Sift flour once before measuring. Mix and sift flour, salt, and
baking powder together.
2. With two table knives or pastry blender, cut shortening into
dry ingredients. Blend until consistency of corn meal.
3. Make a well in center of dry ingredients. Add small amount
of non-fat milk. Blend quickly. Add remaining milk, using as few
strokes as possible to blend two together.
4. On lightly floured board, roll or pat dough out 1/4 to 1/2 inch
thick, handling as little as possible.
5. With unfloured biscuit cutter, cut into desired size rounds.
Place on ungreased cookie sheet.
6. Bake at 450°F. for 12 to 15 minutes.

NO-FAT BUTTERMILK PANCAKES

Yield: batter to serve 2 to 3

Pan: heavy griddle, skillet, or
    electric fry pan, *very* lightly
    oiled with corn oil; or
    greaseless type griddle or
    skillet

1 teaspoon baking soda
1 cup buttermilk
1 egg, beaten

¾ cup all-purpose flour,
    sifted
¼ teaspoon salt

1. Stir soda into buttermilk. Add to beaten egg.

2. Sift flour once before measuring. Mix and sift flour and salt together.

3. Put dry ingredients in pitcher or mixing bowl that pours. Make a well in center of dry ingredients. Add small amount of liquid mixture. Blend quickly. Add remaining liquid mixture, using as few strokes as possible to blend the two together completely.

4. Preheat griddle or skillet *very* lightly oiled with corn oil. When few drops of water sprinkled on hot cooking surface bounce and sputter, the temperature is right (about 400°F. on electric skillet).

5. Pour or spoon batter onto cooking surface in amount for desired size pancake. When top of pancake is well covered with bubbles beginning to burst, turn pancake. *Turn only once.*

6. Serve immediately.

LOW CHOLESTEROL PIE CRUST

Yield: one 2 crust pie, or
  two pie shells

Pan: 8 or 9-inch pie plate

2½ cups all-purpose flour,
  sifted
1½ teaspoons salt

6 tablespoons water
9 tablespoons salad oil
  (vegetable)

1. Sift flour once before measuring. Mix and sift flour and salt together.

2. In mixing bowl, beat water and salad oil together until thickened. Add all at once to flour. Toss lightly with fork until combined completely.

3. Place dough between sheets of waxed paper. Roll out 1/8 inch thick in shape of circle, 11 or 12 inches in diameter.

4. Remove top sheet of waxed paper. Pick up remaining waxed paper with dough and place it on pie plate with paper side up. Peel off paper. Mend any breaks or tears by gently pressing with fingers.

LOW FAT-LOW CHOLESTEROL
WHITE BREAD

Oven temperature: preheat to
425°F.
Baking time: 45 to 50 minutes

Yield: 2 loaves
Pan: 9"x5"x3" loaf pans,
oiled with corn oil

1 cake yeast
¼ cup *lukewarm* water
2 cups non-fat milk, scalded
2 tablespoons granulated
sugar

2 teaspoons salt
6½ cups all-purpose flour,
sifted

1. In bowl large enough to accommodate raised dough, stir yeast into *lukewarm* water to dissolve.
2. Scald milk. Stir in sugar and salt. Cool to *lukewarm*. Add to yeast mixture.
3. Sift flour once before measuring.
4. Add 1/3 of flour. With electric mixer or spoon, beat batter until smooth and satiny. Add remaining flour gradually, changing from spoon or mixer to hands as the dough becomes stiffer.
5. Turn dough onto floured board. Knead until elastic (tight-feeling), smooth and no longer sticky enough to adhere to board, *OR* continue to knead in mixing bowl until all flour and dough are cleaned from sides of bowl by kneading process.
6. Grease bowl with corn oil. Put dough in it. Lightly grease exposed surface of dough with corn oil. Cover bowl with damp cloth, leaving edges on outside of bowl. Let rise in warm place (about 80°F.) until doubled in bulk.
7. When doubled in bulk, punch down the dough. Work the edges to center, turn dough bottom side up, and knead very lightly.
8. Lightly grease again with corn oil, re-cover with damp cloth and let rise again until almost doubled in bulk.
9. Punch dough down and divide into 2 equal parts.
10. Shape dough into loaves. Place in two 9"x5"x3" loaf pans, oiled with corn oil.
11. Brush tops with corn oil. Re-cover with damp cloth. Let rise until center of dough is well-rounded above pan.
12. Bake at 425°F. for 15 minutes. *REDUCE* oven temperature to 350°F. and bake 30 to 35 minutes longer, or until done.

13. Turn out immediately to cool on wire rack or across top of pans.

DIET SKILLET CAKE

A light, fluffy cake for fruit shortcake, or coffeecake.

Cooking temperature: 275°, or low heat
Cooking time: about 30 minutes

Servings: 6 to 8 servings
Pan: electric fry pan, or 9-inch skillet

1 egg, separated
¾ cup granulated sugar
1 cup plus 2 tablespoons cake flour, sifted
1½ teaspoons double-acting baking powder

½ teaspoon salt
3 tablespoons vegetable oil
½ cup skim, or low fat milk
1 teaspoon vanilla

1. Beat egg white in small bowl until frothy. Gradually beat in ¼ cup sugar. Beat until stiff, not dry.
2. Sift flour once before measuring. Mix and sift remaining sugar, flour, baking powder, and salt together. Put in mixing bowl.
3. To dry ingredients, add vegetable oil, milk, egg yolk, and vanilla. Beat until batter is smooth.
4. With pliable rubber scraper or whisk, gently fold in stiffly beaten egg white mixture.
5. Pour batter into lightly oiled electric fry pan, or 9-inch skillet. Cover with domed lid.
6. Cook over low stove heat, or in electric skillet set at 275°. for about 30 minutes.
7. Serve topped with fresh fruit for shortcake. For coffeecake, sprinkle top of unbaked batter with cinnamon, granulated sugar, and brown sugar. Chopped nut meats may be added, too, but they (sad, but true) are fattening!

313

LOW CALORIE DESSERT TOPPING

Made with powdered milk, this delicious topping boasts practically no calories.

½ cup ice water
1 tablespoon lemon juice
1 teaspoon vanilla

½ cup non fat dry-milk powder
3 tablespoons granulated sugar

1.   Chill bowl for whipping.
2.   Place in bowl the ice water, lemon juice, and vanilla. Sprinkle dry-milk powder on top.
3.   Beat with electric mixer or egg beater until stiff (about 10 minutes).
4.   Beat in sugar and continue beating until stiff enough to hold soft peaks (about 5 minutes).
5.   Use in place of any recipe calling for whipped cream topping. Makes 2½ cups.

VARIATIONS

Maple: Omit lemon juice. Substitute brown sugar. Use ½ teaspoon maple extract in place of vanilla.
Coffee: Omit lemon juice. Add 1 teaspoon instant coffee powder with vanilla.

PEANUT BUTTER BALLS

Little work to these healthful no-bakes.

Yield: 24 balls

⅓ cup honey
⅓ cup peanut butter
½ cup instant non-fat dry milk

½ cup gingersnaps, finely crushed
shredded coconut

1.   Blend honey and peanut butter.
2.   Mix in non-fat dry milk and crushed gingersnaps.
3.   Gently form dough into small balls.
4.   Roll in coconut.

314

MODERN MARVELS

Quick Apple Coffee Cake   316
Cheddar Cheese Balls   316
Apple-Lemon Dumplings   317
Quick Brioche   317
Caraway Cookies   318
Cherry-Meringue Cake   319
Individual Chocolate Soufflés   319
Dapple Pie   320
Chocolate Chiffon Cake   321
Devil's Food Crunch Cake   321
Orange Cream Chiffon Pie   322
Lemon Cream Chiffon Pie   323
Drop and Bake Quickies   323
Pudding and Fruit Pie   324
Hot Cross Buns   325
Upside Down Ginger Cake   325
Spice Coffee Cake   326
Pumpkin Pie Topping   327
Mocha Topping   327
Chocolate Dream Topping   327
Fruit Topping   327
Quick Rum Dumplings   327
Quick Walnut Pudding   328
Pineapple Filled Four-Layer Cake   329
Pear and Cheese Foldover Pie   330

The recipes in this section are all made with packaged mixes or ingredients. Most are quick to make, and interestingly new.

QUICK APPLE COFFEE CAKE

In a matter of minutes, make breakfast special.

Oven temperature: preheat to 400°F.
Baking time: 35 to 40 minutes

Yield: 6 to 8 servings
Pan: 9"x5"x3" loaf pan, greased

2 cups packaged biscuit mix
⅔ cup granulated sugar
1 egg, unbeaten
3 tablespoons salad oil or margarine, melted

⅔ cup milk
1 cup apples, cored, pared, and diced
¼ teaspoon nutmeg
1 teaspoon cinnamon

1.   Mix together the biscuit mix and sugar.
2.   Combine egg and salad oil or melted margarine with milk.
3.   Stir biscuit mixture into liquid ingredients. Beat 1/2 minute with electric mixer, or 30 strokes by hand.
4.   Stir in chopped apples, nutmeg, and cinnamon.
5.   Pour into greased 9"x5"x3" loaf pan.
6.   Bake at 400°F. for 35 to 40 minutes, or until done.
7.   Serve warm, or cool and serve.

CHEDDAR CHEESE BALLS

Rich and zippy. Novel to serve with soup.

Oven temperature: preheat to 450°F.
Baking time: 10 minutes

Yield: 2½ dozen balls
Pan: greased cookie sheet

1 cup packaged biscuit mix
½ cup cheddar cheese, grated
2 tablespoons mayonnaise

⅛ teaspoon garlic salt
⅓ cup milk or cream
¼ cup minced parsley
¼ cup minced chives

1.   With fork tines, lightly toss together the biscuit mix, grated cheese, mayonnaise, garlic salt, and milk or cream.
2.   Shape into balls 1/2 inch in diameter.
3.   Roll in mixture of parsley and chives. Place on greased cookie sheet.
4.   Bake at 450°F. for 10 minutes.

APPLE-LEMON DUMPLINGS

A quick dessert with an old-fashioned touch.

Oven temperature: preheat to
   400°F.
Baking time: 25 minutes

Yield: 5 servings
Pan: 10″x6″x2″ baking dish,
   buttered

¾ cup brown sugar,
   firmly packed
1 teaspoon cornstarch
½ teaspoon cinnamon
1 cup water
1 tablespoon lemon juice

1 tube refrigerated
   pan-ready biscuits
2 medium apples, cored,
   pared, and diced
2 tablespoons butter,
   softened
cream for topping

1.   In sauce pan combine brown sugar, cornstarch, cinnamon, and water. Cook until clear (about 5 minutes). Remove from heat.
2.   Add lemon juice.
3.   Stretch each biscuit into circle about 4 inches across.
4.   Put small amount of diced apple in middle of each biscuit. Dot with butter. Gather dough up over apple filling, and seal at center, making dough round and dumpling shaped.
5.   Put dumplings in buttered 10″x6″x2″ baking dish.
6.   Pour syrup around them.
7.   Bake at 375°F. for 25 minutes or until done. Serve warm with cream.

QUICK BRIOCHE

This French delicacy is easy if you begin with a hot-roll mix.

Oven temperature: preheat to
   375°F.
Baking time: 15 minutes

Yield: 18 rolls
Pan: 2½″x1¼″ muffin
   pan, greased

1 package hot-roll mix
¾ cup lukewarm water
3 egg yolks, beaten

melted butter
½ teaspoon lemon rind,
   grated

1. Stir yeast from package into lukewarm water to dissolve.
2. Add beaten egg yolks. Mix well.
3. Thoroughly blend in hot roll mix and lemon rind. Cover with damp cloth. Let rise in warm place (about 80°F.) until dough is double in bulk (about 45 minutes).
4. Shape three-fourths of dough into 18 rolls.
5. Place rolls in greased 2½″x1¼″ muffin pan cups. Press large indention into top of each roll; brush well with melted butter.
6. Divide remaining dough into 18 parts; shape into balls.
7. Press one ball into indention of each roll.
8. Cover with damp cloth and let rise in warm place until light (30 to 60 minutes).
9. Bake at 375°F. for 15 minutes.

CARAWAY COOKIES

Oven temperature: preheat to 350°F.
Baking time: 6 minutes

Yield: approximately 8 dozen small cookies
Pan: greased cookie sheet

1½ cups pancake mix
¾ cup granulated sugar
1 tablespoon caraway seeds
2 egg yolks plus
   1 tablespoon water
½ cup canned applesauce

2 tablespoons butter, melted
½ teaspoon lemon rind, grated
½ teaspoon orange rind, grated

1. Combine pancake mix, ½ cup sugar, and caraway seeds in bowl.
2. Slightly beat egg yolks with water in separate bowl. Blend in applesauce and melted butter.
3. Stir egg mixture into dry ingredients. Mix together very well.
4. Drop by half-teaspoonfuls onto greased cookie sheet.
5. Mix ¼ cup sugar and orange and lemon rinds together. Sprinkle this mixture on top of cookies, being careful not to let sugar fall on cookie sheet.
6. Bake at 350°F. for 6 minutes, or until cookies are slightly brown around edges.

CHERRY-MERINGUE CAKE

Our children shout hurrahs for this cake.

Oven temperature: preheat to 400°F.
Baking time: about 15 minutes

Yield: 8 to 10 servings
Pan: two 8-inch layer pans

1 package yellow cake mix, baked in two 8-inch layer pans
3 egg whites, beaten until stiff, not dry
¼ teaspoon cream of tartar
6 tablespoons granulated sugar
1 No. 303 can pitted Bing cherries

1 tablespoon quick-cooking tapioca
1 teaspoon orange rind, grated
1 tablespoon lemon juice
¼ cup orange juice
¼ cup honey
few drops red food coloring
2 tablespoons butter or margarine

1. Make, bake, and cool cake, following directions on package.
2. Beat egg whites with cream of tartar until almost stiff.
3. Slowly add sugar, continuing to beat egg whites until stiff, not dry.
4. Spread meringue on top and sides of one cake layer. (Save the other layer for another occasion.)
5. Bake at 400°F. about 15 minutes, or until meringue is golden brown.
6. Drain cherries. Stir juice and tapioca in saucepan.
7. Add orange rind, lemon and orange juices, honey, food coloring, and butter or margarine.
8. Cook over medium heat, stirring constantly, until thickened and clear. Add cherries. Remove from heat. Cool.
9. Serve sauce over meringue covered cake wedges.

INDIVIDUAL CHOCOLATE SOUFFLÉS

Finish dinner with a flourish.

Oven temperature: preheat to 350°F.
Baking time: 25 minutes

Yield: 8 servings
Pan: individual custard cups, well greased

319

1 package chocolate pudding
  (not instant type)
¼ teaspoon salt
1¼ cups milk

3 eggs, separated (beat
  whites until stiff, not dry)
1 teaspoon vanilla
coffee cream or chocolate
  sauce for topping

1. In sauce pan, blend pudding mix, salt, and milk. Cook over medium heat, stirring constantly, until mixture is thickened.
2. Beat egg yolks. Slowly beat some of hot mixture into beaten egg yolks, being careful not to curdle mixture.
3. Remove from heat. Add vanilla.
4. With pliable rubber scraper or whisk, gently fold in stiffly beaten egg whites.
5. Pour into well greased individual custard cups. Place cups in pan of hot water.
6. Bake at 350°F. for 25 minutes. Serve hot with coffee cream or chocolate sauce.

DAPPLE PIE

Canned apples and ready mixes are combined to make an interesting dessert.

Oven temperature: preheat to
  400°F.
Baking time: 30 minutes

Yield: 6 to 8 servings
Pan: 9-inch pie plate

9-inch pie shell, unbaked
  (make your own, or use pie
  crust mix)

1 package date-bar mix
4 cups canned apples (two
  No. 2 cans)

1. Place unbaked pie shell in 9-inch pie plate.
2. Mix crumb mixture in one bowl. Mix date filling in another bowl. Add water to each, following directions on date-bar mix package.
3. Stir canned apples and juice into date mixture.
4. Spoon apple and date mixture into pie shell.
5. Top with crumb mixture.
6. Bake at 400°F. for 30 minutes, or until top of pie is golden brown.
Note: This pie is delicious served with vanilla ice cream.

CHOCOLATE CHIFFON CAKE

Marvelous packaged mixes help you make this cake in a jiffy.

Oven temperature and baking
time: follow directions on
cake mix package

Pan: two 8-inch layer pans
Yield: 8 to 10 servings

1 package sponge or chiffon
cake mix, baked in two
8-inch layers
2 ounces chocolate, melted
½ cup granulated sugar
¼ teaspoon salt

1 package dessert topping
mix
½ cup cold milk
½ teaspoon vanilla
½ cup water

1.   Make, bake, and cool cake according to directions on packages.
2.   Melt chocolate in water over low heat.
3.   Add sugar and salt to melted chocolate. Bring to boil and cook
3 minutes, stirring constantly. Cool.
4.   Whip dessert topping with milk and vanilla, following directions on package.
5.   Fold cooled chocolate mixture into whipped mixture. Mix
together well, but carefully.
6.   Split sponge or chiffon layers in half, to make 4 thin layers.
7.   Spread each layer with chocolate fluffy mix, making a four-
layer cake. (There will not be enough fluff for sides of cake.)
8.   Chill 4 hours, or overnight.
Note: If you wish, sprinkle grated chocolate over top.

DEVIL'S FOOD CRUNCH CAKE

A crunchy-coated modern version of chocolate cake.

Oven temperature and baking
time: follow directions on
cake-mix package

Pan: two 9-inch layer pans,
ungreased
Yield: 8 to 10 servings

⅔ cup walnut or almond
meats, chopped
½ cup butter, melted
½ cup granulated sugar
¼ cup brown sugar,
firmly packed
⅛ teaspoon salt

⅔ cup packaged dried bread
crumbs
1 package devil's food cake
mix
½ pint whipping cream,
whipped

1. Combine chopped nut meats with melted butter, sugars, salt, and bread crumbs.
2. Use one-half bread crumb mixture to line bottom of *ungreased* 9-inch layer cake pan. Press crumbs firmly against bottom of pan. Use second half to line bottom of second layer pan.
3. Mix cake batter according to directions on package.
4. Pour batter into crumb-lined cake pans.
5. Bake, following directions on cake-mix package.
6. Cool in pans for 15 to 20 minutes.
7. Remove cake from pans. Cool, crunch-side up.
8. To serve, place one cake layer, crunch-side down. Spread generously with whipped cream. Place second layer, crunch-side up, on top of whipped cream filling. (If you have any whipped cream left, put spoonfuls on top of cake.)

ORANGE CREAM CHIFFON PIE

A celestial concoction!

Yield: 8 servings   Pan: 9-inch pie plate

1 package orange-flavored
  gelatin
1 cup hot water
1 eight-ounce package
  cream cheese
¼ cup granulated sugar

¼ cup orange juice
1 teaspoon lemon juice
½ pint whipping cream
9-inch pie shell, baked (make
  your own or use pie-crust
  mix

1. Dissolve gelatin in 1 cup hot water.
2. With electric mixer or egg beater, beat cream cheese until smooth.
3. Beat in sugar, and orange and lemon juices.
4. Gradually beat in dissolved gelatin. Refrigerate until almost set.
5. When mixture is almost set, beat the whipped cream into gelatin.
6. Pour into cooled, baked pie shell. Refrigerate well before serving.

LEMON CREAM CHIFFON PIE

Use recipe for Orange Cream Pie. Substitute 2 tablespoons lemon juice for juices, and 1 package lemon gelatin for orange gelatin.

DROP AND BAKE QUICKIES

Even when you are rushed, you will have time for biscuits if you begin with a mix.

Oven temperature: preheat to 450°F.
Baking time: 10 to 12 minutes

Yield: 10 to 12 biscuits
Pan: muffin pan or cookie sheet, greased

1 recipe drop biscuit dough

Make as directed on biscuit mix package. Choose variation you wish.

BUTTER-NUT GOLDIES

½ cup brown sugar, firmly packed
¼ cup honey
¼ teaspoon cinnamon

2 tablespoons butter, softened
¼ cup coconut or nut meats, chopped

1. Mix brown sugar, honey, cinnamon, butter, and coconut or nuts together well.
2. Spoon 1 tablespoon mixture into bottom of greased muffin pan cups.
3. Drop biscuit dough by spoonful on top of butter-nut mixture.
4. Bake at 450°F. for 10 to 12 minutes, or until golden brown.

PIMENTO CHEESE QUICKIES

1 four-ounce glass processed pimento cheese spread

2 tablespoons butter

1. In top of double boiler, melt pimento cheese spread. Add butter and mix together very well.
2. Drop biscuit dough onto greased cookie sheet as you would for drop biscuits.
3. Make a small well in center of each biscuit and fill with melted cheese mixture.

1.   Drop biscuit dough by spoonfuls into greased muffin cups. Make a small well in center of each biscuit and fill with variation of your choice:
1 teaspoon raspberry jam, *OR*
½ teaspoon pickle relish and ½ teaspoon chili sauce, *OR*
½ teaspoon honey and sprinkle of nutmeg, *OR*
1 teaspoon drained crushed pineapple plus sprinkle of brown sugar, *OR*
1 teaspoon apricot jam, *OR*
brown sugar mixed with butter, coconut and chopped nuts, *OR*
melted butter mixed with garlic salt and mixed dried herbs, *OR*
1 cube butter and 1 small package cream cheese mixed together.

PUDDING AND FRUIT PIE

There are almost as many versions of this as there are fruits.

Yield: 6 to 8 servings   Pan: 9-inch pie plate

1½ cups milk
1 package vanilla pudding (not instant)
½ cup whipping cream, whipped
9-inch pie shell or crumb crust, baked

2 cups fresh or fresh-frozen whole, blueberries, strawberries, raspberries, peaches or pineapple
1 tablespoon cornstarch, *OR*
2 tablespoons all-purpose flour
¼ cup granulated sugar
¼ teaspoon salt
1 tablespoon lemon juice

1.   Add milk to vanilla pudding mix. Cook, stirring constantly, until thickened. Chill.
2.   Fold whipped cream into cooled pudding. Pour into baked 9-inch pie shell. Refrigerate.
3.   In saucepan mash 1/2 of desired fruit. Add cornstarch or flour, sugar, salt, and lemon juice. Cook, stirring constantly, until thickened and clear. Add remaining half of fruit. Cool.
4.   Spoon fruit over chilled filling. Refrigerate.

HOT CROSS BUNS

So easy to make if you start from a hot-roll mix! Inexpensive, too.

Oven temperature: preheat to 400°F.
Baking time: 15 to 20 minutes

Yield: 16 buns
Pan: 8″x8″x2″ square pan, well greased

1 package hot-roll mix
½ cup seedless raisins
3 tablespoons citron, chopped
2 tablespoons granulated sugar
¼ teaspoon salt

½ teaspoon cinnamon
¼ teaspoon nutmeg
½ cup powdered sugar, sifted
1 tablespoon warm milk
⅛ teaspoon vanilla

1.   Stir together the hot-roll mix, raisins, citron, sugar, salt, cinnamon, and nutmeg.
2.   Prepare dough as directed on roll-mix package, following instructions carefully.
3.   Cover with damp cloth and let rise in warm place (about 80°F.) until dough is double in bulk (about 45 minutes).
4.   When dough is doubled in bulk, shape into 16 ball-like buns.
5.   Place close together in well greased 8″x8″x2″ pan.
6.   Let rise in warm place until dough is doubled in bulk.
7.   When dough is doubled in bulk, cut small cross in each bun with scissors.
8.   Bake at 400°F. for 15 to 20 minutes, or until light golden brown.
9.   Combine powdered sugar, milk, and vanilla. Mix until smooth. Fill crosses with icing.

UPSIDE DOWN GINGER CAKE

This is good with peaches, pears, or pineapple.

Oven temperature: preheat to 375°F.
Baking time: 40 minutes

Yield: 6 servings
Pan: 9″x9″x2″ square pan

¼ cup butter, melted
1 cup brown sugar,
fimly packed
1 No. 2½ can peach or
pear halves, or pineapple
slices, well drained
1 package gingerbread mix
cream for topping or
whipped cream for topping

1. Melt butter. Blend in brown sugar. Spread on bottom of 9"x9"x2" square pan.
2. Arrange pineapple slices or peach or pear halves (cut side up) on top of sugar mixture.
3. Prepare gingerbread mix, following directions on package. Pour over fruit.
4. Bake at 375°F. for 40 minutes. Cool.
5. Cut into squares. Serve fruit side up. Pour coffee cream over top, or top with whipped cream.

SPICE COFFEE CAKE

For breakfast, brunch, or tea.

Oven temperature: preheat to 350°F.
Baking time: 30 to 35 minutes

Yield: 12 to 14 servings
Pan: 13"x9"x2" oblong pan, greased and floured

1 package yellow or
spice cake mix
½ cup butter, softened
2 tablespoons all-purpose
flour

½ cup granulated sugar
1 teaspoon cinnamon
1½ cups walnut or pecan
meats, chopped

1. Prepare yellow or spice cake mix according to directions on package.
2. Pour batter into greased and floured 13"x9"x2" oblong pan..
3. Bake at 350°F. for 15 minutes.
4. Mix together butter, flour, sugar, and cinnamon until crumbly. Add nutmeats. Sprinkle over top of partially baked cake.
5. Continue baking at 350°F. for 15 to 20 minutes, or until cake is done.

PUMPKIN PIE TOPPING

1 package dessert
  topping-mix

½ teaspoon nutmeg
½ teaspoon cinnamon

Whip dessert topping-mix following directions on package. Add spices.

MOCHA TOPPING

1 package dessert
  topping-mix

2 teaspoons instant coffee
3 teaspoons powdered sugar

Whip dessert topping-mix according to directions on package. Add instant coffee and powdered sugar and mix very well.

CHOCOLATE DREAM TOPPING
(For Cakes or Chiffon Pies)

1 package dessert
  topping-mix

2 tablespoons granulated sugar
2 tablespoons cocoa

Whip dessert topping-mix according to directions on package. Add cocoa and sugar to mixture and mix very well.

FRUIT TOPPING

1 package dessert
  topping-mix

¼ cup crushed strawberries

Whip dessert topping-mix according to directions on package. Add crushed strawberries and mix very well.
Note: Crushed pineapple may be used in place of strawberries.

QUICK RUM DUMPLINGS

An interesting variation of bread pudding.

Oven temperature: preheat to
  375°F.
Baking time: 30 minutes

Yield: 6 servings
Pan: 8″x8″x2″ square pan,
  greased

1 tube refrigerated,
  pan-ready biscuits
1 cup syrup from canned
  fruit (water may be
  substituted)

¾ cup brown sugar,
  firmly packed
2 tablespoons butter, melted
1 teaspoon rum extract
cream or whipped cream
  for topping

1.   Arrange pan-ready biscuits in bottom of greased 8″x8″x2″ square pan.
2.   Bake at 375°F. for 6 minutes.
3.   In saucepan mix together syrup or water, brown sugar, melted butter, and rum extract. Bring to boiling point.
4.   Pour liquid mixture over partially baked biscuits.
5.   Bake at 375°F. for 25 minutes more.
6.   Serve warm with cream, or cool to lukewarm and serve topped with whipped cream.

QUICK WALNUT PUDDING

Biscuit mix gives you a head start here.

Oven temperature: preheat to
  375°F.
Baking time: 30 minutes

Yield: 6 servings
Pan: 10″x6″x2″ oblong pan,
  greased

1 cup packaged biscuit mix
½ cup walnut meats, chopped
½ cup light cream
½ cup water
½ cup maple syrup
¾ cup brown sugar,
  firmly packed

2 tablespoons butter
1 teaspoon nutmeg
1 teaspoon cinnamon
coffee or whipped cream
  for topping

1.   Mix together biscuit mix, walnut meats, and cream. Spread unevenly on bottom of greased 10″x6″x2″ oblong pan.
2.   In saucepan, heat to boiling point water, syrup, brown sugar, butter, nutmeg and cinnamon. Pour over dough.
3.   Bake at 375°F. for 30 minutes. Serve warm with cream, or top with whipped cream.

PINEAPPLE FILLED FOUR-LAYER CAKE

A most glamorous torte, yet made from a mix.

Oven temperature and baking time: follow directions on cake mix package

Pan: 8-inch layer pans
Yield: 10 to 12 servings

1 package white-cake mix, baked in two 8-inch layer pans
½ cup granulated sugar
1 tablespoon cornstarch
¼ teaspoon salt
2 egg yolks, unbeaten
2½ cups canned crushed pineapple (No. 2 can),

1 cup marshmallows, cut up
1 cup walnut meats, chopped
¼ cup maraschino cherries, halved
½ cup whipping cream, whipped
1 tablespoon powdered sugar
½ teaspoon vanilla
2 tablepsoons rum or sherry, if desired

1. Make, bake, and cool cake according to directions on package.
2. In saucepan, combine granulated sugar, cornstarch, and salt. Mix together. Add egg yolks. Beat well.
3. Stir in undrained pineapple.
4. Cook over medium heat, stirring constantly, until mixture is thickened. Refrigerate until cold.
5. Split each cooled cake layer, making 4 layers in all.
6. Stir marshmallows, nuts, and cherries into cold pineapple mixture. Spread filling bewteen layers.
7. Whip cream. Stir in powdered sugar, vanilla, and rum or sherry.
8. Top cake with whipped cream. Refrigerate cake for 3 to 4 hours before serving.

PEAR AND CHEESE FOLDOVER PIE

A light, refreshing dessert after a hearty dinner.

Oven temperature: preheat to
  425°F.
Baking time: 30 minutes

Yield: 6 servings
Pan: large cookie sheet,
  ungreased

2 teaspoons orange rind,
  grated
½ cup brown sugar,
  firmly packed
1 teaspoon cinnamon

½ cup sharp cheese, grated
1 package pie crust mix
3 pears, halved, peeled, and
  cored
cream for topping

1. Mix grated orange rind with brown sugar and cinnamon.
2. Add grated cheese to piecrust mixture. Mix according to directions on package.
3. On large ungreased cookie sheet, roll pastry into 20"x10" rectangle ⅛ inch thick.
4. Put peeled and cored pears on half of pastry rectangle.
5. Sprinkle sugar mixture over pears.
6. Fold other half of pastry rectangle over pears. Use spatula to loosen pastry from cookie sheet, if necessary.
7. Press edges together with fork to seal. Prick top to allow steam to escape.
8. Bake at 425°F. for 30 minutes or until done. Cool.
9. Serve with cream flavored with sugar and nutmeg.
Note: Canned pears, drained, may be substituted for fresh pears. *REDUCE* baking time to 20 minutes.

EASY TO MAKE RECIPES
FOR JUNIOR BAKERS

Apple Delight	332
Nut Bread	333
Three-in-One Cake	334
Crazy Cake	336
Orange Coffee Cake and Topping	336
Oatmeal Cookies	338
Chocolate Icing	339
Sugar Cookies	340
Chocolate Sauce	341
Chocolate Cookies	342
Ginger Cookies	343
Guy's Meat Pasties	344
Peanut Drop Cookies	345
Individual Pizzas	346
Hot Dog Roll-ups	347
Joanie's Cheese Pie	348
Foolproof Caramel Icing	349
Pizza Burgers	350
Silver Dollar Pancakes	351
Quick Short Cake	352
Jam Tarts	353
Lunch Box Tarts	354
Easy Waffles	355

APPLE DELIGHT

The flavor is as nice as the name.

START HERE

Heat oven to 375°F.

Grease and flour 9″x9″x2″
square baking pan

When you use measuring spoons, run table knife across top of spoon to make ingredient even with spoon edge.

When you use measuring cups, have ingredient even with measuring mark. Do not shake flour down in cup. Pack brown sugar firmly in cup.

INGREDIENTS YOU'LL NEED

2½ cups applesauce
   (No. 2 can)
2 tablespoons sugar
¼ teaspoon cinnamon
¼ teaspoon nutmeg
½ cup quick-cooking
   rolled oats

½ cup brown sugar, packed
½ cup flour
½ teaspoon double-acting
   baking powder
¼ teaspoon salt
1 cube butter or
   margarine, soft

HOW TO MIX INGREDIENTS

1.   In mixing bowl, mix applesauce, sugar, cinnamon, and nutmeg together.
2.   Pour into greased and floured square baking pan.
3.   In same mixing bowl, put rolled oats, brown sugar, flour, baking powder, salt, and soft butter or margarine.
4.   With fork, or wooden spoon, toss or mix together. Mixture will be crumbly.
5.   Sprinkle crumb mixture over applesauce mixture.

HERE'S HOW TO BAKE AND SERVE IT

1.   Bake at 375°F. for 25 to 30 minutes.
2.   Serve hot with cream if you wish. Makes 6 to 8 servings.

NUT BREAD

A recipe from a 7th grader who "loves to make and eat it!"

START HERE

Heat oven to 350°F.

Prepare 9″x5″x3″ loaf pan; grease bottom and sprinkle lightly with flour

When you use measuring spoons, run table knife across top of spoon to make ingredient even with spoon edge.

When you use measuring cups, have ingredient even with measuring mark. Do not shake biscuit mix down in cup. Pack brown sugar firmly in cup.

INGREDIENTS YOU'LL NEED

2 cups biscuit mix
1/8 teaspoon baking soda
1/4 cup brown sugar, packed
1/4 cup sugar

1/2 cup nut meat pieces
1 egg, beaten
2/3 cup milk

HOW TO MIX INGREDIENTS

1.   In mixing bowl, place biscuit mix, soda, brown sugar, sugar, and nuts. Mix together until blended.
2.   Beat egg and milk together. Add to biscuit mixture. Beat well.
3.   Pour batter into greased and floured loaf pan.

HERE'S HOW TO BAKE AND SERVE IT

1.   Bake at 350°F. for about 1 hour, or until done. Cool.
2.   Serve warm if you wish. Or toast thin slices in pop-up toaster, and serve with butter.

THREE-IN-ONE CAKE

Use this recipe to make gold, chocolate, or spice cake.

START HERE

Heat oven to 375°F.

Prepare two 8-inch layer pans; grease and sprinkle lightly with flour

When you use measuring spoons, run table knife across top of spoon to make ingredient even with spoon edge.

When you use measuring cups, have ingredient even with measuring mark. Do not shake flour or sugar down in cup.

INGREDIENTS YOU'LL NEED

Gold Cake

1 cup sugar
½ cup shortening
2 eggs, beaten
2 cups flour
1½ teaspoons double-acting baking powder

½ teaspoon salt
¾ cup plus 1 tablespoon milk
1 teaspoon vanilla

Chocolate Cake

Use ingredients listed above for gold cake except for the flour. Use 1½ cups flour and ½ cup cocoa.

Spice Cake

Use ingredients listed above for gold cake.
Add ½ teaspoon nutmeg, ¼ teaspoon ground cloves, 1 teaspoon cinnamon, and ½ cup raisins, if you like them.

HOW TO MIX INGREDIENTS

1. In mixing bowl, mix sugar and shortening together until fluffy.
2. Add beaten eggs. Beat very well.
3. Sift flour once before measuring. Measure flour. Add baking

powder and salt to flour. *For chocolate cake,* add cocoa to flour, too. *For spice cake,* add spices to flour.

4.   Add 1/2 of milk to sugar mixture. Beat very hard for 1 minute.

5.   Add 1/2 of flour to sugar mixture. Beat very hard for 1 minute.

6.   Add other 1/2 of milk. Beat. Add other 1/2 of flour. Beat well.

7.   Stir in vanilla (and raisins if you are making spice cake and want to put raisins in it.)

8.   Pour batter into greased and floured cake pans. Cut through batter with table knife to release air bubbles.

HERE'S HOW TO BAKE AND SERVE IT

1.   Bake at 375°F. for 25 to 30 minutes. Do not peek, or bang oven door, during baking.

2.   The cake is done when you touch it lightly on top and it springs back. If your finger leaves a print, the cake needs more baking. You may also use a toothpick, cake tester, or broomstraw for testing to see if a cake is done. Stick the toothpick, cake tester, or broomstraw in the thickest part of the cake. Pull it out. If it is clean and has no sticky batter clinging to it, the cake is done.

3.   Let cake cool in pans for 5 minutes. Turn cake in pans over on a wire rack. Remove pans.

4.   Let cake cool before frosting.

5.   Frost with your favorite icing.

6.   Cake makes about 10 pieces.

CRAZY CAKE

It's crazy and mixed-up, but fun to make because it's so easy.

START HERE

Heat oven to 350°F.   Have ready ungreased 8"x10"
                               cake pan

When you use measuring spoons, run table knife across top of spoon to make ingredient even with spoon edge.

When you use measuring cups, have ingredient even with measuring mark. Do not shake flour down in cup.

INGREDIENTS YOU'LL NEED

1½ cups flour   1 teaspoon vanilla
1 cup sugar   1 tablespoon vinegar
1 teaspoon baking soda   6 tablespoons salad oil
3 tablespoons cocoa   1 cup water

HOW TO MIX INGREDIENTS

1. Into ungreased cake pan sift flour, sugar, soda, and cocoa.
2. Mix with a fork to blend.
3. With a mixing spoon, make three holes in dry mixture.
4. In first hole, place vanilla. In second hole, place vinegar. In third hole, place salad oil.
5. Pour water over all. Stir with fork to make dry ingredients moist. Do *not* beat.

HERE'S HOW TO BAKE IT

1. Bake at 350°F. for about 35 minutes. Cool.
2. Top with any favorite frosting or sauce. Serves 6.

ORANGE COFFEE CAKE AND TOPPING

Try making this for breakfast on Mother's Day, or any special holiday.

START HERE

Heat oven to 425°F.   Grease 8-inch round layer
                               cake pan

When you use measuring spoons, run table knife across top of spoon to make ingredient even with spoon edge.

When you use measuring cups, have ingredients even with measuring mark. Do not shake biscuit mix or sugar down in cup. Pack brown sugar firmly into cup.

INGREDIENTS YOU'LL NEED

2 cups biscuit mix ⅔ ·cup milk
¼ cup sugar ½ cup nut meat pieces
2 eggs, beaten

HOW TO MIX INGREDIENTS

1. In mixing bowl, place biscuit mix, and sugar. Mix.
2. Beat eggs and milk together. Add to biscuit mix mixture. Blend well.
3. Stir in nuts. Make topping while cake is baking.

HERE'S HOW TO BAKE IT

Bake at 425°F. for about 25 minutes.

HOW TO MAKE TOPPING

⅓ cup melted butter ½ cup nut meat pieces
⅔ cup brown sugar, packed ½ cup orange juice
½ cup grated orange rind

1. Mix butter and brown sugar together. Spread over warm cake.
2. Sprinkle grated orange rind and nuts over butter and sugar mixture.
3. Pour orange juice over all.
4. Place under broiler until bubbly.
5. Serve warm. Makes 6 to 8 servings.

OATMEAL COOKIES

Crisp and crunchie goodies.

START HERE

Heat oven to 400°F.   Grease cookie sheet

When you use measuring spoons, run table knife across top of spoon to make ingredient even with spoon edge.

When you use measuring cups, have ingredient even with measuring mark. Do not shake flour or sugar down in cup.

INGREDIENTS YOU'LL NEED

1 cup sugar

1 cup shortening

2 eggs, beaten

4 tablespoons water

2 cups flour

1 teaspoon baking soda

1 teaspoon cinnamon

1 teaspoon ground cloves

½ teaspoon salt

1 cup quick-cooking rolled oats

1 cup raisins

½ cup nut meat pieces

HOW TO MIX INGREDIENTS

1.   In mixing bowl, mix sugar and shortening together until fluffy.

2.   Add eggs. Beat very well. Add water.

3.   Sift flour once before measuring. Measure flour. Add baking soda, cinnamon, cloves, and salt to flour.

4.   Add a little flour to sugar mixture. Stir very well. Add a little more flour and stir well again. Keep adding flour a little at a time and stirring well, until all the flour has been well blended with sugar mixture.

5.   Stir in rolled oats, raisins, and nuts.

HERE'S HOW TO BAKE THEM

1.   On greased cookie sheet, drop rounded teaspoonfuls of dough. Space 2 inches apart.

2.   Bake at 400°F. for 12 to 15 minutes.

3.   Remove from cookie sheet and cool.

4.   There will be about 48 cookies.

CHOCOLATE ICING

Frost your favorite chocolate cake with this easy-make icing.

Have saucepan ready.

When you use measuring spoons, run table knife across top of spoon to make ingredient even with spoon edge.

When you use measuring cups, have ingredient even with measuring mark. Do not shake sugar down in cup.

INGREDIENTS YOU'LL NEED

1 cup sugar	3 tablespoons milk
2 tablespoons cocoa	¼ teaspoon salt
1 egg, beaten	½ teaspoon vanilla
2 tablespoons butter	

HOW TO MIX AND COOK INGREDIENTS

1. In saucepan, put sugar, cocoa, beaten egg, butter, milk, and salt.
2. Place pan on stove burner. Turn on to medium heat.
3. Bring to a rolling boil, stirring all the time. After it comes to a boil, cook 1 minute more.
4. Remove from heat. Let icing cool until it feels barely warm when you touch it.
5. Add vanilla.
6. Beat hard with spoon until icing is creamy and thick enough to spread on cake. It should not be runny.

SUGAR COOKIES

START HERE

Heat oven to 425°F.   Grease cookie sheet

When you use measuring spoons, run table knife across top of
spoon to make ingredient even with spoon edge.

When you use measuring cups, have ingredient even with
measuring mark. Do not shake flour or sugar down in cup.

INGREDIENTS YOU'LL NEED

4 tablespoons butter
1 cup sugar
1 egg, beaten
2 cups flour

1 teaspoon double-acting
  baking powder
¼ teaspoon salt
3 tablespoons milk
1 teaspoon vanilla

HOW TO MIX INGREDIENTS

1.   In mixing bowl, mix butter and sugar together until fluffy.
2.   Add egg. Beat very well.
3.   Sift flour once before measuring. Measure flour. Add baking
powder, and salt to flour.
4.   Add 1/2 of milk to sugar mixture. Beat very hard for 1
minute.
5.   Add 1/2 of flour to sugar mixture. Beat very hard for 1
minute.
6.   Add another 1/2 of milk. Beat. Add other 1/2 of flour. Beat
well.
7.   Stir in vanilla.
8.   Sprinkle bread board with a little flour. Place cookie dough
on floured board. Sprinkle top of dough with flour.
9.   Use rolling pin to roll out dough to ⅛ inch thick.
10. Dip cookie cutter in flour. Cut cookies with floured cookie
cutter.
11. Place on greased cookie sheet. Sprinkle tops with sugar.

1.   Bake at 425°F. for 5 to 6 minutes, or until light golden brown around edges.
2.   Remove from cookie sheet and cool. Makes about 40 cookies.

CHOCOLATE SAUCE

This is yummy over ice cream, puddings, or short cake.

START HERE

Have double-boiler ready.

When you use measuring spoons, run table knife across top of spoon to make ingredient even with spoon edge.

When you use measuring cups, have ingredient even with measuring mark. Do not shake sugar down in cup.

INGREDIENTS YOU'LL NEED

1 cup sugar	3 tablespoons cocoa
4 teaspoons flour	1 cup boiling water
¼ teaspoon salt	1 tablespoon butter

HOW TO MIX AND COOK INGREDIENTS

1.   Put water in bottom half of double boiler (check with mother if you're not sure about the right amount). Place pan on stove burner. Turn on to medium heat.
2.   In top of double boiler, place sugar, flour, salt, and cocoa. Stir together well.
3.   Add boiling water and butter. Stir to blend all ingredients.
4.   Bring to rolling boil, stirring all the time. After it comes to a boil, cook 1 minute more.
5.   Remove from heat.

CHOCOLATE COOKIES

Don't eat too many before dinner. These are so good you will want to.

START HERE

Heat oven to 400°F.   Grease cookie sheet

When you use measuring spoons, run table knife across top of spoon to make ingredient even with spoon edge.

When you use measuring cups, have ingredient even with measuring mark. Do not shake flour or sugar down in cup.

INGREDIENTS YOU'LL NEED

1 cup sugar	½ teaspoon salt
½ cup shortening	½ cup cocoa
1 egg, beaten	1 cup milk
2½ cups flour	1 teaspoon vanilla
2 teaspoons double-acting baking powder	½ cup nut meat pieces

HOW TO MIX INGREDIENTS

1.   In mixing bowl, mix sugar and shortening together until fluffy.
2.   Add egg. Beat very well.
3.   Sift flour once before measuring. Measure flour. Add baking powder, salt, and cocoa to flour.
4.   Add 1/2 of milk to sugar mixture. Beat very hard for 1 minute.
5.   Add 1/2 of flour to sugar mixture. Beat very hard for 1 minute.
6.   Add other 1/2 of milk. Beat. Add other 1/2 of flour. Beat well.
7.   Stir in vanilla and nuts.

HERE'S HOW TO BAKE THEM

1.   On greased cookie sheet, drop rounded teaspoonfuls of dough. Space 2 inches apart.
2.   Bake at 400°F. for 12 to 15 minutes.
3.   Remove from cookie sheet and cool.
4.   There will be about 48 cookies.

GINGER COOKIES

Spicy, molasses tidbits you'll have fun making and more fun eating.

Heat oven to 400°F.   Grease cookie sheet

When you use measuring spoons, run table knife across top of spoon to make ingredient even with spoon edge.

When you use measuring cups, have ingredient even with measuring mark. Do not shake flour down in cup, but pack brown sugar firmly in cup.

INGREDIENTS YOU'LL NEED

1 cup brown sugar, packed	½ cup hot water
1 cup shortening	4½ cups flour
1 cup molasses	1 teaspoon cinnamon
2 teaspoons baking soda	1 teaspoon ginger

HOW TO MIX INGREDIENTS

1.   In mixing bowl, mix sugar, shortening, molasses, soda, and water together until fluffy.
2.   Sift flour once before measuring. Measure flour. Add cinnamon and ginger to flour.
3.   Add a little flour to sugar mixture. Stir very well. Add a little more flour and stir well again. Keep adding flour a little at a time and stirring well, until all the flour has been well blended with sugar mixture.

HERE'S HOW TO BAKE THEM

1.   On greased cookie sheet, drop rounded teaspoonfuls of dough. Space 2 inches apart. Flatten dough with a fork dipped in cold water or fingers dipped in flour.
2.   Bake at 400°F. for 12 to 15 minutes.
3.   Remove from cookie sheet and cool.
4.   There will be about 60 cookies.

GUY'S MEAT PASTIES

Eat them as a sandwich, dipped in ketchup between bites.

Heat oven to 425°F.

Use ungreased medium size
skillet

Have ungreased cookie sheet
ready

When you use measuring spoons, run table knife across top of spoon to make ingredient even with spoon edge.

INGREDIENTS YOU'LL NEED

1 tube refrigerated
pan-ready biscuits
1 pound hamburger
¼ teaspoon salt
¼ teaspoon pepper

¼ teaspoon garlic or
onion salt
1 teaspoon Worcestershire
sauce
dash paprika
5 slices American cheese

HOW TO MIX INGREDIENTS

1.   Brown hamburger in ungreased skillet over medium heat. Stir with spoon all the time so meat will brown all over and not stick to pan.
2.   Add salt, pepper, garlic or onion salt, worcestershire sauce, and paprika to browned meat. Stir well. Cook 5 minutes more.
3.   Sprinkle bread board with a little flour.
4.   Remove biscuits from tube.
5.   Place biscuits on floured board. Sprinkle each biscuit with a little flour.
6.   Use rolling pin to roll each biscuit in shape of oval about 5 inches long.
7.   Place 1/2 slice cheese on each oval.
8.   Place about 2 tablespoonfuls of cooked meat on 5 biscuit ovals.
9.   Cover meat-topped biscuits with remaining 5 biscuits, having cheese face meat on both sides.
10. Pinch edges all around with fingers. Prick top with fork to let steam out during baking.
11. Place on ungreased cookie sheet.

344

HERE'S HOW TO BAKE AND SERVE THEM

1. Bake at 425°F. for about 8 minutes, or until golden brown.
2. Serve hot with ketchup, mustard, or chili sauce. Makes 5 pasties.

PEANUT DROP COOKIES

Just about the best filler-upper there is.

START HERE

Heat oven to 400°F.   Grease cookie sheet

When you use measuring spoons, run table knife across top of spoon to make ingredient even with spoon edge.

When you use measuring cups, have ingredient even with measuring marks. Do not shake biscuit mix down in cup. Pack brown sugar firmly in cup.

INGREDIENTS YOU'LL NEED

2 cups biscuit mix	¼ teaspoon salt
¼ cup soft shortening	1 egg, beaten
1 cup brown sugar, packed	⅓ cup milk
½ teaspoon mace	1 cup chopped peanuts

HOW TO MIX INGREDIENTS

1. In mixing bowl place biscuit mix, shortening, brown sugar, mace, and salt. With fork or wooden spoon, mix ingredients together.
2. Beat egg and milk together. Add to biscuit mix mixture. Blend well.
3. Stir in peanuts.
4. On greased cookie sheet, drop rounded teaspoonfuls of dough. Space 2 inches apart.

HERE'S HOW TO BAKE THEM

1. Bake at 400°F. for 6 to 8 minutes.
2. Remove from cookie sheet and cool. There will be about 75 cookies.

INDIVIDUAL PIZZAS

START HERE

Heat oven to 400°F.

Use ungreased medium size skillet

Have ungreased cookie sheet ready

When you use measuring spoons, run table knife across top of spoon to make ingredient even with spoon edge.

When you use measuring cup, have ingredient even with measuring mark.

INGREDIENTS YOU'LL NEED

1 pound hamburger
½ teaspoon salt
⅓ cup stuffed green olives, cut up
⅔ cup canned tomato sauce
¼ teaspoon garlic salt
¼ teaspoon onion salt

¼ teaspoon ground oregano
8 slices pizza cheese; OR 1 cup pizza cheese, grated
4 brown-and-serve French rolls, OR 4 English muffins, split in half

HOW TO MIX INGREDIENTS

1. Brown hamburger in ungreased skillet over medium heat. Stir with spoon all the time so meat will brown all over and not stick to pan. Add salt.
2. Add cut up olives, tomato sauce, garlic salt, onion salt, and ground oregano to browned meat. Stir well. Cook 5 minutes more.
3. Grate pizza cheese if you do not have slices.
4. Split French rolls, OR English Muffins in half. Place on ungreased cookie sheet.
5. Place about 2 tablespoonfuls of cooked meat sauce on top of split muffin half or French roll half.
6. Place cheese slice or grated cheese over meat.

HERE'S HOW TO BAKE AND SERVE THEM

1. Bake at 400°F. for about 15 minutes or until pizzas look bubbly and done.
2. Serve hot. Makes 8 pizzas.

HOT DOG ROLL-UPS

If you love hot dogs, you'll think these are great.

START HERE

Heat oven to 425°F.   Have ungreased cookie sheet
                                   ready

When you use measuring cup, have ingredient even with measuring mark. Do not shake biscuit mix down in cup.

INGREDIENTS YOU'LL NEED

2 cups biscuit mix   12 hot dogs, uncooked
⅔ cup milk

HOW TO MIX INGREDIENTS

1. Stir biscuit mix and milk together.
2. Sprinkle bread board with a little flour. Place dough on floured board. Sprinkle top of dough with flour.
3. Use rolling pin to roll out dough to ¼ inch thick.
4. With table knife, cut dough in 12 square pieces, a little shorter than hot dogs.
5. Wrap each piece around the center part of hot dog. Leave ends of hot dog uncovered.
6. Place on ungreased cookie sheet.

HERE'S HOW TO BAKE AND SERVE THEM

1. Bake at 425°F. for 15 to 20 minutes, or until biscuit dough is baked.
2. Serve hot with mustard, relish, and olives. Makes 12 roll-ups.

JOANIE'S CHEESE PIE

This is a real glamorous, quick and easy to make version of cheese cake.

START HERE

Heat oven to 350°F.

Have deep 9-inch pie plate
or 9-inch spring-form pan
ready

When you use measuring spoons, run table knife across top of spoon to make ingredient even with spoon edge.

When you use measuring cups, have ingredient even with measuring mark.

INGREDIENTS YOU'LL NEED FOR CRUST

16 graham crackers   ¼ cup sugar
¼ cup butter

1. On waxed paper, roll out graham crackers with rolling pin until they are very fine.
2. Melt butter. Mix melted butter, graham cracker crumbs, and sugar together very well.
3. With back of spoon or fork, press crumb mixture evenly and firmly over bottom and around edges of pan. This forms the pie crust.

INGREDIENTS YOU'LL NEED FOR PIE FILLING

2 eight-ounce packages of   2 eggs
   cream cheese, softened   ½ cup sugar

1. Beat cream cheese, eggs, and sugar together until there are no lumps and the mixture is very fluffy.
2. With spoon, put cream cheese mixture in graham cracker crust.
3. Bake at 350°F. for 20 minutes.

INGREDIENTS YOU'LL NEED FOR PIE TOPPING

½ pint commercial sour   ½ teaspoon vanilla
   cream   cinnamon
¼ cup sugar

348

1. Mix commercial sour cream, sugar and vanilla together very well.
2. When pie is finished baking, take it out of the oven. Sprinkle top with cinnamon.
3. Spread sour cream mixture over cinnamon-topped filling.
4. Return pie to oven. Bake 5 minutes more.
5. This pie will serve 8 to 10 people because it is very rich and the pieces should not be cut as large as regular pieces of pie.

FOOLPROOF CARAMEL ICING

Half the fun of making this icing is licking the pan when you're through.

START HERE

Have saucepan ready

When you use measuring spoons, run table knife across top of spoon to make ingredient even with spoon edge.

When you use measuring cups, have ingredient even with measuring mark. Pack brown sugar firmly in cup.

INGREDIENTS YOU'LL NEED

1½ cups brown sugar, packed
6 tablespoons milk
6 tablespoons butter or
   margarine

¼ teaspoon salt
¾ teaspoon vanilla

HOW TO MIX AND COOK INGREDIENTS

1. In saucepan, put brown sugar, milk, butter or margarine, and salt.
2. Place pan on stove burner. Turn on to medium heat.
3. Bring to a rolling boil, stirring all the time. After it comes to a boil, cook 1 minute more.
4. Remove from heat. Let icing cool until it feels barely warm when you touch it.
5. Add vanilla.
6. Beat hard with spoon until icing is creamy and thick enough to spread on cake. It should not be runny.

PIZZA BURGERS

These are perfect for Saturday lunch.

START HERE

Heat oven to 400°F.

Use ungreased skillet
Have ungreased cookie sheet ready

When you use measuring spoons, run table knife across top of spoon to make ingredient even with spoon edge.

When you use measuring cup, have ingredient even with measuring mark.

INGREDIENTS YOU'LL NEED

1 pound hamburger
4 hamburger buns, cut in half

1 can pizza sauce
4 slices pizza cheese, *OR*
½ cup grated pizza cheese

1. Shape hamburger into 4 patties.
2. Cook hamburger patties in ungreased skillet over medium heat until done.
3. Place hamburger bun bottoms on ungreased cookie sheet.
4. Put 1 cooked hamburger pattie on each bun.
5. With tablespoon put pizza sauce on top of hamburger pattie.
6. Place 1 slice cheese or 1/4 of grated cheese on top of sauce.
7. Put top half of bun over sauce.

HERE'S HOW TO BAKE AND SERVE THEM

1. Bake at 400°F. for about 10 minutes, or until pizza burgers look bubbly and done.
2. Serve hot. Makes 4 servings.

SILVER DOLLAR PANCAKES

You'll eat stacks of these. Make them dollar size or regular size.

START HERE

Heat griddle, skillet, or electric fry pan.

When you use measuring spoons, run table knife across top of spoon to make ingredient even with spoon edge.

When you use measuring cups, have ingredient even with measuring mark. Do not shake biscuit mix down in cup.

INGREDIENTS YOU'LL NEED

2 eggs

2 tablespoons sugar

2 tablespoons salad oil

1 cup milk

2 cups biscuit mix

HOW TO MIX INGREDIENTS

1. In pitcher, or mixing bowl that pours, put eggs. Beat well.
2. Add sugar, salad oil, and milk. Mix.
3. Slowly add biscuit mix to milk mixture.

HERE'S HOW TO COOK THEM

1. When few drops of water sprinkled on skillet, griddle, or electric fry pan, bounce and sputter, it is hot enough for baking.
2. Pour small amounts of batter onto hot skillet, griddle or electric fry pan.
3. When small bubbles appear on top and begin to break, turn the pancakes. Turn pancakes only once. It does not take but a very few minutes for pancakes to cook.
4. Eat pancakes as soon as they are cooked.
5. There is enough batter to serve four people.

QUICK SHORTCAKE

Serve it with fresh fruit topped with whipped cream.

START HERE

Heat oven to 350°F.

Prepare 8"x8"x2" square pan or cupcake pans; grease and sprinkle lightly with flour

When you use measuring spoons, run table knife across top of spoon to make ingredient even with spoon edge.

When you use measuring cups, have ingredient even with measuring mark. Do not shake biscuit mix or flour down in cup.

INGREDIENTS YOU'LL NEED

1½ cups biscuit mix
¾ cup sugar
3 tablespoons shortening, melted

½ teaspoon salt
1 egg, unbeaten
⅞ cup milk
1 teaspoon vanilla

HOW TO MIX INGREDIENTS

1.   In mixing bowl, place biscuit mix, sugar, shortening, and salt. Mix together until blended.
2.   Beat egg and milk together. Add to biscuit mix mixture. Beat well.
3.   Stir in vanilla.
4.   Pour batter into greased and floured pan.

HERE'S HOW TO BAKE AND SERVE IT

1.   Bake at 350°F. for about 30 minutes. Bake cupcakes 20 minutes.
2.   Cool. Cut into squares and serve with fresh fruit and whipped cream or ice cream.

JAM TARTS

These are keen for picnics, camping-out, or lunch boxes.

START HERE

Heat oven to 350°F.   Have ungreased cookie sheet
ready

When you use measuring cups, have ingredient even with measuring mark.

INGREDIENTS YOU'LL NEED

1 cup flour
1 three-ounce package cream
cheese, soft
1 cube soft butter or margarine

1 cup jam (pick out your
favorite flavor or use what
mother has on hand)

1. Sift flour once before measuring. Measure flour.
2. Place *soft* cheese, butter, and flour together in mixing bowl.
3. With fork, or wooden spoon, mix ingredients together.
4. Sprinkle bread board with a little flour. Place tart crust dough on floured board. Sprinkle top of dough with flour.
5. Use rolling pin to roll dough out to 1/4 inch thick.
6. With table knife, cut dough into 2-inch squares.
7. Place one tablespoonful jam in center of each square.
8. Bring four corners of each square to center. Pinch edges together well to seal. Prick crust with fork to let steam out during baking.
9. Place tarts on ungreased cookie shet.

HERE'S HOW TO BAKE AND SERVE THEM

1. Bake at 350°F. for about 20 minutes, or until light golden brown.
2. Cool before removing from cookie sheet.
3. Makes about 8 tarts.

LUNCH BOX TARTS

Pineapple chunks baked in a pie crust envelope.

START HERE

Heat oven to 425°F.   Have ungreased cookie sheet
                             ready

When you use measuring spoons, run table knife across top of spoon to make ingredient even with spoon edge.

When you use measuring cups, have ingredient even with measuring mark. Pack brown sugar firmly in cup.

INGREDIENTS YOU'LL NEED

1 package pie crust mix   3 tablespoons soft butter
flour   2 cups canned pineapple
½ cup brown sugar, packed   chunks (No. 2 can),
½ teaspoon cinnamon   drained

1. Make piecrust following directions on package.
2. Sprinkle bread board with a little flour. Place pie crust dough on floured board. Sprinkle top of dough with flour.
3. Use rolling pin to roll dough out to 1/4 inch thick.
4. With table knife, cut dough into 3-inch squares.
5. With fork, mix brown sugar with cinnamon and soft butter. Mixture will be crumbly.
6. Drain juice from pineapple chunks.
7. Place 1 pineapple chunk in center of each pie crust square. Sprinkle with sugar and butter mixture.
8. Bring four corners of each square to center. Pinch edges together well to seal. Prick pie crust with fork to let steam out during baking.
9. Place tarts on ungreased cookie sheet.

HERE'S HOW TO BAKE AND SERVE THEM

1. Bake at 425°F. for about 10 minutes or until light golden brown.
2. Cool before removing from cookie sheet.
3. Makes 24 tarts.

EASY WAFFLES

Just the thing when mother and dad are going out to dinner.

Heat waffle iron.

When you use measuring spoons, run table knife across top of spoon to make ingredient even with spoon edge.

When you use measuring cups, have ingredient even with measuring mark. Do not shake flour down in cup.

INGREDIENTS YOU'LL NEED

2 cups flour	2 eggs, beaten
4 teaspoons double-acting baking powder	¼ cup salad oil or melted shortening
½ teaspoon salt	1¾ cups milk

HOW TO MIX INGREDIENTS

1.   Sift flour once before measuring. Measure flour. Add baking powder and salt.
2.   In pitcher or mixing bowl that pours, place flour mixture.
3.   Beat eggs, salad oil or melted shortening, and milk together. Add to flour mixture. Beat well.

HERE'S HOW TO BAKE AND SERVE THEM

1.   Be sure waffle iron is hot. When a few drops of water sprinkled on waffle iron plates bounce and sputter, it is hot enough.
2.   Fill heated waffle iron 2/3 full.
3.   Bake about 5 minutes. Do *not* open waffle iron during cooking time.
4.   Serve immediately with melted butter and syrup.

NOTES

Index

Adjustments of Recipes In This
    Book, 10
Almond
    Flavored Butter Cookies, 212
    Cookies, Dutch, 204
    Custard Filling, 173
    Flavored Sheet Cake, 120
    Sherry Custard Filling, 173
Angel Food
    Cake, Deluxe, 155
    Cake, Yellow, 156
    Cake Filling, Heavenly, 173
    Pie, 265
Apple
    Coffee Cake, Quick, 316
    Delight (Junior Bakers), 332
    Fritters, 105
    Fruit Dessert, 302
    Icing, 164
    Lemon Dumplings, 317
    Muffins, 68
    Pie, Darrell's Favorite, 256
    Pie with Cheese Crust, 257
    Pudding, Scalloped, 290
    Tarts, 244
Applesauce
    Cake, 134
    Cake, Party with Icing, 136
    Cookies, 182
    Topping, Low Calorie, 308
Apricot
    Bread, 74
    Custard Filling, 174

Bake-On Icing, 164, 123
Baked Alaska, 288
Baking Powder, Types of, 26
Baking Problems and Solutions
    Cakes, 112
    Cookies, 181
    Pies, 244
    Yeast Breads, 31
Baking, Steps To Good, 16-17
Banana
    Custard Filling, 173

Cream Pie, Hazel's, 267
Fritters, 105
Icing, 164
Nut Bread, Mrs. Lil's, 76
Basic
    Biscuits, 61
    Butter Cookies, 212
    Pie Crust, 248
Berry
    Fruit Dessert, 302
    Pie, 255
    Pudding and Fruit Pie, 324
Biscuit(s), 61-65
    Basic, 61
    Buttermilk, 63
    Cheese, 64
    Cheese Straws, 65
    Cream, 62
    Drop and Bake Quickies,
        323-324
    Herb, 64
    Low-Cholestrol Baking Powder,
        310
    Mix, 64
    Onion, 64
    Parsley, 64
    Suggestions for Successful, 61
    Variations, Other, 64
Bittersweet Icing, 165
Black Bottom Pie, 278
Blender Peanut Butter Icing, 169
Blueberry
    Cobbler, 295
    Dessert with Filling and
        Topping, 288
    Muffins, 69
    Pudding, 294
    Pudding and Fruit Pie, 324
    Pie, 255
    Tarts, 244
Boston Brown Bread, 73
Bran Muffins, 68
Bread Crumb Cookies, 183
Breads, Corn, 85-88

Bread(s), Quick, 59-106
  Apricot, 74
  Banana Nut Bread, Mrs. Lil's, 76
  Biscuits, 61-65
  Boston Brown, 73
  Brioche, 317
  Corn, 85-88
  Cranberry, 82
  Date and Cheese, 75
  Date Nut Loaf, 74
  Doughnuts, 101-104
  Dumplings, 106
  Fritters, 105
  Gingerbread, 78, 138
  Muffins, 66-72
  Nut, Mother's, 79
  Nut, 77, 333
  Orange, 84
  Pancakes, 89-98
  Popovers, 85
  Prune, 82
  Spoon, 86
  Suggestions for Successful, 73
  Tips for Freezing, 60
  Waffles, 98-100
  Walnut, 83
Bread Pudding, 290
  Chocolate, 291
  Chocolate, 298
  Butterscotch, 291
Bread(s), Yeast, 27-58
  Afternoon Tea, 56
  Baking Problems and
    Solutions, 31
  Doughnuts, Raised, 103
  Freezing Tips for, 32
  French, 34
  Griddle Cakes, Whole Wheat or
    Graham, 95
  High Protein, 36
  Low Fat-Low Cholesterol
    White, 312
  Multi-Flour Health, 35
  Orange, Mrs. Bell's, 33
  Rye, 42
  Suggestions for Successful
    Baking, 28-32
  White, 38, 312
  Whole Wheat, Mother
    Miller's, 40

Brioche, 48
  Quick, 317
Brownies (Fudge Squares), 221-231
  Basic Best, 223
  Blonde, 222
  Chocolate Bit, 222
  Cocoa, 224
  Fudge Squares, Cissies, 224
  Tips for Bars and Squares, 221
Brown Betty, 292
Buckwheat Cakes, 94
  Low Calorie-Low Cholesterol,
    308
Butterfly Griddle Cakes, Leila's, 96
Buttermilk
  Biscuits, 63
  Cinnamon Coffee Cake, 80
  Cornbread, 88
  Pancakes, 97
  Pancakes, No Fat, 310
  Waffles, 99
Buns
  Caramel, 54-55
  Cinnamon, 54-55
  Hot Cross, 325
Burnt Sugar Cake with Caramel
  Icing, 137
Butter-Nut Frosting and Filling,
  165
Butternut Goldies, Drop and Bake
  Quickies, 323
Butter Cookies, Basic, 212
Butterscotch
  Bread Pudding, 291
  Chiffon Pie, 278
  Crisps, 206
  Icing, 186
  Sour Cream Pie, 266

Cake(s), 107-162
  Angel Food, Deluxe, 155
  Angel Food, Yellow, 156
  Applesauce, 134
  Applesauce, Party with
    Icing, 136
  Burnt Sugar with Caramel
    Icing, 137
  Cheese, Joanie's (Junior Bakers),
    348

358

Cheese Cake with Strawberry Glaze, 292
Cheese Cakes, Petite, Mother Anderson's, 291
Cherry Meringue, 319
Chocolate, 124-133
Chocolate Bit, Cherry and Date, 151
Chocolate Chiffon, 321
Chocolate, Mrs. Dispence's, 133
Chocolate, Betty's Elegant with Icing, 126
Chocolate, Grandmother Andrew's with Icing, 128
Chocolate, Ken's Continental with Icing, 130
Chocolate Mashed Potato Spice, 132
Chocolate Salad Dressing, 130
Chocolate, Pete's Sour Cream, 124
Chocolate Roll, John's, 158
Chocolate Shower, 118
Cocoa, 129
Coconut, 118
Crazy (Junior Bakers), 336
Creamed, 115-153
Creamed Cake Tips, 115
Cupcakes, 146-149
Dessert Ring with Topping, Mrs. Egan's, 115
Devil's Food Crunch, 321
Diet Skillet, 313
Fruit, 150-153
Fruit, Economy, 153
Fruit, Holiday, 150
Fruit, Old Fashioned Dark, 152
Golden Layer, Quick Method, 121
Fudge, Economy, 125
Gingerbread, Miss Rose's, 138
Ginger Upside Down, 325
Health, 309
Jelly Roll, 157
Lady Baltimore, 117
Lazy Daisy with Topping, 123
Lemon Lady Finger, Virginia's, 301
Man's, A, 140
Maple Nut, 141

Marble Halowe'en, 139
Nut Fudge, Lee's, 127
Peach Upside Down, 142
Pineapple Upside Down, 142
Pineapple, Four Layer, Filled, 329
Poppy Seed Cake, 116
Pound Cake, 124
Powdered Sugar Cake, 119
Pumpkin, Mark's, 143
Scripture, 144
Shortcake, Quick (Junior Bakers), 352
Sour Cream, 124, 134
Spice, 145
Spice (Junior Bakers), 334
Spice, Little, 146
Sponge, 154-162
Sponge and Variations, 161
Sponge, Four Egg, 162
Sponge, Orange, 162
Sponge, Tips for, 154
Suggestions for Successful Baking, 110
Three-In-One (Junior Bakers), 334

Tips for Freezing, 113-114
Torte, Mocha, 159
Torte, Viennese, 160
Upside Down Ginger, 325
Upside Down Pineapple or Peach, 142
Whipped Cream, 135
White, 115-121
White Sheet, One Bowl, 120
White, Two-Layer, 120
Yellow, 121-124
Yellow, Three Layer with Filling and Icing, 122
Candy Bar Cookies, 184
Can Sizes, Standard, 24-25
Caramel
Bread Pudding, 290
Buns (Foundation Sweet Dough), 54
Dumplings, 294
Icing, 166
Icing, Foolproof (Junior Bakers), 349

359

Icing with Burnt Sugar
Cake, 137
Caraway Cookies, 318
Carrot
Cookies, 184
Pie, 269
Cheese
Balls, Cheddar, 316
Biscuits, 64
Cake with Strawberry
Glaze, 292
Cakes, Mother Anderson's
Petite, 291
Crust, Apple Pie with, 257
Pie, Joanie's (Junior Bakers), 348
Pie Crust, 251
Pimento Drop and Bake
Quickies, 323
Straws, 65
Wafers, Cocktail, 251
Cherry
Chocolate Soufflé, Italian, 296
Cobbler, 295
Crunchies, 214
Fritters, 105
Fruit Dessert, 302
Meringue Cake, 319
Pie, Canned, 258
Pie, Fresh, 258
Pie, Frozen, 260
Pudding, 294
Tarts, 244
Chocolate
And Vanilla Pinwheels, 206
Bars, Chewy, 232
Bread Pudding, 291, 298
Bit Brownies, 222
Bit, Cherry and Date Cake, 151
Cake, Betty's Elegant with
Icing, 126
Cake, Grandmother Andrew's
with Icing, 128
Cake, Ken's Continental with
Icing, 130
Cake, Mrs. Dispence's, 133
Cake, Pete's Sour Cream, 124
Cake, Salad Dressing, 130
Changeable Treats, 232
Cherry Italian Soufflé, 296
Chiffon Cake, 321

Chiffon Pie, 277
Cookies (Junior Bakers), 342
Cream Meringue Pie, 268
Cream Filling, Quick, 174
Custard Filling, 174
Dream Topping, 327
Drop Cookies, 188
Frosting, Cream Cheese, 166
Fudge Sponge Cupcakes, Dee's
With Icing, 147
Glaze, 175
Icing, Freezer Perfect, 167
Icing or Filling, Easy, 166
Icing (Junior Bakers), 339
Marble Bars, 231
Pie, 266
Pie, Marvelous, 264
Powdered Sugar Icing, 167
Potato and Spice Cake, 132
Roll, John's, 158
Sauce (Junior Bakers), 341
Sauce or Frosting, 168
Shower Cake, 118
Soufflés, Individual, 319
Waffles, 98
Walnut Treats, 233
Cinnamon
Buns (Foundation Sweet
Dough), 54
Sugar Balls, 216
Buttermilk Coffee Cake, 80
Citrus
Glaze with Carrot Cookies, 184
Roll-ups with Filling and
Frosting, 50
Cobbler, Cherry, 295
Cocoa
Brownies, 224
Cake, 129
Coconut
Bake-On Icing, 164
Breakfast Rings with Filling
and Glaze, 52
Cake, 118
Cookies, El's, 188
Custard, 297
Custard Pie, Hazel's, 267
Macaroons, 185

Seven Minute Icing, 171
Coffee Cakes
  Apple, Quick, 316
  Cinnamon Buttermilk, 80
  Deluxe, 78
  German, with Topping, 53
  Grandma Grace's, 76
  Individual, 84
  Orange Marmalade, 80
  Orange with Topping
    (Junior Bakers), 336
  Spice, 326
Coffee (flavored)
  Cup Cakes, 149
  Eggnog Chiffon Pie, 280
  A Man's Cake, 140
  Topping, Low Calorie, 314
Contents, 7-8
Cookie Crumb Pie Crust, 252
Cookie(s), 177-235
  Almond Basic Butter, 212
  Applesauce, 182
  Baking Problems and
    Solutions, 181
  Bars and Squares, 221-231
  Bars and Squares, Tips for, 221
  Basic Butter, 212
  Black Walnut Refrigerator, 209
  Brownies, Best Basic, 223
  Brownies, Blonde, 222
  Brownies, Chocolate Bit, 222
  Brownies, Cocoa, 224
  Bread Crumb, 183
  Butterscotch Crisps, 206
  Butterscotch Date with
    Icing, 186
  Candy Bar, 184
  Caraway, 318
  Carrot with Glaze, 184
  Changeable Chocolate
    Treats, 232
  Cherry Crunchies, 214
  Chocolate and Vanilla Pin-
    wheels, 206
  Chocolate Bars, Chewy, 232
  Chocolate (Junior Bakers), 342
  Chocolate Marble Bars, 231
  Chocolate Walnut Treats, 233
  Cinnamon Sugar Balls, 216
  Coconut, El's, 188

Coconut Macaroons, 185
Cottage Cheese, 212
Date Cereal Surprises, 234
Date Filled, 215
Date Flake Nuggets, 233
Date Macaroons, Nutty, 187
Date Pinwheels, 205
Date Refrigerator, 207
Drop, 182-203
Drop Cookie Tips, 182
Dutch Almond, 204
Fruit Compote, 186
Fry Pan, 235
Fudge Squares, Cissie's, 224
Ginger (Junior Bakers), 343
Ginger, Drop, 190
Ginger, Refrigerator, 210
Gum Drop Bars, 226
Hermits, Drop, 192
Hermits, Refrigerator, 208
Kifflings, 213
Lace, 190
Lacy Wafers, 191
Lemon Basic Butter, 212
Macaroons, 185, 187
Meringue Squares, 225
Mincemeat Bars with Butter
  Icing, 230
Mocha Squares, 225
Molasses Chocolate Bit, 192
Oatmeal (Junior Bakers), 338
Oatmeal, Easy, 194
Oatmeal, 194
Orange with Frosting, 200
Peanut Butter, 217
Peanut Butter Balls, 314
Peanut Cluster, 195
Peanut Drop, 193
Peanut Drop (Junior
  Bakers), 345
Peanut Raisin, 196
Pecan Kisses, 189
Pecan Supremes, 197
Pineapple Nut, 201
Puffed Wheat Cereal Bars, 236
Pumpkin, 203
Quick-Change with Varia-
  tions, 220
Raisin, Mother's, 199
Raisin Squares, Frosted, 228

Refrigerator, 204-210
Refrigerator, Tips for
Baking, 204
Rice Cereal, Crispy, 202
Rolled or Molded, 211-221
Rolled or Molded, Tips for, 211
Rum Balls, 236
Sour Cream with Variations, 198
Spiced Drop, 202
Spiced Molasses Nuggets,
Paul's, 216
Spritz, Swedish, 221
Sugar, Classic, 218
Sugar, (Junior Bakers), 340
Sugar, Drop, 198
Sugar, Grandmother's, 219
Swedish, Nut Crescents, 218
Tips for Freezing, 181
Toffee Bars, Rocky
Mountain, 228
Toffee Squares, English, 234
Toll Oats, 196
Uncooked, 232-237
Vanilla Wafers, Refrig-
erator, 210
Walnut Bourbon Balls, 237
Whatcha Callit, 229
Corn
Bread, 87
Bread, Sour Cream or Butter-
milk, 88
Bread, Suggestions for
Baking, 85
Fritters, 105
Muffins, 87-89
Sticks, 88
Corn Meal
Griddle Cakes, 91
Raisin Muffins, 88
Spoon Bread, 86
Cottage Cheese Cookies, 212
Cottage Pudding, 298
Cranberry
Bread, 82
Dessert, 299
Crazy Cake (Junior Bakers), 336
Cream
Biscuits, 62
Cheese Chocolate Frosting, 166

Cheese Cake or Pie, 291, 293,
348
Puffs, 300
Crispy Rice Cereal Cookies, 202
Crumb Crusts for Pies, 252-253
Cereal (cornflake, wheat flake,
crisp rice cereal), 253
Cookie (vanilla wafer, chocolate
wafer or gingersnap), 252
Graham Cracker, 252
Nut Crumb, 253
Nut Crust (pecan, peanut,
walnut, brazil, or almond), 253
Zwieback, 253, 292
Crumb Pie, Pennsylvania, 276
Cupcakes, 146-149
Coffee, 149
Fudge Sponge, Dee's with
Fudge Icing, 147
Golden, 148
Puff Cakes, 148
Pumpkin, 143
Tips for, 146
Custard, Baked, 297
Coconut, 297
Maple, 297
Party, 297
Honey, 297
Custard Filling, 173, 289
Almond, 173
Apricot, 174
Chocolate, 174
Banana, 173
Pineapple, 173
Sherry Almond Marshmallow,
173
Custard Pie, 268

Dapple Pie, 320
Date
And Cheese Bread, 75
Cereal Surprises, 234
Cookies, Filled, 215
Cookies, Refrigerator, 207
Flake Nuggets, 233
Nut Loaf, 74
Nut Pudding, 300
Pinwheels, 205

Deep Dish Pie, How to Make, 244
Dessert, Favorite Fruit, 302
Desserts, 287-305
  See also Cakes, Pies, Puddings
  Ring, Mrs. Egan's, 115
Diet Baking, 307-314
Diet Skillet Cake, 313
Doughnuts, 101-104
  Drop, Orange or Plain, 102
  New England, 101
  Raised, 103
  Sour Cream, 104
Drop and Bake Quickies, 323-324
Dumplings
  For Chicken or Meat Stews, 106
  Apple-Lemon, 317
  Caramel, 294
  Quick Rum, 327

Easy
  Chocolate Icing or Filling, 166
  Lemon Icing, 168
  Oatmeal Cookies, 194
  To Make Recipes for Junior
    Bakers, 331-355
  Waffles, 355
Eclairs, 300
English Muffins, 43
Equivalents, Table of, 20-22

Feathery Light Rolls, 46
Filling(s) for Cakes, 173-175
  Almond Custard, 173
  Almond-Sherry Custard, 173
  Angelfood, Heavenly, 173
  Apricot Custard, 174
  Banana Custard, 173
  Butternut, 165
  Caramel for Burnt Sugar
    Cake, 137
  Chocolate Cream, Quick, 174
  Chocolate Custard, 174
  Chocolate, Easy, 166
  Custard with Variations, 123
  Date Filling, 215
  Lemon Custard, 174
  Orange-Almond, 167
  Orange for Three-Layer Yellow
    Cake, 122

Pineapple Custard, 173
Pineapple Cake with, 329
Raisin Nut, 175
Foreign Measurements, Interpret-
  ing, 23
Foundation Sweet Dough, 54
  Caramel Buns, 54
  Cinnamon Buns, 54
Freezer
  Perfect Chocolate Icing, 167
  Chart, 17-20
Freezing
  Baked Goods, General Rules
    for, 17
  Cakes, Tips for, 113
  Cookies, Tips for, 181
  Pie Crust, Tips for, 246
  Pies, Tips for, 247
  Quick Breads, Tips for, 60
  Yeast Breads, Tips for, 32
French
  Bread, 34
  Pancakes, Dorothy's, 93
  Pastry Pie Crust, 250
Frenchmint Pie, Margie's, 279
Fritters, 105-106
  Corn, 105
  Fruit, 105
Frostings and Fillings, 163-175
Frostings, 163-172
  Apple, 164
  Bake-on, 164
  Banana, 164
  Bittersweet, 165
  Butter with Mincemeat
    Bars, 230
  Butternut, 165
  Butterscotch with Cookies, 186
  Caramel, 166
  Caramel with Burnt Sugar
    Cake, 137
  Caramel, Foolproof (Junior
    Bakers), 349
  Citrus with Three-layer Yellow
    Cake, 122
  Citrus with Roll-ups, 50
  Chocolate (Junior Bakers), 339
  Chocolate Cream Cheese, 166
  Chocolate, Easy, 166

Chocolate, Freezer-Perfect, 167
Chocolate Glaze, 175
Chocolate Powdered Sugar, 167
Chocolate with Betty's Elegant
    Cake, 126
Chocolate with Grandmother
    Andrew's Cake, 128
Chocolate with Ken's Con-
    tinental Cake, 130
Fudge, Minute, 164
Fudge Cup Cakes, with, 147
Fudge, Sauce or, 168
Lemon, Easy, 168
Marmalade-Butter, 168
Mint Jelly, 171
Mocha, 169
Orange-Almond, 167
Orange Cookies with, 200
Orange Butter Cream, 169
Orange with Three-layer Yellow
    Cake, 123
Peanut Butter, Blender, 169
Penuche, 170
Pineapple, 170
Raisin-Nut with Applesauce
    Cake, 136
Raisin Squares, with, 228
Salted Peanut, Ground, 225
Sea Foam, I, 172
Sea Foam, II, 172
Seven Minute, I, 170
Seven Minute, II, 171
Seven Minute, Coconut, 171
Seven Minute, Lemon, 171
Seven Minute, Orange, 171
Seven Minute, Peppermint, 171
White, 171
Fruit
    Compote Cookies, 186
    Dessert, Favorite, 302
    Fritters, 105
    Pies, 255-263
    Tarts, 263, 244
    Topping, 327
Fruit Cake(s), 150-153
    Chocolate Bit, 151
    Economy, 153
    Holiday, 150
    Old Fashioned Dark, 152
Fry Pan Cookies, 235

Fudge
    Cake, Economy, 125
    Icing, Minute, 164
    Nut Cake, Lee's, 127
    Sauce or Icing, 168
    Sponge Cup Cakes, Dee's
        with Icing, 147
    Squares, Cissies, 224

Garlic and Herb Rolls, 44
German Coffee Cake with
    Topping, 53
Ginger
    Cake, Upside Down (Junior
        Bakers), 325
    Cookies, (Junior Bakers), 343
    Cookies, Drop, 190
    Cookies, Refrigerator, 210
Gingerbread
    Miss Rose's, 138
    White, 78
Glaze(s)
    Chocolate, 175
    Citrus with Carrot Cookies, 184
    Citrus with Breakfast
        Roll-ups, 50
    Coconut with Breakfast
        Twists, 52
    Sugar with Hot Cross Buns, 325
    Strawberry with Cheese-
        cake, 292
    Vanilla with Foundation
        Sweet Dough, 54
Golden
    Cupcakes, 148
    Layer Cake, Quick-Method, 121
Goose Berry Pie, 259
Grape Pie, Concord, 260
Graham Cracker
    Pie Crust, 252
    Pudding, 302
Graham Griddle Cakes, 95
Griddle Cakes (see Pancakes),
    89-98
    Corn Meal, 91
    Graham, 95
    Leila's Butterfly, 96
    Whole Wheat, 95
Gum Drop Bars, 226

Health Cake, 309
Hermits
    Drop, 192
    Refrigerator, 208
High Altitude
    Baking, Why It Is Different,
        9-10
    Cities and Towns, 11-14
    Cooking Definitions, 14-16
    Conversion Tables, 10
High Protein Bread, 36
Honey Custard, 297
Hot Cross Buns, 325
Hot Dog Roll-Ups (Junior
    Bakers), 347
Hot Water Pie Crust, 250

Icings, See Frostings
Ingredient Substitutions, 22-23
Introduction, 9-10

Jam Tarts (Junior Bakers), 353
Jelly Roll, 157
Junior Bakers, Easy to Make
    Recipes for, 331-355

Kifflings, 213
Kolacki with Filling, 57
Lace Cookies, 190
Lacy Wafer Cookies, 191
Lazy Daisy Cake with
    Topping, 123
Lemon
    Angel Pie, 270
    Cake, Virginia's Lady
        Finger, 301
    Cream Chiffon Pie, 323
    Custard Cake Filling, 174
    Icing, Easy, 168
    Meringue Pie, 271
    Rocky Mountain Dream Pie, 275
    Seven Minute Icing, 171
    Flavored Sheet Cake, 120
Lemonade Chiffon Pie, 280
Lime
    Chiffon Pie, 282
    Pie, Florida Frozen, 282
Limeade Chiffon Pie, 280
Low Calorie
    Apple Sauce Topping, 308

Coffee Topping, 314
Dessert Topping, 314
Maple Topping, 314
Low Calorie-Low Cholesterol
    Buckwheat Cakes, 308
Low-Cholesterol
    Biscuits, 310
    Pie Crust, 311
Low-Fat
    Low Cholesterol White
        Bread, 312
Lunch Box Tarts, 354

Macaroons, Coconut, 185
Man's Cake, A, 140
Maple
    Custard, Baked, 297
    Low Calorie Dessert
        Topping, 314
    Nut Cake, 141
Marble
    Cake, Halowe'en, 139
    Bars, 231
Marmalade
    Butter Frosting, 168
    Orange Coffee Cake, 80
Meat Pasties, Guy's, 344
Meringue
    Cookie Squares, 227
    Lemon Angel Pie, 270
    Pie, Chocolate Cream, 268
    Pie Shell, 254
    Puff Crust Cream Pie, with, 274
    Rocky Mountain Dream Pie, 275
    Suggestions for Successful, 245
    Topping, 2-egg and 3-egg, 254
    Shells, Individual, 268
Mincemeat, 261
    Chiffon Pie, 284
    Cookies, Quick Change, 220
    Bars with Butter Icing, 230
Mint Jelly Icing, 171
Mix
    Biscuit, 64
    Muffin, 67
Mixing Tips For
    Cakes, 111
    Cookies, 180
    Pie Crusts, 241
    Yeast Breads, 29

Mocha
  Icing, 169
  Squares, 225
  Torte, 159
  Topping, 327
Modern Marvels, 315-330
Molasses Chocolate Bit
  Cookies, 192
Muffins, 66-72
  Apple, 68
  Blueberry, 69
  Bran, 68
  Corn, 87
  English, 43
  Fruit, 67
  Fruit Nut, 67
  Mix, 67
  Nut, 67
  Orange, 67, 70
  Raisin Cornmeal, 88
  Sally Lunn, 70
  Spice, 67
  Streusel Smacks, 72
  Suggestions for Successful, 66
  Whole Wheat, 71
Multi-Flour Health Bread, 35

New England Doughnuts, 101
Nesselrode Chiffon Pie, 281
Nut
  Bread (Junior Bakers), 333
  Bread, 77, 79
  Crescents, Swedish, 218
  Fudge Cake, Lee's, 127
Nutty Date Macaroons, 187

Oatmeal
  Cookies (Junior Bakers), 338
  Cookies, 194
  Cookies, Easy, 194
  Pancakes, 98
Orange
  Almond Filling and
    Frosting, 167
  Bread, 84
  Bread, Mrs. Bell's, 33
  Butter Cream Frosting, 169
  Cookies, with Frosting, 200
  Coffee Cake (Junior Bakers), 336
  Cream Chiffon Pie, 322

  Drop Doughnuts, 102
  Flavored Sponge Cake, 162
  Flavored Sheet Cake, 120
  Marmalade Coffee Cake, 80
  Muffins, 67, 70
  Seven Minute Icing, 171
Oven Temperatures, 23

Pancakes, 89-98
  Pancakes, 90
  Pancakes for Two, 92
  Buckwheat Cakes, 94
  Buckwheat Cakes, Low Calorie-
    Low Cholesterol, 308
  Butterfly Griddle Cakes,
    Leila's, 96
  Buttermilk, 97
  Buttermilk, No Fat, 310
  Cornmeal Griddle Cakes, 91
  Dorothy's French, 93
  Graham Griddle Cakes, 95
  Oatmeal, 98
  Silver Dollar (Junior
    Bakers), 351
  Suggestions for Successful, 89
  Whole Wheat Griddle Cakes, 95
Party Baked Custard, 297
Peach
  Betty, 303
  Crumble Pie, 262
  Crunch, 304
  Fruit Dessert, 302
  Upside Down Cake, 142
Peanut Butter
  Balls, 314
  Cookies, 217
  Icing, Blender, 169
Peanut
  Cluster Cookies, 195
  Drop Cookies, 193
  Drop Cookies, (Junior
    Bakers), 345
  Frosting, Ground, Salted, 225
  Raisin Cookies, 199
Pear and Cheese Foldover Pie, 330
Pecan
  Kisses, 189
  Pie, Debby's, 270
  Supremes, 197
Penuche Icing, 170

Pie(s), 239-285
  Angelfood, 265
  Apple with Cheese Crust, 257
  Apple, Darrell's Favorite, 256
  Baking Problems and
    Solutions, 244
  Baking, Timetable for, 246
  Baking Tips, General, 245
  Banana Cream, Hazel's, 267
  Berry or Fruit, 255-264
  Black Bottom, 278
  Butterscotch Chiffon, 278
  Butterscotch Sour Cream, 266
  Carrot, 269
  Cheese, Joanie's (Junior Bakers),
    348
  Cherry, Canned, 258
  Cherry, Fresh, 258
  Cherry, Frozen, 260
  Chiffon Pies, 277-285
  Chocolate, 266
  Chocolate Chiffon, 277
  Chocolate Cream Meringue, 268
  Chocolate, Marvelous, 264
  Coconut Custard, Hazel's, 267
  Coffee Eggnog Chiffon, 280
  Concord Grape, 260
  Cream or Custard, 264-277
  Custard Pie, 268
  Dapple Pie, 320
  Deep Dish, 244
  Frenchmint, Margie's, 279
  Gooseberry, 259
  Lemon Angel, 270
  Lemonade Chiffon, 280
  Lemon Cream Chiffon, 323
  Lemon Meringue, 271
  Lime Chiffon, 282
  Lime, Florida Frozen, 282
  Limeade Chiffon, 280
  Meringues For, 254
  Mincemeat For, 261
  Mincemeat Chiffon, 284
  Mixing Tips for, 241
  Nesselrode Chiffon, 281
  Orange Cream Chiffon, 322
  Peach Crumble, 262
  Pecan, Debby's 270
  Pear and Cheese Foldover, 330

  Pennsylvania Crumb, 276
  Pineapple Cream, 272
  Pudding and Fruit, 324
  Puff Crust Cream, 274
  Pumpkin Chiffon, 283
  Pumpkin, Jerry's Favorite, 272
  Pumpkin, Old Fashioned, 269
  Raisin Cream, 273
  Rhubarb Cream, 276
  Rocky Mountain Dream, 275
  Strawberry, Fresh, 262
  Strawberry, Chiffon, 285
  Suggestions for Successful
    Baking, 240
  Tarts, Fruit, 263, 244
  Tips for Freezing Pies, 247
  Turnovers, to Shape, 244
Pie Crusts, 248-253
  Angelfood Pie for, 265
  Basic, I, II, 248-249
  Cheese, 251, 257
  Crumb, 252-253
  French Pastry, 250
  Glazes for, 243
  Hot Water, 250
  Low Cholesterol, 311
  Meringue, 254, 268, 270
  Puff, 274
  Quick, 249
  Tarts, For, 263
  Tips for Freezing, 246
  Tips for Rolling Out, 242
Pimento Cheese Quickies, 323-324
Pineapple
  Cake, Filled Four-Layer, 329
  Cream Pie, 272
  Custard Filling, 173
  Fritters, 106
  Fruit Dessert, 302
  Fruit Topping, 327
  Icing, 170
  Nut Cookies, 201
  Pudding Pie, 324
  Upside Down Cake, 142
Pizza Burgers (Junior Bakers), 350
Pizzas, Individual (Junior
  Bakers), 346
Popovers and Corn Breads, 85-88

Popovers, 86
Popovers, Suggestions for
 Baking, 85
Poppy Seed Cake, 116
Pound Cake, 124
Powdered Sugar Cake, 119
Preface, 5-6
Prune
 Bread, 82
 Whip, Johnstown, 304
Pudding
 and Fruit Pie, 324
 Apple, Scalloped, 290
 Bread and Variations, 290, 298
 Cherry, 294
 Chocolate Bread, 291, 298
 Cottage, 298
 Date-Nut, 300
 Graham Cracker, 302
 Rice, 305
 Walnut, Quick, 328
Puff Cakes, 148
Puff Crust Cream Pie, 274
Puffed Wheat Cereal Bars, 236
Pumpkin
 Cake, Mark's, 143
 Cookies, 203
 Cup Cakes, 143
 Chiffon Pie, 283
 Pie, Jerry's Favorite, 272
 Pie, Old Fashioned, 269
 Topping, 327
Quick
 Apple Coffee Cake, 316
 Brioche, 317
 Crazy Cake, 336
 Breads, 60-106
 Chocolate Cream Filling, 174
 Change Cookies with Varia-
  tions, 220
 Method Golden Layer Cake, 121
 Pie Crust, 249
 Rum Dumplings, 327
 Shortcake, 352
 Walnut Pudding, 328
Quickies, Drop and Bake, 323
 Butter-Nut Goldies, 323
 Pimento Cheese, 323
 Other Variations, 324

Raised Doughnuts, 103
Raisin
 Cookies, Mother's, 199
 Corn Meal Muffins, 88
 Cream Pie, 273
 Nut Filling, 175
 Peanut Cookies, 196
 Squares, Frosted, 228
Refrigerator Cookies, 204-210
 Black Walnut, 209
 Butterscotch Crisps, 206
 Chocolate and Vanilla Pin-
  wheels, 206
 Date, 207
 Date Pinwheels, 205
 Dutch Almond, 204
 Ginger, 210
 Hermits, 208
 Vanilla Wafers, 210
Refrigerator Rolls, 49
Rhubarb Cream Pie, 276
Rice
 Crispy Cereal Cookies, 202
 Pudding, 305
Rocky Mountain Dream Pie, 275
Rolls, Yeast, 43-49
 Brioche, 48, 317
 Caramel, 54
 Cinnamon, 54
 Citrus Roll-Ups with Filling
  and Frosting, 50
 Coconut Breakfast Rings with
  Filling and Glaze, 52
 English Muffins, 43
 Feathery Light, 46
 Foundation Sweet Dough, 54
 Garlic and Herb, 44
 How to Shape, 30-31
 Kolacki, 57
 Mother Anderson's
  Wonderful, 47
 Refrigerator, 49
 Sour Cream with Filling, 57
 Whole Wheat, Mother
  Miller's, 40
Rum
 Balls, 236
 Dumplings, Quick, 327
Rye Bread, 42

Sally Lunn, 70
Scripture Cake, 144
Sea Foam Icing
  I, 172
  II, 172
Seven Minute Icing
  I, 170
  II, 171
  Coconut, 171
  Lemon, 171
  Orange, 171
  Peppermint, 171
Shortcake, Quick,
  (Junior Bakers), 352
Soufflé(s)
  Date Nut, 300-301
  Individual Chocolate, 319
  Italian Cherry-Chocolate, 296
Sour Cream
  Cake, 134
  Chocolate Cake, Pete's, 124
  Cookies, Coconut, Raisin-Nut
    and Spice, 198
  Corn Bread, 88
  Doughnuts, 104
  Nut Bread, Mother's, 79
  Pie, Butterscotch, 266
  Rolls with Filling, 57
  Topping for Cheese Cake,
    291, 293, 348
Spice
  Cake, 145
  Cake (Junior Bakers), 334
  Cake, Little, 146
  Chocolate Mashed Potato
    Cake, 132
  Coffee Cake, 326
  Drop Cookies, 202
  Muffins, 67
Spiced
  Molasses Nuggets, Paul's, 216
Sponge Cake(s), 154-162
  Cake, 161
  Four-Egg Cake, 162
  Orange, 162
Spoon Bread, 86
Strawberry
  Glaze for Cheesecake, 293
  Pie, Chiffon, 285
  Pie, Fresh, 262

Sugar Cookies
  Classic, 218
  Drop, 198
  Grandmother's, 219
  (Junior Bakers), 340
Suggestions for
  Baking Corn Bread, 85
  Baking Popovers, 85
  Successful Biscuits, 61
  Successful Cake Baking, 110-113
  Successful Muffins, 66
  Successful Pancakes, 89
  Successful Pie Baking, 240
  Successful Quick Breads, 73
  Successful Waffles, 89
  Successful Yeast Breads, 28-32
Swedish
  Nut Crescents, 218
  Spritz, 221
Sweet Dough, Foundation with
  Icing, 54
Sweet Rolls, Yeast, 50-57

Tarts
  Fillings, 264
  Fruit, 263, 244
  How to Shape, 244
  Jam, 353
  Lunch Box, 354
Tea Bread, Afternoon, 56
Three-in-One Cake (Junior
  Bakers), 334
Toffee
  Bars, Rocky Mountain, 228
  Squares, English, 234
Toll Oat Cookies, 196
Toppings
  Blueberry, 289
  For Deluxe Coffee Cake, 78
  Fruit, 327
  With German Coffee Cake, 53
  Low Calorie Applesauce, 308
  Low Calorie Dessert, Coffee,
    Maple, 314
  For Grandma Grace's Coffee
    Cake, 76
  For Individual Coffee Cakes, 85
  Meringue, 254
  Mocha, 327
  For Mrs. Egan's Dessert

Ring, 115
For Orange Coffee Cake, 337
Pumpkin Pie, 327
Streusel, 72
Torte
Mocha, 158
Viennese, 160
Turnovers, to Shape, 244

Upside Down Cake
Ginger, 325
Peach, 142
Pineapple, 142

Vanilla Wafers, Refrigerator, 210
Viennese Torte, 160

Waffles, 98-100
Basic, 100
Buttermilk, 99
Chocolate, 98
Easy (Junior Bakers), 355
Suggestions for Successful, 89
Walnut
Bread, 83
Bourbon Balls, 237
Pudding, Quick, 328
Whipped Cream Cake, 135

White
Bread, 38, 312
Cake, Lady Baltimore, 117
Cake, Two Layer, 120
Cake, Sheet, One Bowl, 120
Icing, 171
Whole Wheat
Bread, Mother Miller's, 40
Griddle Cakes, 95
Muffins, 71
Rolls, Mother Miller's, 40
Wonderful Rolls, Mother
Anderson's, 47

Yeast
Breads, 27-58
Coffee Cakes, 50-58
Raised Doughnuts, 103
Rolls, 43-49
Sweet Rolls, 50-58
Whole Wheat or Graham
Griddle Cakes, 95
Yellow
Cake, Angel Food, 156
Cake, Three-Layer with Filling
and Icing, 122

Zwieback Crumb Crust, 253, 292